the complete guide to

SPRING TRAINING

2nd edition

Warm breezes, blue skies, and cold beer: Getting the most from your baseball spring training experience

by kevin reichard

 August Publications

Minneapolis, Minnesota

For Courtney

The Complete Guide to Spring Training, 2nd Edition
Kevin Reichard

August Publications
527 Marquette Av., Suite 800
Minneapolis, MN 55402
612.343.5207
augustpublications.com
Copyright © 2008 August Publications

Notice of Rights

Notice of Liability

ISBN 978-0-9752706-6-0

9 8 7 6 5 4 3 2 1

Design (cover and interior): Natalie Nowytski

Printed and bound by Sentinel Printing, St. Cloud, Minnesota, USA.

→ table of contents

→ table of contents (continued)

→ acknowledgments

This is the first book (of many, we hope) to be published under the August Publications name.
   – From the first edition of *The Complete Guide to Spring Training*

The first line of the Acknowledgements to the first edition to this book was, as it turns out, prophetic. Little did the many, many buyers of that tome realize how early August Publications was in its formative history: it was, basically, a one-person shop chugging out a guide to spring training and hoping for the best.

And the best did happen: August Publications is now a thriving, on-going commercial concern. We've moved from a home office to a fairly comfortable office suite. We've published several other books since then and launched a dozen sports-oriented Websites; all are successful on many levels.

Much of the credit for this success must go to the many buyers of the first edition of *The Complete Guide to Spring Training*: They proved there's a market for a well-done, informational guide to spring training. Launching a publishing company with books as a key component when the world is moving to the Internet takes a certain amount of recklessness. Luckily for me, my wife Courtney a) probably doesn't realize how reckless it is, and b) doesn't really care because she trusts and loves me. I can ask for no more.

A little background on August Publications. The company is named for my grandfather, August Reichard. I'd like to think that somewhere he knows his ordeals in coming to America from Germany at the turn of the century were not in vain; his descendents are doing quite well, thank you.

Thanks also go to my kids — Sean, Rachel, and Sarah — who find themselves being dragged to every manner of ballpark big and small all spring and summer long, and Jo Ward and Jack and Cathy Kurtz for putting me up during spring training (it does pay to have kin and friends in Florida and Phoenix when you're producing a book on spring training). The staff at August Publications is top-notch: Creative Director Natalie Nowytski is responsible for the clear, readable design, and Senior Editor Dave Wright added his considerable editorial touch to the text. Jim Robins added several other photos within these pages.

And, most of all, thanks to the loyal readers of Ballpark Digest, a Website I launched on the side in 2002 that's blossomed into a full-time job. Not everyone can turn their passion into their career, and I'm lucky enough to say I've done so.

—Kevin Reichard
June 2008

→ introduction

Warm Breezes, Cold Beer, Sunny Skies

People ask me what I do in the winter when there's no baseball. I'll tell you what I do. I stare out the window and wait for spring.
— Rogers Hornsby

Spring training is America's annual transformation from darkness to light, from cold to warm, when millions of baseball fans — both hardcore and casual — descend upon warmer climes to shed their winter blues. For those of us living north of the Mason-Dixon line, baseball's spring training is not a luxury but a necessity, our reward for living in climates filled with overcast skies, snow, ice, and rain.

Beer and brats in hand, we arrive in Florida and Arizona every February and March to soak up some sun and catch some baseball. We wait months for that first whiff of freshly mown grass at the ballpark, that first foul ball, that first inevitable sunburn. Who cares whether the starting pitcher is some kid who will likely begin the season in Double-A? As long as the drinks are cold and the dogs are hot, all is right with the world.

We begin planning our winter getaways months in advance, juggling airline schedules and hotel openings to ensure the maximum number of games. We show up to morning workouts just to stand by the fence and feel like we're part of the action. And we take spring-training performances a lot more seriously than do the players and managers.

This book is both for the hardcore baseball fan who goes to spring training to scout out his favorite team in depth as well as the more casual fan who heads to spring training more in search of the perfect suntan than this year's spring phenom. In fact, the casual fans are more likely to get something out of this book: While the hardcores just want to know the shortest route between their hotel and the ballpark, the casual fan knows that the richness of spring training is augmented with visits to local restaurants, shopping areas, and area attractions.

Previous books covering spring training have centered on the Florida experience. Rich with history and tradition, spring training in Florida is a spectacle that every American should experience. But focusing on the Grapefruit League leads one to ignore the vibrant spring-training scene that's developed in Arizona's Cactus League.

The two spring-training experiences tend to be different. Spring training in Florida is a relaxed, sprawling affair; though many teams train in the Tampa and Orlando areas, spring training takes place throughout the state. You tend to focus on a team or two in a specific area and then schedule other activities around an afternoon exhibition game. It's a very laid-back environment.

Compare that with Arizona, where eleven teams train in Phoenix and three in Tucson; the concentration of fourteen teams into just nine facilities makes for baseball nirvana, as you can hit a large number of games with relatively little fuss. A spring-training game in Florida's Lakeland or Kissimmee tends to be a subdued affair rich with tradition, but a spring-training game in Peoria or Mesa tends to be a rowdier affair, with kids romping through the outfield berm and college co-eds teasing young men. Florida is your father's spring training and Arizona is party central — not that there's anything wrong with either, and you can certainly find rowdy parties at Florida ballparks and subdued atmospheres in Arizona, particularly down in Tucson.

This book is divided into two sections: a Florida guide and an Arizona guide. They're not structured exactly the same. As mentioned, Florida spring training sprawls across the entire state, and most fans tend to stick in one place (in other words, they won't be traversing the width of the state often), so there's plenty of information about each spring-training city. Most visitors to the Cactus League spend the vast majority of their time in the Phoenix/Scottsdale or Tucson areas, and our Arizona coverage focuses on those areas.

Finally, a word or two of warning. When it comes to restaurants, things can change quickly. The listings here were current as of September 2008, but it would not be surprising if a restaurant listed in this book did not go out of business in the meantime. Also, there's always a little flux associated with spring training from baseball's end: Schedules tend to change even up to the last minute (in 2007 the master schedule was still being revised as late as February), so things could indeed change. When in doubt, check this book's Website, **springtrainingonline.com**, for up-to-the-minute information.

Spring Training: An American Tradition

How popular is spring training? In 2007, MLB teams drew more than 3 million fans to spring-training games, a record. And spring training continues to boom as an economic boost for hosting communities. For example, a study commissioned by the Arizona Office of Tourism estimates fans spent a total of more than $310 million within Arizona in 2007, a 54 percent increase from 2003. More than 1.3 million fans attended Cactus League games in 2007. Leading the way were the Chicago Cubs, averaging over 12,000 fans per game. The same sort of growth was experienced in the Grapefruit League, which set a record for attendance in 2007 when 1.7 million fans attended games. Leading the way: the New York Yankees, who averaged 10,311 fans per game.

Though the beginning of spring training marks the official beginning of the baseball season, teams prepare for training camp months in advance. Planning starts at the end of the prior season, when team equipment managers start laying in supplies in advance of spring training, and team officials begin mapping out spring-training schedules.

Things are slow until after the Christmas holidays. In January managers will begin packing in anticipation of sending the equipment to training camp via semi trailer. For instance, the Oakland A's send 22,000 pounds of equipment to Phoenix and ship 30,000 pounds back to Oakland.

PLANNING YOUR TRIP

Major League Baseball does not make it easy for you to schedule your spring-training vacation. Schedules are not released until the World Series is concluded, and many of you will be reading this book way before then. Plus, the early schedules tend be more like suggestions than written-in-stone plans: In 2007 teams were shifting their schedules as late as February to accommodate games overseas.

So how should you plan? With flexibility in mind.

Generally, pitchers and catchers begin reporting around the 15th of February, give or take a few days, with position players reporting four or five days later. Full workouts begin a couple of days after position players report. Although some of these early workouts are open to the public, they're dreadfully dull for the average fan unless you like watching players stand around in line, waiting to practice sacrifice bunts: You're better off postponing your trip and attending the actual games. You can assume that spring-training games will begin in earnest by the first weekend of March. In 2009 the spring-training season will run between Feb. 26 and March 28.

You can also assume that most teams are wrapping up their spring-training games by the last full weekend of March. Sometimes teams wrap up spring-training earlier in order to play exhibition games overseas, while others head home a little early to play exhibition games in their home ballparks: Both the Dodgers and Angels, for example, break camp early to play a freeway exhibition series in Dodger Stadium and Angel Stadium.

Other than those parameters, it's all a crapshoot when you try to arrange early travel. If you head for your favorite team's spring-training base for a two- or three-day stretch, you can assume with a great level of confidence that at least one game will be played in that time. Teams do not go on lengthy road trips in spring training, and a large number of split-squad games (where teams split into two squads, with both playing in a day) early in the month increase the sheer number of games played in March.

It's clear, then, that you should arrange your travel first and then scout for tickets later. But don't wait too long after tickets go on sale before buying a set: By the beginning of February, many games at popular venues — like Scottsdale Stadium and HoHoKam Park — are sold out, particularly those on weekends.

One more thing to note when scheduling your time: most spring-training games are played in the afternoon.

If you want to save a tree or two, you can utilize our electronic resource. Just send an email to **info@springtrainingonline.com** and we'll put you on a mailing list that sends out important information about team schedules and spring-training news. (Privacy note: Email addresses sent to this address will be used strictly for mailing out spring-training schedule announcements and will not be shared with any third parties.) There is also a form at Spring Training Online (**springtrainingonline.com**) that will place you on the list as well. Finally, Spring Training Online will post spring-training schedules as they become available.

How to Order Tickets

When teams announce their spring-training schedules, they also announce when tickets will go on sale. Generally, single-game tickets don't go on sale until after the beginning of the year — which means that January and February tend to be mad scrambles for tickets to March games.

Still, tickets are available from a variety of sources. Most people assume that only MLB teams sell tickets, but that's not always the case. MLB does sell the majority of spring-training tickets, but there are usually some alternative ways to come up with ducats for a popular match.

For sheer convenience, however, your search for tickets should begin with the MLB teams. They're set up best to sell massive amounts of tickets in a short amount of time, as the beginning of spring-training ticket sales can best be described as a feeding frenzy, with tens of thousands of fans rushing to obtain tickets for specific games.

There are four ways to order spring-training tickets directly from MLB teams: via telephone, via the Internet, in person, and via the U.S. mail. We'll describe each.

→ **Via telephone.** Most tickets are sold via phone sales. This can be a frustrating way of doing things, as you're likely to encounter some busy signals or long wait times when tickets first go on sale. Don't bother calling before the tickets are technically on sale: All you'll do is waste your time and irritate the ticket reps. They can't help you until the tickets are actually on sale; they won't call you back, and they won't put you on a secret list to be hauled out when tickets are on sale. When the tickets do go on sale — and you'll find a complete listing of when tickets go on sale at the **springtrainingonline.com** team pages — be prepared to call early in the day for popular games, like the Boston-New York matchups. You'll also pay a "ticketing fee" for the convenience of buying tickets.

→ **Via the Internet.** Every team sells spring-training tickets via the Internet. There are some pluses and minuses to this approach. On the one hand, you can bypass clogged phone

lines and make your purchases directly (although Ticket-master has implemented the equivalent of telephone wait times when you buy popular tickets online). But the ticketing systems are not very sophisticated: you enter a price range and take whatever tickets the system presents: you can't order specific seats or see a list of available seats within a price range and select the ones you want. And yes, you'll also pay a ticketing fee for the convenience of buying tickets.

→ **In person.** Most teams sell spring-training tickets at their main ticket office at the major-league ballpark, the spring-training ticket office, or local team stores. The Colorado Rockies, for example, sell spring-training tickets at all six Rockies Dugout Stores. There are three big advantages to buying tickets in person: You can usually get a good idea of the range of available tickets, you can request specific seats, and you won't need to wait too long in line. Plus, the major-league box office and the spring-training box offices are the only locations where you won't incur evil handling fees.

→ **Via U.S. mail.** Some teams sell tickets via the mail. You send in your money for a price range, and you take whatever tickets the team decides to send you. Will you receive the best tickets in your price range? Depends on the whims of a ticket rep with the team. The advantage, however, is that these orders tend to be filled first, so you are virtually assured of receiving tickets to the game of your choice. But not every team offers this service.

insider's tip

If you order tickets and plan on picking them up at the ballpark, make sure you have the confirmation number and an ID with you. Ticket-office personnel are instructed to make sure that the right person is picking up tickets. More than once have we waited in line in the Will Call line and cooled our heels while the party in front of me argues in vain with the ticket staff over disputed tickets.

Teams also offer two ways to obtain bulk tickets that may fit your needs: season tickets and group sales.

If you think you'll be attending many games, consider a season ticket. Season-ticket packages go on sale weeks before single-game tickets. Usually season tickets are the province of locals and brokers, but if you really, really want some tix for the Red Sox-Yankees games and realize that you have no chance of obtaining a ticket via convention means, spring for the season ticket and then try to sell tickets to some of the other games via eBay or StubHub.

Other teams offer a break to groups of 25 or more. Again, this won't apply if just you and your buddies are in a group, but there may be opportunities where you could put together a group (via a church organization, an Internet chat site, etc.) that could buy discounted tickets to a game or two.

insider's tip

If you can, schedule a game on St. Patrick's Day. It's the only real holiday in the month, and most teams do something to commemorate it, whether it be cheap green beer, green uniforms, or the giveaway of something green (such as the Pittsburgh Pirates' annual giveaway of green Pirates caps). You can also bet watering holes close to the ballparks will have some St. Patrick's Day drink specials as well.

Working with Brokers

There is another way to obtain a single-game ticket: through a ticket broker. This is indeed American capitalism at its finest: Good brokers tend to have decent tickets to the best games, and they're not afraid to charge extra for them. They're also not shy about telling the world about the availability of the tickets, so if you want to go to a game badly enough, chances are good that one of them will step up with a ticket. We work with a vendor to offer after-market tickets at **ballparkdigesttickets.com**. Of course, we'd recommend you start there.

WHERE TO STAY

If you lack friends or family in Arizona or Florida, you'll need to arrange housing for your stay. There are a few ways to go.

The obvious choice is a hotel. Virtually every spring-training site is located in an urban or suburban area and features easy access to a slew of hotels. You'll pay more to stay near the more popular ballparks; in our guides to each venue we list the closest hotels to each ballpark and tell you if it's worth staying near the ballpark. (In most cases, it's not.) There are

some baseball fanatics that insist on staying within walking distance of a spring-training facility, but they a) tend to spend the entire day at the facility, and b) don't want to spring for the cost of a car.

Here are the 800 numbers for the major hotel chains found near spring-training sites in Florida and Arizona. We also list the local numbers for hotels located close to the ballparks in each chapter of this book.

→ **AmeriHost:** 800/434-5800
→ **AmeriSuites:** 877/774-6467
→ **Baymont Inn:** 866/999-1111
→ **Best Western:** 800/447-4728
→ **Candlewood Suites:** 800/HOLIDAY
→ **Clarion Hotels:** 877/424-6423
→ **Comfort Inn:** 877/424-6423
→ **Country Inn & Suites:** 800/456-4000
→ **Courtyard by Marriott:** 800/321-2211
→ **Crestwood Suites:** 877/EXTENDED
→ **Crowne Plaza:** 800/HOLIDAY
→ **Days Inn:** 800/329-7466
→ **Doubletree:** 800/222-TREE
→ **EconoLodge:** 877/424-6423
→ **Embassy Suites:** 800/EMBASSY
→ **Exel Inns:** 800/FOR-EXEL
→ **Extended Stay America:** 800/EXT-STAY
→ **Fairfield Inn:** 800/321-2211

→ **Fairmont Hotels:** 800/257-7544
→ **Four Points:** 888/625-5144
→ **Hampton Inn:** 800/HAMPTON
→ **Hawthorn Suites:** 800/527-1133
→ **Hilton:** 800/HILTONS
→ **Holiday Inn:** 800/HOLIDAY
→ **Homewood Suites:** 800/CALL-HOME
→ **Howard Johnson:** 800/446-4656
→ **Knights Inn:** 800/843-5644
→ **La Quinta:** 866/725-1661
→ **MainStay Suites:** 877/424-6423
→ **Marriott:** 800/321-2211
→ **Microtel Inn:** 888/222-2142
→ **Motel 6:** 800/466-8356
→ **Omni Hotels:** 800/THE-OMNI
→ **Park Inn:** 800/670-7275
→ **Peabody:** 800/PEABODY
→ **Prime Hotels & Resorts:** 866/864-3649
→ **Quality Inn:** 877/424-6423
→ **Radisson:** 800/333-3333
→ **Ramada Inn:** 800/272-6232
→ **Red Roof:** 800/RED-ROOF
→ **Renaissance Hotels:** 800/HOTELS-1
→ **Residence Inn:** 800/321-2211
→ **Ritz-Carlton:** 800/241-3333
→ **Rodeway Inn:** 877/424-6423
→ **Sheraton:** 888/625-5144
→ **Sierra Suites:** 888/695-7608
→ **Sleep Inn:** 877/424-6423
→ **Springhill Suites:** 800/321-2211
→ **Staybridge Suites:** 800/HOLIDAY
→ **Summerfield Suites:** 877/999-3223
→ **Super 8:** 800/800-8000
→ **Travelodge:** 800/578-7878
→ **TownePlace Suites:** 800/321-2211
→ **Wellesley Inn and Suites:** 877/774-5345
→ **Westin:** 888/625-5144
→ **Wingate Inns:** 800/228-1000
→ **Wyndham:** 877/999-3223

Only in rare situations will you be shut out of an affordable hotel room for spring training — provided that you can be flexible about where you stay. In Phoenix, for instance, there's not a time when all the hotel rooms are sold out during spring training. Sure, the hotels on the west side of town (Peoria, Glendale, Surprise) may be sold out, but there will usually be rooms available downtown or near the airport. In both cases you'll want to rent a car — but you'd need to do so in Phoenix anyway, as Phoenicians drive everywhere.

You can also investigate a package deal involving a hotel. Most teams and many hotels now offer package deals, which combine a hotel stay with tickets to a game or two.

But there are some alternatives to daily-stay hotels. If you're planning on an extended stay, consider renting a condo or RV. In this book we list RV resorts close to the spring-training facilities.

Almost every area listed in the book has condos or timeshares for rent. We're not going to delve heavily into the topic (quite honestly, we've never rented a condo or participated in a timeshare), but there are places in this book where we note the availability of condos or timeshares.

There are many folks who visit spring training in the comfort of their own RV; they're the ones setting up shop three or four hours before a game, grilling their pre-game sandwiches. Though you can't park overnight at a ballpark parking lot, most communities hosting spring training also have several RV parks, especially when you're dealing with the smaller communities in Florida (like Lakeland, Bradenton, Kissimmee or Clearwater) and the Phoenix suburbs (like Mesa) or Tucson.

You don't even need to own an RV to use one for spring training: Companies like Cruise America rent RVs by the day or week from hundreds of locations across the United States. Today's RV is not like yesterday's RV: They have considerably more amenities (like showers, decent bathrooms, and air conditioning) and are more reliable than in the past. And RV parks can be amazingly upscale, with shaded parking, wireless networking, and more.

Making Your Way to the Ballpark:
Planes, Trains, and Automobiles

Getting to the city hosting spring training is one thing. Making your way to your hotel room and the ballpark is another.

The ballparks of spring training, in general, aren't easily accessible via public transit. For every ballpark like Scottsdale Stadium (which is well-served by public transit and a dedicated ballpark bus for Giants games) or Disney World's Champion Stadium (served by the Disney bus system) there are 10 others like Tempe Diablo Stadium or Port St. Lucie's Tradition Field, where public transit is spotty or nonexistent. For Yankees or Red Sox fans used to hopping a bus or subway to the game, forget about it: ain't no subway running down in the sands of Florida.

So, in most cases, you'll need to resign yourself to an inevitable cost of attending spring training: springing for a car. Sure, you could drive your own car to spring training — and trust us, plenty of folks do just that, as evidenced by the large number of Michigan license plates in the Joker Marchant Stadium parking lot — but if you're committed to flying, you're going to be forced to rent a car.

Luckily for you, rental cars are cheap and plentiful in Florida and Arizona. Both are tourist destinations, so you should have no problem in obtaining a rental car at a convenient price.

ATTENDING A GAME: SOME GENERAL GUIDELINES

Now that you actually have a game ticket, a plane ticket, a hotel room, and a car, you're ready to actually attend a spring-training game. Congratulations.

There are some things you should know:

→ Most spring-training ballparks open two hours before game time, and they generally run the same schedule for a 1:05 p.m. game start: home team takes batting practice first, followed by the visitors. This is usually the best time to score autographs: players are relaxed during their warmups and are happy to wander over to the stands and sign away. Or you could head to the practice facility in the morning and try to score some autographs there.

→ Many of the ushers at spring-training games are volunteers, usually senior citizens living in the area. Don't hassle them: they're volunteering at the game because they love baseball. Some of them can be a little on the officious side, but remember their job is to make sure fans are in their proper seats. In Bradenton, almost 100 locals volunteer their services at Pittsburgh Pirates games. In Peoria, 581 "Diamond Backers" in the Peoria Diamond Club work Seattle and San Diego games as ushers, program sellers, parking-lot attendants, and more.

→ You're not always assured of seeing a superstar or even a famous player at a spring-training game. Teams are notorious for leaving their best players at home. There is a rule that each team must send four regulars on the road to play in an exhibition game, but that rule is not truly enforced, and some teams — like the New York Yankees — don't even make a pretense of following that rule.

"B" Games

You don't need to shell out the big bucks to see major leaguers in action during spring training.

If you're willing to put up with a few creature discomforts like a lack of seatbacks, concessions, and restrooms, you can hit a "B" game held on a satellite field in a spring-training complex. These are pure practice games, usually held in the morning. There's no scoreboard tracking the action or an announcer announcing the players, so you should know a little about the players to get anything out of the experience.

And you can't be too much of a purist. As said, these are true practice games: Players bat out of order and wander in and out of the lineup depending on the situation.

But these games are also excellent places to see the real major leaguers work on their game: You're never going to be closer to a superstar working on one specific part of their game. Hard-working players are legendary for using these games to work on their swings or on specific pitches.

In the past, teams held "B" games almost daily, but they seem to be going by the wayside. Last spring, the Arizona teams held only five or six "B" games. Call the team's local box office to see if a "B" game is scheduled for a given day (they are not subject to a published schedule), but your best bet may to be wander around a facility in the morning and see if there's any action on a field.

You can also see the stars of tomorrow at a minor-league spring-training game. These games are also played on a satellite field and are open to anyone wandering through the facility. Unlike "B" games, minor-league games are subject to a schedule: They begin a few weeks into spring training and feature all the teams in an organization taking on all the teams from another organization. For instance, the Class AAA and Class AA from the Arizona Diamondbacks will take on the Class AAA and Class AA teams from the San Diego Padres at the satellite fields at Peoria Stadium. In the minors, there are four levels of teams in training camp (AAA, AA, High A and Low A); if the AAA and AA teams are home, the A teams will be away, and vice versa. Again, these games are run on a casual basis, and most of the better players will be with the parent team, but they offer a very intimate view of some of tomorrow's superstars. Schedules for these games are released after the beginning of the year. Check **springtrainingonline.com** for a complete list of minor-league schedules.

Weather

You can tell a spring-training rookie by his beet-red face and sunburned shoulders. If you've spent the last four months cooped up in a climate dominated by snow and ice, you're going to do the logical thing and bask for hours on end in the warm spring sun.

Don't.

Yes, you'll hear from everyone the importance of slathering on some suntan lotion before hitting your first spring game. But the advice is sound: Even a mildly overcast day can scorch your skin to the painful point, and you don't want to ruin your trip with a bad sunburn.

Otherwise, you should expect perfect weather for your spring-training sojourn. Here are the average high and low temperatures during March for popular baseball destinations in Florida and Arizona:

Average Highs/Lows (F)

City	March 1	March 10	March 20	March 30
Phoenix	71/49	73/50	75/52	78/54
Tucson	70/43	72/44	74/46	77/47
Orlando	76/53	78/55	80/57	81/58
Tampa	74/56	75/58	77/59	78/60
Ft. Lauderdale	78/61	79/62	79/64	80/65
Ft. Myers	78/57	80/59	81/60	82/61

What can I bring into the ballpark?

Forget about bringing much into the ballpark past a medium-sized bag. There's a uniform MLB policy regarding what you can bring into a ballpark. First, everything must fit within a backpack, cooler, or diaper bag no larger than 16 inches by 16 inches by 8 inches. Non-alcoholic beverages must be in sealed, plastic containers. Food must be stored in sealed, clear-plastic containers. If you're carrying any sort of backpack or larger bag, you will be asked to open it up for inspection. Most teams are pretty mellow about backpacks and oversized bags, even if you're bringing in some peanuts or snacks. The key is to have sealed water and food: it's a way to ensure you're not sneaking booze into the ballpark.

So forget about bringing a six-pack of cans or bottles into the park. You can't bring Fido or Fluffy with you unless your dog is a certified seeing-eye or helper dog. And you certainly are not allowed to bring any weapons into the ballpark.

What if it rains?

If it rains, you'll be able to exchange your ticket for a ticket to a future game; some teams also refund unused tickets in case of game cancellations due to weather. You will not be refunded any service or parking fees, however.

→ history

A Short History of Spring Training

The best evidence points to spring training first taking place in 1870, when the Cincinnati Red Stockings and the Chicago White Stockings held organized baseball camps in New Orleans. By 1886 spring training had spread throughout professional baseball, with at least four professional teams holding a formal training camp, and *The Sporting News* lauded the development in its inaugural March 17, 1886, issue:

> *The preparatory work now being done by two or three prominent clubs in the county marks one of the most sensible departures from the old rut in base-ball that has ever been made. It has always been a matter of wonder to professional and amateur athletes that men having thousands of dollars invested in a business of which so much depends on the physical condition of their men, should pay so little attention to the matter of training these people for the arduous work that was expected of them during the six months covering the championship season. Take these same men and let them put the money that they have invested in base-ball in horse-flesh. Would they dare send their horses out on a trotting or running circuit in the spring without training them....*
>
> *Man is the superior animal and really needs more care and attention than the horse. Yet for years ball players have been sent out in the spring with muscles soft and flabby, carrying from ten to twenty pounds of extra flesh, and told to "play ball." Well, they have played ball, but the games have been "yaller," and many a man has come in from a first game with a shoulder, a leg or an arm that has impaired his effectiveness for an entire season....*

That season saw the Chicago White Stockings go to Hot Springs, Arkansas, for spring training, while the Philadelphia Phillies headed for Charleston, S.C., for some games against local talent. The White Stockings were owned and managed by A.G. Spalding, who told *The Sporting News* of his plans to literally "boil" the members of his team in Hot Springs for two weeks:

> *"It's a great scheme," said Mr. Spalding yesterday, leaning back in his chair and stroking his forehead. "I wonder whatever*

made me think of it. All the boys are enthusiastic about it and all want to go. I have written to a professor down there, and he is making arrangements to build a vat in which he can boil the whole nine at once....I boil out all the alcoholic microbes which may have impregnated the systems of these men during the winter while they have been away from me and Anson....If that don't work I'll send 'em all over to Paris and have 'em inoculated by Pasteur."

By 1900, spring training was firmly established as a baseball ritual, with most American and National League teams heading out of town so players could train and managers could evaluate. In those days spring training was a considerably looser affair: Players would gather in a Southern (or sometimes Western) city, work out for a few days, sweat out the winter booze, perhaps sample some of the local delights (many teams held spring training in Hot Springs, Ark., with the city's notable gambling establishments as an inducement to report), and then make their way back to their homes while barnstorming daily against local teams.

Crescent Park still exists and hosts college games; see our Tampa overview for more information.

Even so, spring training was never a strenuous activity in the past. Take the Cleveland Indians of the 1920s, who trained in Lakeland, Fla. Most teams worked out only once a day, either for an hour or two; the rest of the time the players were free to play golf and carouse — which many of them did. In the 1924 *Reach Guide*, Jack Ryder reported that Indians manager Tris Speaker was a firm believer in a single, brief but intense daily workout.

Other teams of that era were more intense. The Brooklyn Dodgers were known for their three-hour workouts, while Pat Moran, manager of the Cincinnati Reds, held 10 a.m. and 2 p.m. workouts. Ryder seemed to approve of the Reds' schedule:

It is the observation of this writer that the policy of Manager Moran is the best of those outlined. Ball players are young men, many of them merely boys, full of pepper and anxious to work.

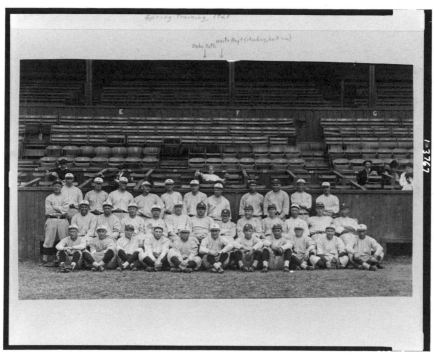

The New York Yankees training in New Orleans, circa 1922-1923. Note Babe Ruth in the middle of the photo. (Library of Congress, LC-US262-103767)

They all enjoy the spring training after the long lay-off of the winter. They do ask to be coddled or favored with light labor. In fact, the more work they can get, provided it is not up to the point of exhaustion, the better they like it. Furthermore, the policy of two sessions a day of practice leaves the boys less time to themselves and keeps them together more, which is always a good thing for a team. They have less temptation to get into bad habits or bad company and the younger recruits are more apt to follow the good example set by the veterans on the team. It must not be understood that Manager Moran is a hard driver or forces his players too far, quite the reverse. If he sees that any ones of the athletes is lazy or inclined to shirk, he is after him at once with a sharp stick, but there are not many such cases. In most instances, the Red leader has to curb the ambition of his men instead of urging them on. This he constantly does, not allowing any man to get an inch beyond the limit of his strength.

901 WATERFRONT PARK, TRAINING QUARTERS OF ST. LOUIS CARDINALS, ST. PETERSBURG, FLORIDA

Waterfront Park gave way to Al Lang Field, which was used through Spring Training 2008.

Small Florida communities were suddenly known across the nation because of the allure provided by major-league baseball: St. Petersburg. Plant City. Orlando. Lakeland. Vero Beach. Fort Lauderdale. Sarasota. Bradenton.

Teams jockeying for good spring-training facilities is nothing new. If anything, things were more cutthroat in the 1920s, when teams would demand new facilities but did not need to make a long-term commitment to a city. Whoever made the best offer to a team in January usually landed the spring training in March.

Case in point: tiny Bogalusa, Louisiana, which hosted the St. Louis Browns spring training in 1921. The city lured the Brownies to their fair city with the construction of a new grandstand and inexpensive accommodations at the Pine Tree Inn. The *Bogalusa Enterprise and American* of March 10, 1921 reported how pleased the Brownies were with the facilities:

> *"When we ask for something at the hotel," said one of the best known players in the American League, "we are not told that 'it will be looked into,' but within a shorter time than one would expect in the best hotel in America, we are served. I never saw people so hospitable in all my life, they simply go out of their way*

in Bogalusa to make it enjoyable for us and I know there is not a member of the team who will not leave Bogalusa with regret when we finish our training, and I also know that if it was left to the members of the team as to where we would train next spring, that it would be Bogalusa by 100 percent."

Manager Coleman of the Terre Haute, Ind. team of the Central League, and former manager of the Mobile club, said that the club house built here for the Browns was by far better than any club house on the American League circuit and that it passed Detroit, which had the best in the league. "The grounds," said Mr. Coleman, "are great and by next year they can be made as good as any in the country."

All of this, apparently, was not enough: the Brownies never returned to Bogalusa for spring training, heading in 1922 for Mobile, Alabama.

Each team has a unique spring-training history, and we present some of the highlights in each team chapter. There was one period in spring training that bears further discussion, however: spring training during the war years. We all associate spring training with warmer climes, but there was a period when major-league teams trained close to home. Travel restrictions during World War II kept teams north of the Ohio River and east of the Mississippi River; the St. Louis Browns and Cardinals were exempted and trained in the greater St. Louis area.

The former Al Lang Field.

As a result, teams trained in such exotic locales as Evansville and French Lick, where both the Chicago Cubs and Chicago White Sox trained in 1943 and 1944. The East Coast teams didn't stray too far from home, either: The Brooklyn Dodgers trained at the West Point fieldhouse between drills, and the Boston Braves trained at Choate School in Wallingford, Conn.

When the war ended, normalcy resumed — and that included baseball, which returned to springs spent mostly in Florida and Arizona. As travel and demographics changed, so did spring training. Rather than writing off spring training as a necessary expense, baseball teams saw spring training evolve into a profit center: Rather than being limited to boozy journalists and clubby insiders, spring training became open to everyone with enough money for admission.

And the reason for spring training changed as well, from a team-building exercise to a month-long advertisement. Today very few roster spots are decided in spring training, and in the era of multimillion contracts players work out in the winter, coming into camp already in shape. Very few major-league teams need six weeks to round into shape and determine rosters, but spring training is so profitable and such a great advertisement for baseball that it would be impossible to scale back.

florida and the grapefruit league

For many people, Florida is synonymous with spring training. Since the 1920s Florida has been the psychic home of spring training, with virtually every major-league team, save the modern expansion franchises, spending some time in the warm Florida sun

It's easy to see the allure of Florida, particularly going back to the days when major-league baseball's westernmost team was in St. Louis and most franchises were in the north and the east. For residents of Pennsylvania or New York or Massachusetts, there was nothing as magical as spring training, that sudden rush of warm air when departing from the three-day train ride, or the realization for the carbound that the snowline is firmly in the rear-view mirror and the outside temperature is fast approaching short-sleeve territory. Folks from Minnesota or Detroit still feel that rush today when they walk off the airplane and inhale that first whiff of scented spring air.

Over time Florida became fused with America's Pastime, providing all of us sustenance at the end of a long winter. And that's the power of the Grapefruit League: It provides a long, rich tradition at a time when Americans are increasingly in search of stability and tradition in their lives.

In this section we'll cover the teams of the Grapefruit League. Our coverage will focus on four areas: Fort Myers/Port Charlotte (spring home of the Boston Red Sox, Minnesota Twins, and Tampa Bay Rays), Tampa/St. Pete (spring home of the Cincinnati Reds, New York Yankees, Philadelphia Phillies, Pittsburgh Pirates, and Toronto Blue Jays), Orlando (spring home of the Atlanta Braves and the Houston Astros), and the Treasure Coast (spring home of the Baltimore Orioles, Florida Marlins, New York Mets, St. Louis Cardinals, and the Washington Nationals).

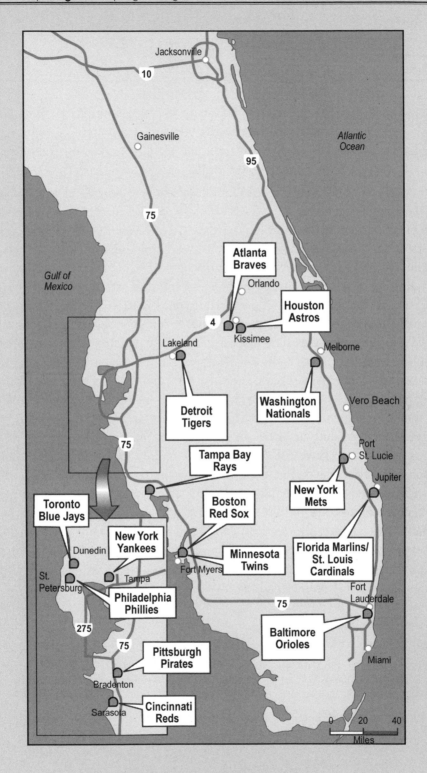

→ fort myers / port charlotte

The greater Fort Myers area is the southernmost point for spring training on the Gulf Coast, and three teams train in the general area: the Tampa Bay Rays in Port Charlotte and the Boston Red Sox and Minnesota Twins in Fort Myers. If you go, you may feel a little isolated from the rest of spring training, as it's 125 miles up the coast to Tampa/St. Pete but less than that to Bradenton (spring-training home of the Pittsburgh Pirates) or Sarasota (spring-training home of the Cincinnati Reds, at least through 2009).

Indeed, the tourism types stress the relative isolation and the scenic seashore when they sell Fort Myers and Port Charlotte as vacation destinations. It's a tropical area with relatively unspoiled beaches on the Gulf Coast, so you should not plan on lining up a series of frenetic activities aimed at keeping the kids occupied.

For the purposes of this section we're discussing the entire Port Charlotte/Fort Myers/Naples area, with a special focus on Fort Myers. These cities along the Gulf Coast run the gamut of restaurants, hotels, and demographics. In the north, Port Charlotte is more of a working-class territory, with a slightly more rural feel and offerings geared toward the locals. Fort Myers is a thriving city with a solid downtown, relying heavily on the tourist trade with plenty of attactions. Naples, to the south, has some ties to the Twin Cities that make it feel like Minnesota South: Many Minnesotans winter in Naples, and popular Twin Cities restaurants like Campiello have Naples outposts. And Naples features the best shopping in the area, by far. In this section we'll focus on Fort Myers because most baseball tourists set up shop there.

Just because the area isn't a little isolated doesn't mean it's unoccupied, however. Indeed, one of the dirty secrets of the area — especially Fort Myers and Naples — is how built up it really is. You will, unfortunately, spend a lot of time just getting from Point A to Point B because of the many locals and the influx of snowbirds. Add to that thousands of baseball fans and you have the recipe for congested roads, crowded restaurants, and hard-to-find affordable hotel rooms. Scenic, yes; bucolic, no. (Speaking of hotels, we will cover hotels in association with each spring-training complex. The needs of the Rays fans will not be the same as those of the Twins fans when it comes to accommodations, and you want to be

33

as close as you can be in order to minimize the amount of time spent in the car.)

Still, you should be prepared for days of baseball, nature, shopping, and history. The Florida Everglades are located in the southern part of the

TERRY PARK

Though the Boston Red Sox, Minnesota Twins, and Tampa Rays are relatively recent transplants to the Fort Myers/Port Charlotte area when it comes to spring training, the area has hosted squads for almost a century, mostly at Terry Park.

Terry Park was named for Dr. Marshall Terry and his wife, Tootie McGregor Terry, who turned a cow pasture into the Fort Myers Yacht and Country Club in 1906. That venture didn't work out, and the land was donated to Lee County. In 1914 the American Association's Louisville Colonels set up spring training at the Country Club grounds, utilizing a small clubhouse and large playing field. The Colonels practiced twice a day, charging 25 cents for admission, and played host to the Philadelphia A's and the St. Louis Browns.

(That small clubhouse, by the way, later served as spring offices for the Kansas City Royals and was eventually demolished in 1980.)

The Louisville Colonels never returned, but by 1923 Fort Myers was ready to make another pitch for spring training and approached Philadelphia A's owner/manager Connie Mack, guaranteeing $6,000 and a new 1,500-seat ballpark if he moved spring operations from Montgomery, Alabama. The shrewd Mack knew a good deal once he saw it, so he sent down ballfield specs and began play at the new wooden grandstand in 1925.

In those days spring training was a considerably more fluid proposition than it is today, and stars didn't necessarily play every day with their own teams. In 1925, for instance, Babe Ruth suited up for the A's in an exhibition match against the minor-league Milwaukee Brewers. Around 5,000 fans crammed into the 1,500-seat ballpark — a figure even more impressive when you consider at the time the total population of Fort Myers was 6,774. In 1927 Mack pitched batting practice to inventor Thomas Edison (who was 80 years old at the time); Edison made good enough contact to smack the ball to Ty Cobb, who feigned surprise at the ferocity of the hit. Olympic star Babe Didriksen pitched an inning against the Brooklyn Dodgers in 1934, and the barnstorming House of David team played a memorable game against the A's in 1935.

By 1936 the A's were gone, replaced by the Cleveland Indians in 1940. Times apparently were a little rougher: whereas the A's were guaranteed $6,000, area, stretching all the way to the southern coasts of the state. Sanibel and Captiva Islands are known for their long expanses of white beaches and mangrove forests, as well as many biking and hiking trails. In fact, over half of the islands are preserved as wildlife sanctuaries, and you could

the Indians were guaranteed $4,000. The Indians' tenure in Fort Myers didn't last long: in 1942 MLB teams moved training bases close to home to save resources for World War II.

The original Terry Park wooden grandstand burned down in 1943 — a not uncommon fate for wooden sports structures — but by 1954 a new 2,500-seat steel grandstand was erected, and in 1955 the Pittsburgh Pirates set up shop. In a nice move, the Pirates' first game was against the Philadelphia A's, with the 92-year-old Connie Mack throwing out the first pitch. The Pirates left after spring training 1967 for Bradenton, to be replaced by the expansion Kansas City Royals. Over the years the Royals are a steady attraction, but spring training was changing, and by 1987 the Royals were ready to move on to a state-of-the-art complex in Haines City. (So much for state of the art: that complex has already been leveled, and there's a certain amount of irony in seeing Terry Park live on and Baseball City gone.) Except for a 1989 exhibition game involving the Texas Rangers and Edison Community College and its use in 1990 as the minor-league camp for the Minnesota Twins while the Hammond Stadium complex was under construction, Terry Park was done as a pro training facility.

But not as a baseball mecca. In many ways the Terry Park complex is more popular than ever before, as the grandstand was rebuilt in 2004 in a slimmed-down 1,000-seat configuration. Around 2,000 games are played at the complex each spring and summer, and if you visit today you'll probably see a game of some sort, as many colleges schedule games there in February and March. You will probably have some downtime if you're in the area to see a Red Sox, Twins, or Rays game, and there's something grand about watching baseball played on a field where Ty Cobb, Jimmy Foxx, Roberto Clemente, George Brett, and Bob Feller spent serious time in the course of their long and illustrious careers.

Terry Park, 3410 Palm Beach Blvd., Fort Myers. Palm Beach Boulevard (also marked as Highway 80) runs northeast from downtown Fort Myers. The ballpark complex is located on the south side of Palm Beach Boulevard; there's a small field for parking west of the ballpark. Virtually every game in February and March is free and open to the public.

The Twins usually play well-attending night games during spring training. Courtesy of the Fort Myers Miracle.

spend days wandering through the area in search of the perfect beach. The folks at the Lee County Visitor & Convention Bureau recommend the following beaches:

→ Boca Grande on Gasparilla Island is known for the Boca Grande lighthouse, still used to guide ships through the Boca Grande Pass. The lighthouse area also features a maritime museum.

→ Coya Costa State Park requires a ferry-boat ride to a seven-mile-long island, but the remote nature of the park — no electricity and few buildings — makes it an attractive day trip, while some prefer staying overnight and setting up camp in a primitive cabin or in a tent on the beach. The area is also noted for its great shelling because of its remote location. Don't lose track of time: The last ferry leaves at 3:30 p.m.

→ Lighthouse Beach on Sanibel Island is one of the easiest beaches to reach — it's the first one you reach after crossing the Sanibel Tollway — but it's also the one where the parking lot fills rapidly. You can watch the dolphins from the white-sand beach.

→ Fort Myers Beach is the most developed of the beaches in the area, so it's an attractive area for those who want to combine a stroll on the beach with a cocktail or two.

This is by no means an exhaustive list of beaches in the area. If you're in the area, the best advice is to ask a few locals where they like to hang out — and hope they're gracious enough to give up their secrets. Lee County Visitor & Convention Bureau, 800/237-6444; **fortmyerssanibel.com**.

Also recommended by the locals: the Six Mile Cypress Slough Reserve. A 1.2-mile boardwalk takes you into a nature preserve, where there are opportunities galore for wildlife viewing. Birders adore the conditions here. Six Mile Cypress Slough Reserve, 7751 Penzance Crossing, Fort Myers; 941/432-2004; **leeparks.org/sixmile**. Open 8 a.m. to sunset daily.

If you want a little of the sea without actually getting sand in your shoes, check out the Bailey-Matthews Shell Museum. (Yes, there actually is a shell museum in Florida.) While this may smack of the naked tourism found in backwater Florida, the Bailey-Matthews Shell Museum is actually a serious endeavor: It publishes the definitive academic journal on malacology (the study of mollusks), and while there's a little whimsy in the exhibits (you can see shell valentines created by the women of the Barbados in the early 19th century for sailors to take home to their loved ones), most of the public area concerns the history of shells and mollusks. Bailey-Matthews Shell Museum, 3075 Sanibel-Captiva Rd., Sanibel; 888/679-6450; **shellmuseum.org**. *Open daily 10 a.m.-5 p.m. Adults $7, kids (5-16) $4.*

Fort Myers is also known as the former winter home of both Thomas Edison and Henry Ford, with their estates located on the Caloosahatchee River. (City of Palms Park is located a short distance from both.) Inventor Edison started wintering in Fort Myers in 1885 and built a small estate,

Hammond Stadium is a busy place during spring training.

"Seminole Lodge," as a winter retreat and lab. Industrialist Ford followed suit in 1915 and built his own winter home, "The Mangoes," to be near his friend Edison. The two houses sit on 17 acres of riverfront property and are open for tours. The buildings are maintained in the style of the era, while a reproduction of Edison's original lab is open for showing as well. You can tour both homes as well as the lab and an adjoining museum, or you can just visit the museum and lab. Edison & Ford Winter Estates, 2350 McGregor Blvd., Fort Myers; 239/334-7419; **efwefla.org**. *Open daily 9 a.m.-5:30 p.m. Tours: Adults $20, children (6-12), $22. Laboratory and museum: Adults $12; children (6-12), $5.*

On the less serious side is the prototypical Florida roadside attraction, Everglades Wonder Gardens, located near Naples in Bonita Springs. When you go, you'll be impressing upon the kids the importance of conservation and the preservation of wildlife; they will be pumped to see the alligator feeding frenzy. So there's something for everyone. Everglades Wonder Gardens, 27180 Old U.S. 41, Bonita Springs; 239/992-2591. *Open 9 a.m.-5 p.m. daily.*

Just down the road from the Twins training complex is Sun Harvest Citrus, a processing plant for Indian River citrus. Watching citrus processing isn't very exciting — basically, oranges, grapefruit, and tangerines are sorted, washed, and packed — so the large store is the main draw. You can jostle for free samples of juice and citrus, but they're worth a few sharp elbows, or you can load up on bags of fresh produce. The lines for the café can be a bit long, as the orange soft serve is a big hit. Sun Harvest Citrus, Six Mile Cypress at Metro, Fort Myers; 800/743-1480; **sunharvestcitrus.com**. *Open M-Sat 8 a.m.-7 p.m., Sunday 10 a.m.- 6 p.m.*

Fort Myers Restaurants

Being in a beachfront area, you'll want to eat seafood at a beachfront restaurant.

Take the kids to The Bubble Room Restaurant, where the décor is strictly kitsch: Christmas lights, over 2,000 movie stills, memorabilia from the 1930s, and a seven-foot-high Mickey Mouse from a 1930 Disney float. Oh, the place is known for the food as well, especially the

The exterior of Hammond Stadium is impressive.

seafood and the desserts. No reservations are taken, so be prepared to wait in line. Bubble Room Restaurant, 15001 Captiva Dr., Captiva Island; 239/472-5558; **bubbleroomrestaurant.com**.

The Mucky Duck is somewhat of an anomaly: a British-style pub in a converted beach house. But it's popular with the locals, who seem to enjoy playing darts and eating duck fingers (strips of duck breast meat) after a day on the beach. Mucky Duck, 11546 Andy Rosse Lane, Captiva Island; 239/472-3434; **muckyduck.com**.

There's a little bit of the Key West spirit in the Fort Myers area, so it's no surprise that Jimmy Buffett reportedly wrote "Cheeseburger in Paradise" while dining at the Cabbage Key Restaurant, renowned for its cheeseburgers. You can't drive there: Cabbage Key on Pine Island Sound is accessible only via boat, helicopter, or seaplane. (Boats make the run to Cabbage Key from Punta Gorda, Captiva Island, and Pine Island.) Call 239/283-2278 or visit **cabbagekey.com/restaurant.html** for more information.

For cheap eats, the locals hit Farmer's Market Restaurant, which specializes in Southern delicacies like biscuits, black-eye peas, country-fried steaks, catfish, and fried chicken gizzards. Farmer's Market Restaurant, 2736 Edison Av., Fort Myers; 239/334-1687; **farmersmarketrestaurant.com**.

You'll need to pay a toll to access Sanibel Island, but it's worth the money if you're seeking out a good restaurant or two. They're all of the same sort, really: slightly upscale with outside seating options. We've eaten at the Mermaid Kitchen and Cake Factory (2055 Periwinkle Way) and can recommend any of the sweets, including the Red Velvet Cake. Catering to families is the Hungry Heron (2330 Palm Ridge Rd., Sanibel Island), where everyone in the group can find someone on the absurdly huge menu to please them. You can expect a line at the Island Cow Eatery (618 N. Yachtsman Dr., Sanibel Island), but the wait will be worth it. But really, you can't go wrong at many of the restaurants on Sanibel Island with a nice glass of wine and a sunset in front of you.

Other Sports

With all the Minnesotans living in the area, it's no surprise the success enjoyed by the minor-league Florida Everblades is one of the best draws in the ECHL. Germain Arena holds 7,181, and crowds approaching that number aren't uncommon. The ECHL is a decent hockey league, and the Everblades put on a good show. Florida Everblades, Germain Arena, 11000 Everblades Pkwy., Estero; 239/948-7825; **floridaeverblades.com**.

Flying In

Fort Myers is home to South Florida International Airport (**swfia.com**) and is served by most major airlines, including Delta, Continental, Frontier, Northwest, Southwest, United, US Airways, AirTran, JetBlue, and American.

You may also want to consider flying into Tampa or Sarasota and then driving to Fort Myers if the fare is significantly cheaper. The drive from Tampa is 125 miles and 75 miles from Sarasota, but as Tampa Bay is home to several other spring-training facilities, you can combine several visits to games with the excursion to Fort Myers. Then again, if you're a Boston Red Sox fan, you probably don't give a damn about any other teams — the only reason you'd venture outside of Fort Myers would be to see the Bo-Sox trample the likes of Pittsburgh in Bradenton.

→ boston red sox

CITY OF PALMS PARK

Capacity	7,700
Year Opened	1992
Dimensions	330L, 385LC, 410C, 385RC, 330R
Surface	Grass
Local Airport	Ft. Myers
Dugout Location	First-base side
Phone	1-877-RED-SOXX (1-877-733-7699)
	or 1-239-334-4700
Address	2201 Edison Av., Ft. Myers

From I-75, take Exit 23 West onto Martin Luther King Blvd., turn left on Fowler St. and then right on Edison Avenue.

A Little New England on the Gulf Coast

No, it's not as though Legal Seafoods or the T can be found on every street corner in the surprisingly bustling Fort Myers. But there's a definite Boston flavor to the city when the Red Sox begin spring-training workouts, as thousands of members of Red Sox Nation can be counted on to show up for a simple practice or line up ten deep in hopes of snaring a ticket to a high-profile spring game. The Red Sox are surely the most popular draw in spring training: Their fans follow the team on the road like no others (giving teams like Toronto some of their only sellouts during the spring-training season), and Boston has no problem selling out virtually every seat in City of Palms Park for the month of March.

In fact, many of the seats are sold out long before the Red Sox release single-game tickets to the public. During our most recent visit we snared seats behind the Sox' dugout and were surrounded by a sea of New England retirees, whose only purpose in investing in Fort Myers retirement condos was to buy spring season tickets to the Red Sox. They were there every day, spending as much time discussing Jon Lester's spring performances as their own assorted and ongoing health ailments.

These people are the backbone of the Red Sox spring-training experience, though: passionate and educated. Arrive two hours before a Red Sox spring match and you'll find hordes of fans already milling around City of

One of the best seats in the house: Behind the Red Sox dugout.

Palms Park and filling the large parking lot to the west. If you don't have a ticket, don't worry — surely one of the many, many ticket scalpers cruising the area would be happy to get you into the gates (at a nice markup, of course: This is a milieu where $24 tickets go for at least $100).

To say the Red Sox in Fort Myers represents all that's good about spring training is an understatement. You have a small, quaint ballpark surrounded by palm trees — showing that Fort Myers is indeed the city of palms — and set in the midst of a quiet neighborhood, a move by former city leaders to try to clean up the area. (The jury is still out as to whether it worked.) The local Rotary Club still manages the parking lot, and volunteers man the concession stands. True, you know you're at a Major League game because of the high concession prices — $4 for a rather ordinary hot dog (not even a Fenway Frank!) is pretty steep — but that fresh smell of floral spring is a continual reminder of where you are. The sense of place at City of Palms Park is overwhelming, and during March there's no better place for a baseball fan than in Section 105, Row 3, Seat 5.

insider's tip

The Red Sox do not train at City of Palms Park; rather, workouts take place at the Fort Myers Minor League Facility, located 2.5 miles east of City of Palms Park on Edison Avenue. The Red Sox and the city limit parking access at the complex, so don't park on the street: The cops will indeed tow you if you're parked illegally, and there's very little legal parking in the area. Instead, you're encouraged to park at the ballpark and take a $2 bus to the workouts, which are free but come with a price of sorts: The Red Sox have managed to sell sponsorships to practices, so be prepared to stare at a Dunkin' Donuts outfield panel. Workouts begin at 9 a.m., but fans will begin taking the shuttle at 7:30 a.m. to snare a good position along the fence. That's right, along the fence: There is minimal bleacher seating at the practice facility, and fans are positioned outside the barricades. Some practices attract thousands of fans, so be prepared for some sharp elbows and cramped quarters. On the plus side, vendors are usually on hand selling hot dogs and soda, so you won't go hungry. Be patient when trying to score autographs at practices: players won't sign on their way out to workouts, but they'll sign on their way back to the clubhouse.

Once games start the team works out mornings at City of Palms Park, but these workouts are not open to the public.

ABOUT THE BALLPARK

Fort Myers in Lee County has been the spring-training home of the Boston Red Sox since 1993, when the team moved from Winter Haven. There's nothing particularly Boston-like in the ballpark, as it's certainly no miniature Fenway Park: No Green Monster, no Fenway Franks, no Yawkey Way. However, there are a few homages to the Red Sox tradition. Enter the front gates and you'll be greeted by a larger-than-life statue of Ted Williams, who never actually played at City of Palms Park; he played during the era the Red Sox trained in Sarasota. You'll also be able to buy a Boston paper from a box outside the park if you want to keep up-to-date with what's happening at home.

The stadium is done in a pure Florida style, with a main covered grandstand and palm trees past the outfield fence. There are two sections separated by a concourse: The section closest to the action contains box seats, and the section past the concourse contains bleachers. The complex contains a 9,000-square-foot visiting-team clubhouse and four enclosed batting tunnels.

City of Palms Park has been expanded in the last several years to hold 7,700 fans, but that's not close to filling demand — we imagine the Red Sox could build a 20,000-seat ballpark and barely fill the spring demand — and the Red Sox cap season ticket sales at 3,000 (the waiting list is three years). We don't say this to dissuade you from making the trip to Fort Myers to watch the Sox, but seeing the Red Sox in spring is such a challenge, and it will definitely need some planning on your part. Tickets to some games, such as for the Yankees' annual visit to Fort Myers, are virtually impossible to acquire, as are traditional highlights like the St. Patrick's Day match. The only advice here is either to work the phones or the Internet when tickets go on sale or be willing to pay extra to a ticket broker.

insider's tip

There are two games that do not immediately sell out. Traditionally, the Red Sox play a day-night doubleheader against Boston College and Northeastern early in March. Despite the fact tickets for these games are offered at half price, they don't sell out, as most fans correctly deduce the chance of seeing more than one or two Red Sox stars in action are between slim and none; you're basically watching minor leaguers take the field. Still, the Sox are the Sox, and we've found these games to be as delightful as most early-spring games.

In fact, unless you know a retiree or two in the area, you can forget about sitting in the best seats for a Red Sox game unless you go through a broker like **ballparkdigesttickets.com**. The seating in City of Palms Park is set up in a traditional manner, with box seats closest to the action and reserved seats in back of a small walkway that extends down each line. A small second level includes a large press box and a few suites. In general, the second level and a large canopy shade the third-base seating and much of the seating behind home plate. If you want to sit near the Red Sox dugout, be prepared to lather on the sunscreen.

insider's tip

The Red Sox put 200 or so tickets on sale the day of the game at 9 a.m. As you might expect, be prepared to queue early for these tickets.

A small berm area and bleachers are located down the right-field line, while a newer deck is located beyond right field. This is definitely a sun field: Bring the sunscreen and the sunglasses. Still, it's the hottest party area in the ballpark, thanks to the 400 barstool seats and freestanding bar.

All concessions are located behind the grandstand. This is also the place to grab some shelter should you encounter a spring shower.

insider's tip

The Red Sox do not conform with MLB guidelines regarding food in the ballpark: The Red Sox say no outside food or drink allowed no matter how it is packaged. However, we've found the folks at the front gates to be a little more liberal than the rules indicate, and we've brought in peanuts and unopened water containers. Just be discreet; don't attempt to bring in a soft-sided cooler, for instance.

The large canopy provides plenty of shade, especially on the third-base side.

Even visiting players are eager to sign autographs at City of Palms Park.

The Minnesota Twins also train in Fort Myers, making for a nice little rivalry when the teams square off multiple times during the first few weeks of spring training. The Tampa Bay Rays shifted spring operations to nearby Port Charlotte, which should give them an attendance boost when the Red Sox visit.

SPRING TRAINING HISTORY

The Boston Red Sox have trained in the following locations: Charlottesville, Va. (1901); Augusta, Ga. (1902); Macon, Ga. (1903-1906); Little Rock (1907-1908); Hot Springs, Ark. (1909-1910); Redondo Beach, Cal. (1911); Hot Springs, Ark. (1912-1918); Tampa (1919); Hot Springs, Ark. (1920-1923); San Antonio (1924); New Orleans (1925-1927); Bradenton (1928-1929); Pensacola, Fla. (1930-1931); Savannah (1932); Sarasota (1933-1942); Medford, Mass. (1943-1944); Atlantic City (1945); Sarasota (1946-1958); Scottsdale (1959-1965); Winter Haven (1966-1992); Fort Myers (1993-present).

BALLPARK HISTORY

The Red Sox have been training at City of Palms Park since the ballpark opened.

THE SPRING-TRAINING BALLPARK EXPERIENCE

Concessions

City of Palms Park is not known for a plethora of interesting concessions. For some reason, the team does not offer Fenway Franks or anything reminiscent of Fenway Park; instead, the fare veers toward the tried-and-true: hot dogs, burgers, pizza, soda, beer (Kirin and Sam Adams in bottles, Bud products on tap), etc. Most concessions are located in the walkway within the grandstand, but a freestanding bar is located in the right-field bench. Picnic tables are located on the first-base side of the walkway should you want to sit down and eat before entering the ballpark.

Parking

Parking is adjacent to the ballpark and costs $7. There is some free parking in the surrounding neighborhood, but you'll need to arrive pretty early to snare a decent spot.

Autographs

City of Palms Park used to be one of the hardest places to score an autograph, as the dugouts lead directly to the clubhouses, so unless a player is in the mood to be mobbed near the stands, they don't need to interact with fans before or after the game. In recent years the Red Sox players have seemed more cognizant of their responsibilities in terms of fan support, so you can find a few signing autographs next to the dugout before the game, especially at the tail-end of batting practice. The same goes for visitors: Our most recent visit was a Mets/Red Sox sellout, and New York's Johan Santana — of all people — was happily greeting fans and signing autographs. You can also try stalking players in the parking lot before the game, but security tends to frown on that.

IF YOU GO

What to Do Outside the Ballpark

Many Red Sox fans head over to Hammond Stadium to watch the Minnesota Twins play, even if Boston isn't the opposing team. The schedules are usually arranged so one of the two teams is in town. We expect many Red Sox fans to make the relatively short drive to Port Charlotte to see the Red Sox in action. And, of course, many Red Sox fans follow their team no matter how far the drive. In fact, we're sure so many readers of this book will follow the Red Sox on the road we've put together this handy little chart so you can plan your drive from Fort Myers. Distance and driving time doesn't always add up in Florida; taking the back roads can be an infuriating process, so it quite often takes less time to drive 140 miles than it does 109 miles when you're comparing a freeway route versus backroads.

Fort Myers to:	Distance	Time
Sarasota (Cincinnati)	83 miles	1.5 hours
Bradenton (Pittsburgh)	95 miles	1.75 hours
Jupiter (Cards/Marlins)	109 miles	3 hours
Port St. Lucie (Mets)	133 miles	3 hours
Clearwater (Philadelphia)	135 miles	2.25 hours
Tampa (Yankees)	138 miles	2.25 hours
Dunedin (Toronto)	138 miles	2.5 hours
Fort Lauderdale (Baltimore)	139 miles	2.25 hours
Lakeland (Detroit)	150 miles	2.5 hours
Lake Buena Vista (Atlanta)	190 miles	3 hours
Kissimmee (Houston)	200 miles	3 hours
Viera (Washington)	245 miles	3.75 hours

Since many Red Sox spring games are now televised, you should be able to find a bar with a Red Sox game on the dish when the team is on the road. Several bars in tonier Naples market to Boston expats.

As you would expect from the name, Boston Beer Garden markets to Boston sports fans, showing games on 30 plasma and two big-screen TVs. Bar food and cheap drinks all the way. Boston Beer Garden, 2396 Immokalee Rd., Naples; 239/596-BEER (2337); **bostonbeergardennaples.com**.

Along the same lines is the Foxboro Sports Tavern, which markets to Boston sports fans in then same manner: Lots of Boston sports on big-screen TVs and lots of references to Boston sports teams on the walls. Foxboro Sports Tavern, 4420 Thomasson Dr., Naples; 239/530/BEER (2337); **foxborotavern.com**.

Sal's Longshot Lounge in downtown Fort Myers brings in former Red Sox greats each spring for autograph sessions; past greats included Bill Lee and a natural, Luis Tiant. As you can imagine, there's a lot of market-ing at Sal's toward Red Sox Nation. Sal's is part of four interconnected bars attracting a diverse clientele. Sal's Longshot Lounge, 1508 Hendry St., Fort Myers; 239/337-4662; **cigarbarlive.com**.

In general, it's hard to go wrong hitting the bars of downtown Fort My-ers: Imagine a great bar crawl in (probably) warmer weather than you've been experiencing at home. Patio De Leon, a historic plaza, itself features a range of dining and drinking establishments: The Envie Lounge is a bit more upscale, the outdoor seating area at Patio 33 is a great environment for dinner and cocktails, and the Indigo Room features over 100 kinds of beer and a busy dance floor. We cover more Fort Myers hotspots in the previous chapter.

Where to Stay

Be warned hotel rooms are on the expensive side during spring training, and chances are pretty good you'll be fairly discomfited when paying more than $200 for what would be a $80 room in almost any other circumstance. So shop around and jump on any bargains. It's a very competitive market within the greater Fort Myers area, though you can save a whole lot of money if you're willing to drive in from Port Charlotte or Naples.

There's only one hotel within walking distance of City of Palms Park: the Holiday Inn Downtown Historic, a Quality Inn renovated in the fall of 2007. While the surrounding neighborhood isn't the greatest — don't stay out too late at night — the location of the hotel just three blocks from the ballpark makes it the best choice for Red Sox Nation, especially fans willing to shell out upwards of $300 for a hotel room. Holiday Inn Downtown Historic, 2431 Cleveland Av., Fort Myers.

Otherwise, you will drive to the ballpark. If you feel compelled to stay in the general area, a number of chain hotels can be found in North Fort Myers, Port Charlotte (which we'll cover in our Tampa Bay chapter), and in the southern part of Fort Myers, closer to the Minneso-

The concourse is small but functional.

49

ta Twins training facility (which, naturally, we'll cover in our Minnesota Twins chapter).

RV Parks

There are no RV parks within walking distance of the ballpark. Two RV parks are located within a close drive of the ballpark: Cypress Woods RV Resort (5551 Luckett Rd., Fort Myers; 888/299-6637; **cypresswoodsrv.com**) and Tice Courts (541 New York Dr., Fort Myers; 239/694-3545; **ticemobilehomecourt.com**). Cypress Woods RV Resort is located southeast of City of Palms Park, while Tice Courts is located northeast of downtown Fort Myers. There are other RV resorts closer to the beaches as well.

→ minnesota twins

HAMMOND STADIUM

Capacity	7,800
Year Opened	1991
Dimensions	330L, 404C, 330R
Surface	Grass
Local Airport	Ft. Myers
Home Dugout Location	Third-base side
Ticket Line	612/33-TWINS; 800/33-TWINS
Web Site	www.twinsbaseball.com
Address	14100 Six Miles Cypress Pkwy., Fort Myers. From I-75, take the Daniels Road exit west 2 miles to Six Miles Cypress Parkway; go south and the stadium is on the right.

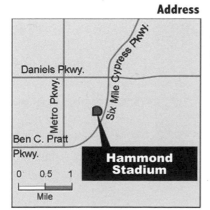

Fort Myers: From Pastures to Pennants

The Lee County Sports Complex in Fort Myers has been the spring-training home of the Minnesota Twins since 1991. It's a facility designed for the entire organization, with five full fields, two half fields, and a stadium serving as the home of the Fort Myers Miracle (Class A; Florida State League) and the Gulf Coast League Twins.

All the streets within the complex are named for Twins greats, a welcoming sight for Minnesota snowbirds who undoubtedly are disoriented by the lack of snow on the ground.

Hammond Stadium is an interesting ballpark, as it features an outside façade designed to invoke the feeling of Louisville's Churchill Downs. And while it's not in the most scenic of locales, Hammond Stadium does have enough little things to make a visit interesting even if you're not a Twins fan. A large fountain and waterfall are located directly outside the main gates of the ballpark, while another fountain in right field entertains fans.

Twins superfan Thomas Hovde, a fixture at Hammond Stadium.

There are only two levels of seats for spring training: box and reserved bleachers. Twins fans are passionate and annual attendees: Season tickets are strong, and there are frequently sellouts — especially when a strong draw like the Boston Red Sox is visiting. There is no escaping the presence of Red Sox Nation at Hammond Stadium, though: Red Sox fans will take in a Twins game if the Red Sox are out of town, and during a Red Sox/Twins matchup there's almost an even split between the loyalties in the stands. It would be interesting to see how the Twins would draw if the Red Sox were to ever leave Fort Myers. Sure, remaining would be hardcores like Thomas Hovde (one of the most notable presences in the stands; you can see him near the dugout, a loyal season-ticket holder), but it's not clear whether sellouts would be the norm.

But to give Lee County credit, they've worked to improve Hammond Stadium in recent years. When the Twins moved spring training in 1991 to Fort Myers, it was located out in the country; The land beyond the out field wall formerly was pastureland for cattle. Today there's development around the ballpark, but the end result was encroachment that probably means the ballpark will never be expanded too much, so the county and the Twins have worked on a few ways to spiffen up the experience. Most notable was the addition of a party deck in right field. While Hammond Stadium will probably never be one of these newer ballparks with a wraparound concourse and lots of places for standing and mingling, the addition of the deck did allow for a more casual baseball viewing experience.

And there are some other spots away from the action designed for mingling. If you're tired of your seats far down the line, head to the back of the concourse and pull up a chair at a bar and have a beer. Really, most spring-training games aren't important by the seventh or eighth innings, and a beer or two while perched on a bar stool wouldn't be the worst thing in the world.

The Twins recently signed a lease extension to stay at Hammond Stadium through the 2020s, not a surprise when you consider the team rarely moves spring-training facilities. The team has trained in Florida since their days as the Washington Senators: 1936 to the present (except for the war years of 1943-45, when the team trained in College Park, Maryland). Most of those years were spent training in Orlando's Tinker Field — 1936 through 1990 — while their minor-league teams trained in nearby Melbourne from 1964-1989 and Terry Park in 1990. The minor- and major-league camps were combined in Lee County in 1991. (We discuss Tinker Field, which still stands, in the Orlando chapter.)

The ballpark was named for Bill Hammond, the assistant director for Lee County who was a prime mover in attracting the Twins to Lee County.

The Boston Red Sox also train in Fort Myers, though much closer to downtown. As a result, you can expect to see many Twins/Red Sox scrimmages and games during the first month of spring training.

BALLPARK HISTORY

The Lee County Sports Complex has been the home of the Twins for its entire history, while Fort Myers has been home to several major-league clubs in its spring-training history. Nearby Terry Park Stadium is possibly the oldest surviving spring-training stadium in Florida; we discuss it ear-lier in the Fort Myers section.

THE SPRING-TRAINING BALLPARK EXPERIENCE

Concessions

The food served at Twins spring-training games is a little more upscale than the average spring-training facility. Why? Probably because of the demographics of spring season-ticket holders. Fort Myers is located near Naples, a rather affluent area of the state. Specifically, there's a community of moneyed Minnesotans who winter in Naples and then make their way north for a host of spring-training games. In addition to the normal ball-park fare (hot dogs, burgers, nachos, pop, and a wide selection of beer), the Twins also offer smoked turkey legs, freshly made pizza (none of that frozen stuff for the Naples crowd), ice-cream treats, and small bottles of merlot, Chardonnay and pinot grigio wines.

Autographs

There are no special areas within the ballpark to score autographs, and access to the practice fields is limited. However, Twins players are known for being very accessible before games, so you can expect a few to wander over to the grandstand to sign.

Parking

Parking costs $5 and is located next to the ballpark.

IF YOU GO

What to Do Outside the Ballpark

Fort Myers is in southwestern Florida, far away from the madding crowds of Tampa or Orlando. The closest foes for the Twins are the Boston Red

Lots of shade in the back of the Hammond Stadium grandstand.

Sox (who also train in Fort Myers) and the Tampa Bay Rays (who train in nearby Port Charlotte). It's 125 miles up the coast to Tampa/St. Pete and less than that to Bradenton (spring-training home of the Pittsburgh Pirates) or Sarasota (spring-training home of the Cincinnati Reds), so you're quite a ways down the coast.

We cover many of the local hotspots in our Fort Myers overview. You can sometimes find Twins players — usually rookies — at Potts Sports Café (6900 Daniels Pkwy., Fort Myers; 239/768-5500). It's a typical Florida sports bar: Virtually every one touts their wonderful grouper sandwich, and Pott's is no different. Even if no Twins are on the premises, it's a good place to stop after the game.

Otherwise, south Fort Myers is filled with every kind of chain restaurant imaginable along Tamiami Trail, which runs north-south through Fort Myers (eventually north to Port Charlotte, making it the route to take to go to spring-training facilities for the Boston Red Sox and Tampa Bay Rays). You won't starve if you head out of the ballpark and north onto Tamiami Trail, unless you're forever stuck in traffic — one of the unfortunate realities of March in Fort Myers.

Where to Stay

There's nothing within easy walking distance of the ballpark, due to its location on a fairly major throughway. Hotels closest to the ballpark include Crestwood Suites (7071 Lakeridge Court SW., Fort Myers; 239/415-8440; **crestwoodsuites.com**), Fairfield Inn (7090 Cypress Terrace, Fort Myers; 239/437-5600; **marriott.com**), and Homewood Suites (5255 Big Pine Way, Fort Myers; 239/275-6000; **hilton.com**). Traditionally the Twins have stayed at the Crowne Plaza (13051 Bell Tower Dr., Fort Myers; 239/482-2900; **holiday-inn.com**).

SPRING-TRAINING HISTORY

The Minnesota Twins/Washington Senators have held spring training in the following locations: Phoebus, Va. (1901); Washington, D.C. (1902-1904); Hampton, Va. (1905); Charlottesville, Va. (1906); Galveston, Texas (1907); Norfolk, Va. (1910); Atlanta (1911); Charlottesville, Va. (1912-1916); Atlanta (1917); Augusta, Ga. (1918-1919); Tampa (1920-1929); Biloxi, Miss. (1930-1935); Orlando (1936-1942); College Park, Md. (1943-1945); Orlando (1946-1990); Fort Myers (1991-present).

→ tampa bay rays

CHARLOTTE COUNTY SPORTS COMPLEX

Capacity	7,500 (6,000 fixed seats, 1,500 berm seating)
Year Opened	1986; renovated 2009
Surface	Grass
Local Airport	Fort Myers
Address	2300 El Jobean Road, Port Charlotte

From I-75, take Exit 170 for Highway 769/Kings Highway toward Port Charlotte. Turn left onto Highway 769/Kings Highway, and then things get a little complicated: You'll want to turn left at Peachland Boulevard, right at Birchcrest Boulevard, right at Bachmann Boulevard, and then a left on Veterans Boulevard, which will turn into El Jobean Road. You'll go down El Jobean for almost seven miles. The complex will be on your left.

The old ballpark was stripped to the girders and rebuilt.

Moving South

At first, it seems like an odd move for the Tampa Bay Rays to abandon one of the cushiest spring-training setups in baseball and leave scenic Al Lang Field in downtown St. Petersburg for a spring-training site once abandoned by the Texas Rangers.

But appearances can be deceiving, and there's a reason teams like to get away from home for spring training: It's hard for a team to bond when everyone is heading for home after each practice and game. Plus, major-league teams increasingly want to locate everything — practice fields, spring ballpark, multiple clubhouses, year-round minor-league operations — in the same facility, and the split nature of Rays spring training at Al Lang Field and the Naimoli Complex split operations under several roofs.

And then there's the issue of the Rays being taken for granted because spring training wasn't considered by locals to be too special: Why make a point of heading for an afternoon game in March when the team would be safely ensconced at Tropicana Field for the season? It was at the point where the Rays weren't even the biggest draw in their own town, as both the Yankees and Phillies outdraw the Rays in spring training, and so the decision was made to relocate operations where a more receptive audience would turn out in droves for spring baseball.

That receptive audience, Rays officials hope, is in Port Charlotte, the northern part of the growing Fort Myers area. True, Port Charlotte is the more working-class part of the area, and the Rays' new spring home, Charlotte County Sports Complex, isn't close to much of anything, really. But the Rays and Charlotte County are extensively renovating the former spring home of the Texas Rangers, a nondescript facility for most of the decade-plus Texas was a tenant, while the rest of the complex will serve as an extended spring-training base and potentially the home of a Class A Florida State League. Over $27 million was spent on a complete makeover of the ballpark and the rest of the complex. The ballpark was stripped down to its concrete base and was remade with new seating, a center-field tiki bar, outfield berms, a restaurant, new suites, and family picnic areas down each line. In addition, a new entrance will greet visitors with a festive atmosphere.

Players will appreciate the new 40,000-square-foot clubhouse, full-size major-league practice field, one half field, and four full-size minor-league practice fields. In addition, there's parking for 1,500 cars. It should provide quite the Florida experience: Alligators have been known to patrol the ponds surrounding the ballpark.

The Tampa Bay Rays have had the unfortunate luck of always operating under another team's shadow, especially in spring training. The move to Charlotte County will give the Rays a chance to create their own traditions and identity in what will basically be a new facility.

The setting is pure Florida: water next to the ballpark, with a chance of alligators.

BALLPARK HISTORY

Charlotte Sports Complex was formerly the spring home of the Texas Rangers from 1986 through 2002, when the team shifted operations to Surprise, Arizona. In 2007 it served as the home of the best-drawing team in the independent South Coast League, the Charlotte County Redfish. For the Rays, the ballpark was stripped down to its concrete base and rebuilt. We're guessing area baseball fans and former Rangers spring-training attendees won't recognize the place.

THE SPRING-TRAINING BALLPARK EXPERIENCE

It is a little hard to preview what will happen in the future when it comes to things like concessions and such (as this book went to press, the Rays were still working out the details themselves), so we'll just say parking shouldn't be an issue at the complex — there's plenty in the surrounding area.

IF YOU GO

The Boston Red Sox and the Minnesota Twins train in nearby Fort Myers. In addition, the Cincinnati Reds train up the freeway in Sarasota, and the many teams training in the Tampa-St. Pete area are a two-hour drive away.

The team's former spring-training home, Al Lang Field.

What to Do

Charlotte County Sports Complex isn't exactly situated in the midst of a scenic Florida locale. True, a four-lane highway provides easy access for fans. But the livestock expo across the highway and a nearby motorcycle repair shop really don't add much to the ambiance.

Port Charlotte is located on the northern part of the Fort Myers metro area and is considered to be the more working-class area: Whereas Naples and Lee County attracts the bigger buck residents, most of Port Charlotte's main strip — Hwy. 41 — is made up of strip malls and big-box retailers. If you're coming down from Tampa-St. Pete or up from Fort Myers, don't expect a scenic drive in Charlotte County.

Like most Florida cities on the Gulf Coast, Port Charlotte is oriented toward the waterfront, and it's there you'll find restaurants and nightlife. Places like the Portside Tavern (3636 Tamiami Trail, Port Charlotte; 941/629-3055) and Patio 33 (33 Patio de Leon, Port Charlotte; 239/461-2727) feature DJs and drink promotions, while downtown hot spots like EnVie (2213 Main St., Port Charlotte; 239/337-0909) feature live music and Portofino (23241 Bayshore Rd., Port Charlotte; 941/743-2800) advertises both casual and upscale dining with views of the harbor. Nearby Punta Gorda and Fisherman's Village features a downtown and somewhat more upscale nightlife scene as well; Benedetto's (300 Retta Esplanade, Punta Gorda; 941/639-9695; **benedettossteakhousemartinibar.com**) hits all the trends by billing itself as an Italian steakhouse/martini bar.

There's also an artsy side to the area: The Charlotte Symphony Orchestra is a fixture at the Charlotte Center for Performing Arts & Education (941/625-5996; **charlottesymphony.com**).

Where to Stay

There is nothing within walking distance of the ballpark. Most chains are represented in downtown Port Charlotte, which is a little more than three miles west of the ballpark, while other accommodations can be found eight miles away in Punta Gorda.

RV Parks

The closest RV park is about 10 miles away on the east side of I-75. The Riverside RV Resort & Campground is on the Peace River and offers heated pools and pontoon rentals. Riverside RV Resort & Campground, 9770 SW. Co. Rd. 769 (Kings Highway), Arcadia; 800/795-9733; **riversidervresort.com**.

SPRING-TRAINING HISTORY

The Tampa Bay Rays trained at historic Al Lang Field in downtown St. Petersburg from 1998 through 2008. Al Lang Field was the most historicball-park in the Grapefruit League, as the site has been used as a spring-training venue since 1916, when the Philadelphia Nationals first trained here from 1916-1921. Other teams calling Al Lang Field spring-training home include the Boston Braves (1922-1924), the New York Yankees (1925-1937), and the St. Louis Cardinals (1938-1997). The Al Lang moniker dates from the Cardinals era — 1947, to be exact — and comes from the original Al Lang, St. Petersburg's local "father of baseball," the mayor of the city who worked effortlessly to bring spring training to town. When the Cardinals left, the Rays became the first MLB team to train in its hometown since the 1919 St. Louis Cardinals and Philadelphia Athletics (save the wartime years of the 1940s, when spring training was interrupted). The ballpark is slated to be torn down; the Tampa Bay Rays want to use the site for a new major-league ballpark to replace Tropicana Field.

orlando

Orlando: More than the Magic Kingdom

Orlando relies heavily on the tourist economy and is synonymous with theme parks. It's never been a major hub for spring training, although the Washington Senators/Minnesota Twins were mainstays in Tinker Field for decades, and smaller venues like Sanford Stadium were pressed into service occasionally as training facilities. Today, only two teams — Atlanta and Houston — train in the immediate area, while Washington's home, Space Coast Stadium, is only a short drive away, and the many camps in the greater Tampa area — for the Tigers, Yankees, Phillies, and Blue Jays — are less than 90 minutes away. As a tourism hub, there's a lot to love about Orlando, and it makes a great home base for spring training, especially if you have kids.

If you attend spring training to spend 12 hours at the training complex and soak up every minute of time tracking the exploits of kids who will likely end up in Single-A ball at the start of the season, then Orlando is a waste of time for you: You're best off staying at the cheapest hotel closest to the training complex and not worrying about frills like amusement-park rides. (Don't worry, we'll tell you where these hotels are as well.) But for many of us, spring training is a renewal on many levels: A renewal of our baseball passion and a renewal of our general spirits. After a long, cruel winter we need some time in the sun, and that doesn't automatically mean baseball: It means baseball and more.

And more is in abundance in Orlando — conveniently located on the southwest side of town, as all three major Orlando attractions are located along Interstate 4. (Interstate 4 also leads directly to Tampa to the south, making it a handy route to Orlando for those attending spring-training games in Tampa and Lakeland.) The theme-park area is only 10-15 miles away from Orlando International Airport and features Disney World, Universal Orlando, and Sea World. Disney World is the closest theme park to the Atlanta and Houston training camps — in fact, Atlanta trains *inside* Disney World — so many fans will use the most popular theme park in the world as a base of operations. Also close to the Atlanta and Houston complexes are the bustling International Boulevard mélange of hotels and attractions, the Hwy. 192 strip, and the town of Celebration. We'll cover

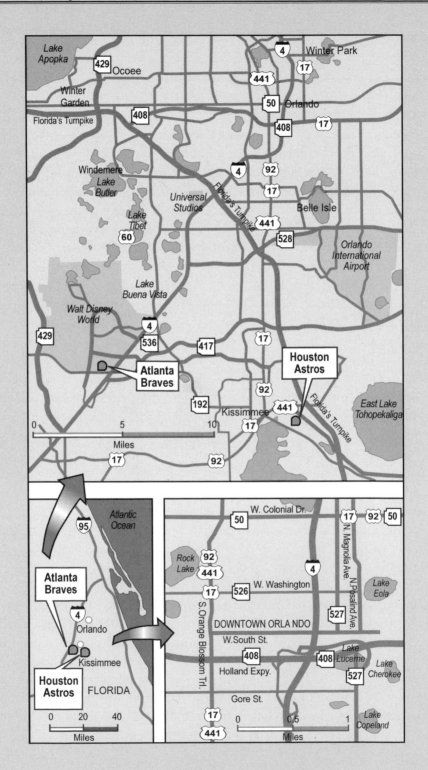

them all here, making recommendations for hotels and restaurants along the way.

The House of Mouse

Disney World is either the personification of all that is bad in America or one of the most wonderful places on the planet.

The truth is somewhere in between. Disney World can be a frustrating experience: The folks at Disney are well-versed in the art of customer manipulation, and waiting in line for a popular attraction isn't anyone's idea of a good time. And while the vision of Walt Disney can be hackneyed and clichéd at times, you never feel cheated after spending $200 on the family for an entire day at the Magic Kingdom or EPCOT. You truly do understand the magic of the Magic Kingdom when you have kids.

Of course, this certainly isn't the most original advice or a secret to most of you — after all, Disney World is one of the most popular places on the planet — but we're here to tell you the parks are worth the steep admission prices, and there's such a wide range of lodging, dining, and entertainment options that a stay there should be high on your priority list as you cast the perfect spring-training experience.

First, a general overview. To say that Disney World is a sprawling complex is an understatement: It encompasses more than 30,000 acres and still hews to the original vision set forth by Walt Disney, who decided on Orlando for a new theme-park location after studying highway maps and touring the area via helicopter. It features four theme parks, two water parks, literally tens of thousands of hotel rooms, a major retail and entertainment complex, and a wide range of restaurants and smaller attractions. It is a world unto itself, with its own transit system and police squad.

The Atlanta Braves train at the Wide World of Sports complex, located on the south side of the park. The ballpark has been known by several names — Cracker Jack Stadium, the Ballpark at Wide World of Sports — but a recent naming-rights deal means it's now Champion Stadium, as in the clothing manufacturer Champion. The Houston Astros train at Osceola County Stadium, located on Hwy. 192 in Kissimmee, east of Disney World. How much you decide to interact with Disney World depends on what team you follow: Dealing with the Mouse is mandatory if you're a Braves fan and less so if you're an Astros fan.

There are four theme parks under the Disney World umbrella:

➔ **The Magic Kingdom**, which is a re-creation and expansion of the original Disneyland in Los Angeles. It's divided into four "lands" — Frontierland, Fantasyland, Tomorrowland, Adventureland — and includes its own Main Street. Disney stalwarts like Pirates of the Caribbean, Space Mountain, Splash Mountain, Big Thunder Mountain, and It's a Small, Small World are located here. There's something for everyone here: The smaller kids will enjoy the Winnie the Pooh and Peter Pan rides, while teenagers will appreciate Splash Mountain and Space Mountain.

→ **EPCOT**, which combines visions of tomorrow in Future World and a World's Fair-type pavilion of nations in World Showcase. Some of the rides show their age, but in a good way: They're close to the same as when EPCOT opened in 1982, which makes for great nostalgia for you and a new experience for your kids. The newer rides, such as Mission: Space and Test Track, are worth the wait; they add an element of speed to what has traditionally been a laid-back theme park.

→ **Disney's Hollywood Studios**, where a slew of movie-themed attractions (Indiana Jones, Star Wars), thrill rides (Tower of Terror, Rock 'n Roller Coaster), and live shows featuring Playhouse Disney staples (Little Einsteins, Handy Manny) appeal to a wide variety of ages. (This theme park was formerly known as MGM/Disney Studios.)

→ **Animal Kingdom**, which transforms the swamps of Florida into a credible Serengeti Plain. The park is divided into geographic entities (Africa and Asia) as well as themes (like Dinoland USA). For the smaller kids, the Kilimanjaro Safari provides a safe, upclose look at a raft of exotic animals, while older kids will appreciate the thrilling Dinosaur (Countdown to Extinction) ride. (If you go on the Kali River Rapids ride, bring along a change of clothes — you will be drenched.)

It takes at least a half a day to get the most out of a Disney World park. Since most spring-training games start at 1:05 p.m., you can easily hit the ballpark early and catch a morning workout, watch the game, and be back at a theme park for a late night. (How late? In recent years Disney has instituted an Extra Magic Hours program, where certain parks open earlier and stay open later for those staying at a Disney resort. In the case of the Magic Kingdom, closing time can be as late as 2 a.m., depending on the day of the week. As a bonus, the crowds thin out and attractions are more accessible.) If you do this you'll need to plan ahead and purchase a Park Hopper pass for an additional fee, and you'll need to stay at a Disney resort. We'll cover the offerings at the Wide World of Sports complex in the Atlanta Braves chapter; it has its own small set of attractions besides the ballpark.

insider tips

→ Plan your meals in advance. The dining options at most of the theme parks can be limited, and if you don't want to eat fast food twice a day, you'll want to make reservations for sit-down restaurants in advance. Call 407/WDW-DINE for reservations and availability.

→ You could combine two parks in a day using a Disney Park Hopper pass — hitting Magic Kingdom in the morning and early afternoon and then EPCOT in the late afternoon for dinner and the fireworks. Recently, Disney extended the theme-park hours for those staying onsite in Disney resorts, sometimes as late as 2 a.m.

→ Disney offers a FastPass system, where you can sign up to come back later to a ride and cut to the front of the line. This works well for popular rides: You can check in for a Space Mountain jaunt in a couple of hours and then hit some other rides in the meantime.

→ If you have smaller children, check out the character dining options. At EPCOT, the revolving Garden Grill Restaurant features Mickey Mouse and friends, while the Norwegian restaurant, Akershus Royal Banquet Hall, is home to a princess dinner twice daily. In Magic Kingdom, the highlight of breakfast and lunch at Cinderella's Royal Table is a visit from Cinderella, while the Crystal Palace features visits from Winnie the Pooh and friends, and Liberty Tree Tavern features visits from Minnie Mouse.

→ Not everything carries a price tag at Disney World. If you want the Disney experience without the high admission prices, head over to Downtown Disney. Yes, the world's largest Disney-merchandise store is here, but the hip Virgin Megastore makes up for it. There are also some good restaurants, including a Wolfgang Puck Cafe (go for the meatloaf), House of Blues, and Bongo's Cuban Cafe. Pleasure Island is an adults-only area that features eight clubs with a wide variety of offerings, including dance clubs, comedy clubs, and bars. Wandering around Downtown Disney is free. There's a cover charge for Pleasure Island.

→ Also free: the late-afternoon feeding at the Animal Kingdom Lodge (located adjacent to the theme park). The resort is spectacular, and the feeding attracts zebras, giraffes, and other exotic animals from throughout the park.

Your first big decision, after you've decided to stay in Orlando, is whether or not to stay at Disney World. Astros fans may not be compelled to do so: Unless you want to watch your boys taking on the Braves at Disney World, you can have a lovely time on vacation without setting foot on Disney soil. If you're a Braves fan, we'd recommend looking seriously at staying at a Disney World resort. Yes, it will be more expensive than staying at the Comfort Inn on International Drive, and rooms in Disney resorts tend to be on the smaller side, but how many times are you going to be at spring training? The extended hours at the theme parks offered only to resort guests is also a persuasive argument for staying onsite.

insider's tip

A big decision is whether or not to rent a car for a Disney World visit. The transportation system in Orlando basically consists of a lot of cabs, some limited bus service, and the Disney transit system. There are lots of families who rely on Disney buses to take them from the airport to a resort, and then to a theme park. In spring training, you can also rely on those buses to get you around, though you may end up waiting a long time for service. (For the impatient, there are cabs.) So, it's very possible to do a spring-training trip without a rental car. Just be prepared for queues.

And be prepared to pay tolls. While I-4 is not a toll road, there are several in Orlando, including the Florida Turnpike and the two main highways leading to the airport. It is theoretically possible to make your way to and from Orlando International Airport without paying a toll, but it requires patience and a knowledge of the Orlando road system. Be sure to have some cash; you'll need around $5 each way for tolls.

Disney does make it easier by offering hotel rooms in four price ranges: Deluxe Villa ($399+ nightly), Deluxe ($355+ nightly), Moderate ($150+ nightly), and Value ($150 nightly). (Room rates at Disney World go up in March, but that's because of the prevalence of spring breaks during the month, not because of the hordes of spring-training fans.) Luckily, the resorts in the Value range are also the ones closest to the Wide World of Sports complex. Baseball fans and their families will like Disney's All-Star Sports Resort: There's a section with a baseball theme, and the swimming pool is in the shape of a baseball diamond. The All-Star Movies Resort features two swimming pools and a Hollywood theme throughout. The All-Star Music Resort features pools shaped like a guitar and a piano, as well as rooms with different musical genres. Now, under most circumstances these resorts are outliers, located far away from the four theme parks. But in the world of spring training these resorts truly are All-Stars.

If staying within walking distance of a theme park is a bigger concern for you, then be sure to check out the Deluxe accommodations close to the Magic Kingdom, EPCOT, or Animal Kingdom.

Eating at Disney World

Staying in Disney World means taking in a meal or three there. Surprisingly, the food options are mixed. The resorts all have restaurants of some sort — food courts in the Value resorts, five-star dining in the Deluxe resorts — but food in the theme parks can be hit or miss.

The best (and some of the most expensive) restaurants in Disney World are located in EPCOT's World Showcase: Recommended are Le Cellier Steakhouse in the Canada Pavilion, Restaurant Marrakesh in the Morocco Pavilion, and Rose & Crown Dining Room in the United Kingdom Pavilion. Also recommended: Coral Reef in Future World's Living Seas attraction, where you can sit next to one of the largest aquariums in Florida and watch the sharks swim by; and Garden Grill, where younger kids can meet a slew of Disney characters as they wait for their meals.

The food levels fall off dramatically outside EPCOT. The best restaurant in Disney's Hollywood Studios (past the ridiculously expensive Brown Derby) is the Sci-Fi Dine-In Theater, where families sit in cars and watch old science-fiction clips on a big screen as in a drive-in theater. OK food, terrific atmosphere. And in the Magic Kingdom, fast food rules.

As we mentioned, each resort does have some sort of restaurant, whether it be the food court at Disney's All-Star Sports Resort or a Todd English restaurant at the Swan and Dolphin. Beware: You'll find it difficult to walk out of a decent resort restaurant without paying $30 or $40 for a meal for two. You will pay for the convenience of dining onsite anywhere in Disney World, and nowhere is that more true than in a resort.

Disney World, 407/WDW-MAGIC (939-6244); **disneyworld.com**. *A one-day pass for a single park costs $71 for an adult, $60 for a child (3-9), free for 2 and under. A four-day Park Hopper pass costs $257 for an adult, $223 for a child (nine years old and younger). Discounts apply if the tickets are purchased in advance.*

The Universal Orlando Resort isn't quite as large and sprawling as Disney World, but there are some high-end on-site venues there. The young and hip will want to check out Hard Rock Hotel, while the more staid will want to look at Portofino Bay Hotel or Royal Pacific Report, which are both Loews properties inside Universal. The two theme parks at Universal — Universal Studios and Islands of Adventure — are aimed at a hipper demographic slightly older than the Disney demographic: Whereas Disney has a few thrill rides throughout its four parks, Universal has several with Marvel Comics themes (Spider-Man, The Hulk) at Islands of Adventure, and movie-themed attractions (Men in Black, The Terminator) at Universal Studios. For younger kids, there's a Dr. Seuss island at Islands of Adventure and a Nickelodeon Studios area at Universal Studios. The Universal CityWalk area is similar to Downtown Disney, with restaurants, bars, and shopping.

Universal Studios, 1000 Universal Studios Plaza, 407/363-8000; **universalstudios.com**. *A one-day pass to Universal Studios purchased in advance costs $73 for an adult, $61 for a child (3-9), free for 2 and under. A two-day Orlando ticket that includes unlimited admission to Universal Orlando, Islands of Adventure, and Wet 'N Wild Orlando costs $99.99 for both adults and children 3-9. An Orlando flex ticket that includes unlimited admission to Sea-World Orlando, Aquatica, Universal Orlando, Islands of Adventure, and Wet 'N Wild Orlando costs $234.95 for adults, $194.95 for a child (3-9).*

Sea World Orlando may not be as glitzy as Universal Orlando or large as Disney World, but it's perhaps a more authentic Florida experience. Sea World combines tried-and-true attractions, like Shamu the Killer Whale, with a plethora of dining options including an underwater grill and some amusement rides, such as Kraken (the largest roller coaster in Orlando) and Journey to Atlantis, billed as a combination roller coaster and water coaster. The Waterfront at Sea World combines restaurants with shopping and other attractions.

Discovery Cove is a high-end, intensive water-park experience where you can swim with dolphins, hang out with rays, snorkel in a coral reef, and more. Admission is limited to 1,000 visitors a day, so you won't feel suffocated by swarms of people.

Sea World Orlando, intersection of Interstate 4 and Bee Line Expressway, 407/351-3600; **seaworld.com**. *A one-day pass costs $69.95 for an adult, $59.95 for a child (3-9), free for 2 and under. Admission to Sea World and Discovery Cove costs $242.* Past the Big Three in Orlando attractions, there are a host of alternatives for family entertainment. There's a long tradition of tourist traps in the Orlando area, and many of them can be found along Route 192 in Kissimmee. Want to see the world's largest orange-shaped building? Then Route 192 is the place for you.

For the ultimate in old-school Orlando, there's Gatorland. All gators all the time, Gatorland features gators jumping for chickens at meal time, gators wrestled by gator wranglers, and gators pretending to attack Gatorland workers. Gatorland has been around since 1949, and while it features family-oriented activities like a water park and petting zoo, Gatorland is really a celebration of the great reptile that can scare the crap out of small kids.

Gatorland, 14501 S. Orange Blossom Trail, Orlando; 800/393-JAWS; **gatorland.com**. *Adults, $22.99; children (3-12), $14.99.*

WonderWorks is one of the odder attractions in a town full of them. Basically, the premise of this attraction on International Drive is that a top-secret lab in the Bermuda Triangle was uprooted by a hurricane and deposited upside down in Orlando. The experiments in the lab survived and are available for use by visitors. Throw in some laser tag, dinner theater, and a magic show, and you've got an experience for the whole family.

WonderWorks, 9067 International Dr., Orlando; 407/351-8800; **wonderworksonline.com**. *Adults, $18.45; children, $13.45.*

Finally, families will enjoy a trip out to Kennedy Space Center: It's a straight shot down the Bee Line Expressway toward the Space Coast. We cover the Kennedy Space Center in our section on the Washington Nationals, who train at Space Coast Stadium.

Orlando Hotels

One of the nicer things about Orlando is the plethora of hotel options, especially on the western side of town, close to Disney World, Sea World, and Universal Studios. International Drive is a popular destination, and it contains a wide variety of hotel options, ranging from $55-per-night Econo Lodge to the $400-per-night Rosen Plaza. There's such a multitude of hotels that a listing here would be futile: You're best off checking out Travelocity, Expedia, or Hotels.com for a fuller listing of available properties. The great thing about Orlando is that spring training doesn't generate enough traffic to significantly drive up hotel prices in the area. You can find a wide number of properties in any price range, and some hotels you assume are expensive — like a Peabody or a Gaylord — can be moderate thanks to the competition.

For those attending spring training, your best bet is a hotel either within the city of Lake Buena Vista or in the southwest quadrant of Orlando. Besides the resorts in Disney World, there are a ton of hotel rooms in the greater Orlando/Kissimmee area. World Center Drive is technically within the grounds of Disney World, but the hotels along the drive are run by outside vendors and include such names as Hilton, Doubletree, Sheraton, and Best Western. You'll rarely spend more than $275 a night on World Center Drive, with most of the rates at the $150-$185 range. The prices go down even more once you leave the Disney World grounds. The Orlando and Kissimmee areas around Disney World (especially those on International Drive and Hwy. 192) feature a slew of decent hotels with room rates under $125, with family suites at a hotel like the Clarion Suites running $140 or so a night. The family may enjoy Nickolodeon Family Suites (14500 Continental Gateway, Orlando; 407/387-5437; **nickhotel.com**), where every room is a family suite and you can dine with the likes of Jimmy Neutron or SpongeBob Squarepants. You may also want to check out resorts from the likes of Radisson and Hyatt. Virtually every brand-name hotel is represented between Sea World and Disney World. You may want to consider staying in Celebration, a Disney-planned community southeast of Disney World. We're not going to get into the politics of Celebration (let's just say Disney has exerted a level of control over Celebration that has been dissected elsewhere), but Celebration is a very attractive community. The Celebration Hotel (700 Bloom St., Celebration; 407/566-6000; **celebrationhotel.com**) is located at the end of Celebration's main street and overlooks a small lake. It's decorated in a Florida plantation style — worth a look.

We will cover hotels close to Osceola County Stadium in the Houston Astros chapter.

The International Drive Area

Spend time with locals and they'll probably have some strong feelings about the sprawl on International Drive, a seemingly endless row of hotels, strange attractions, and "outlet" shops alongside I-4 between Sea World and Disney World. The density of the attractions can be overwhelming, and the general tackiness of many can add a depressing air to what is generally a festive town.

But the International Drive area serves a useful purpose: It provides an affordable level of accommodations for families of all sizes. Again, some of the least expensive tourist accommodations in the Orlando area can be found on International Drive, and we're talking about reasonably well-kept hotels. Locals may hate the area, but it's perfectly fine for you.

SPRING-TRAINING HISTORY

History and ballpark buffs will want to make the pilgrimage to Tinker Field, the former springtime home of the Washington Senators and Minnesota Twins.

Tinker Field is the former home of the Orlando Rays, who left much behind when they left town.

Baseball has been played at the Tinker Field site since 1914, and the stadium was named after Joe Tinker — he of "Tinker to Evers to Chance" fame — who came to Orlando after his playing days and made his mark as a developer and land speculator. The original 1,500-seat wooden Tinker Field was built in 1923 and served as the spring-training home of the Cincinnati Reds from 1923 through 1933, and the Brooklyn Dodgers trained there in 1934 and 1935. In 1936 Clark Griffith moved the Senators' spring training to Tinker Field, and for many years the Twins' AA affiliate played there as well. Almost 1,000 of the seats were moved to Tinker Field from Griffith Stadium when that Washington landmark closed. Those seats are still there, as is a bust at the front entrance honoring Griffith. Over the years it served as home to various Florida State League and Southern League teams, and it now serves as a high-school baseball site and the home of a summer-collegiate Florida State Collegiate League team.

Even though baseball has been played at Tinker Field since 1914, the present Tinker Field configuration dates back to 1963 and has been updated several times since. It features an open design: The press box is totally open to the crowd, and a spacious concourse allowed fans to mill around during the game. The FSCL team has cleaned up the place, and it's now a pleasant place to take in a game. Since area high schools still use the facility, there's a good chance you'll see some baseball if you drop by.

UCF's Jay Bergman Field.

We definitely recommend visiting Tinker Field during the day. Its Orlando neighborhood is not the best part of town, and the area around the Citrus Bowl can feel a little cut off at times.

Tinker Field, 287 South Tampa Av., Orlando. *The ballpark is part of the Citrus Bowl complex, right off the East-West Expressway (which, unfortunately, is a toll road). Just take the Citrus Bowl exit north and the ballpark is to your left, on the west side of the complex.*

Boston Braves fans will remember the days when Sanford Stadium was the team's spring-training home. Built in 1926, the ballpark has been immaculately maintained over the years and now hosts high-school tourneys every spring and a Florida State Collegiate League each summer. It's still a lovely place to take in a game. While we don't recommend you make a special trip to see the place because of the toll charges — unless you have fond memories of attending games there in springs past and want to revisit those times — it's located close to the Sanford airport, a worthy diversion if you're flying into this secondary airport. Historic Sanford Stadium, 1201 S. Mellonville Av., Sanford.

COLLEGE BASEBALL IN THE AREA

If you fly down to Orlando, chances are good some sort of traveling baseball or softball team will be sharing the plane with you. Florida is a mecca for college teams in March, and many of them end up at college ballparks or former spring-training complexes to cram in as many games as they can during a spring-break trip.

Two major colleges are located in the Orlando area, and their ballparks are worth the drive. (Interestingly, they are both located northeast of downtown Orlando, right off University Boulevard.) The University of Central Florida (UCF) Knights play at Jay Bergman Field, named for former Knights coach Jay Bergman. The athletic facilities at UCF are located in the northwest corner of campus, and the ballpark is situated next to a new arena and a new football stadium. It's a nice, small, facility, seating less than 1,000 fans, and if a big-name school is in town, there's a chance the game could be a sellout. So arrive early and claim a seat in front of the small press box. After you do that, walk around the small ballpark. There's plenty of interesting mosaic tilework in the concourse, and a small concession stand will keep you fed. Jay Bergman Field, 4000 Central Florida Blvd., Orlando; **ucfathletics.cstv.com**.

Rollins College is a small liberal-arts college in nearby Winter Park known for its academics and elite admissions standards, but it's no slouch on the baseball side, as the Tars regularly contend in the surprisingly tough D-II Sunshine State Conference (which includes the University of Tampa, which we discuss in our Tampa chapter, and Florida Southern, which we discuss in our Lakeland chapter) and is the smallest school to ever compete in the College World Series. (Former major leaguers John Castino and Clay Bellinger played for Rollins.) The team's home isn't actually on campus, but rather off the main Fairbanks Avenue drag. Alfond Stadium at Harper-Shepherd Field, the home of the Tars since 1983, is a smaller, quaint facility where seating is located on a raised grandstand, giving you a great view of the action. Every March Rollins hosts a very good tournament, Baseball Week, bringing in some of the better teams from around the country. It's worth checking out the schedule if you're a college baseball fan. Alfond Stadium at Harper-Shepherd Field, 801 Orange Av., Winter Park.

OTHER SPORTS

Baseball isn't the only game in town in March. The Orlando Magic (NBA) play at the downtown Amway Arena, as do the Orlando Predators of the Arena Football League. Amway Arena was built before arenas became the equivalent of a 18,000-seat rec room; it's a functional facility, but it lacks the extensive restaurants and amenities you find in newer arenas. See it now before the Magic and Predators move to a new downtown arena. Amway Arena, 600 W. Amelia St., Orlando; 407/849-2020; **orlandovenues.net**.

KISSIMMEE

When you envision tourist-trap Florida, chances are good you're envisioning Kissimmee. Located to the south of Orlando, Kissimmee contains a host of roadside attractions hearkening back to the old days when tacky and outrageous attractions (see the gators eat chickens! look at the giant orange!) vied for the attention of skeptical tourists. There's a rich tradition of hucksterism in Florida, and while much of its has abated throughout the state as fewer people take the back roads, it's alive and well in Kissimmee.

We'll spend more time on the peculiar charms of Kissimmee in our chapter on the Houston Astros — who train there — but here we'll highlight some Kissimmee restaurants for anyone attending spring training in the greater Orlando area.

Florida barbeque tends to be on the bland side — as anyone who's eaten at Sonny's knows — but Fat Boys' Bar-b-que bucks the trend with flavorful ribs and brisket. Fat Boys' Bar-b-que, 1606 W. Vine St., Kissimmee; 407/847-7098.

Azteca's is renowned for its authentic Mexican food by local restaurant critics. Any restaurant with beef tongue on its menu is OK by us. Azteca's, 809 N. Main St., Kissimmee; 407/933-8155; **aztecasmexrestaurant.com**.

Kissimmee Steak Company: Red meat and lots of it. Orlando isn't known as a great steak town, but this is a notable local outpost. Kissimmee Steak Company, 2047 East Irlo Bronson Memorial Hwy., Kissimmee; 407/ 847-8050.

Everett's Old Tymes Eatery serves liquor, but it really shines as a breakfast spot. The portions are huge and the prices are low. Everett's Old Tymes Eatery, 2754 N. Orange Blossom Trail, Kissimmee; 407/933-4400.

Located on the grounds of the Gaylord Palms Resort on the western edge of Kissimmee (fairly close to Disney World), the Old Hickory Steakhouse is made up to look like an old backwoods Florida restaurant, complete with a faux Florida swamp setting. Despite the themey decor, the food is excellent, if not a little on the French side: Your choice of meat (steak, bison tenderloin, veal, venison, capon) comes with a choice of sauces (bearnaise, au poivre, bordelaise). 6000 W. Osceola Pkwy., Kissimmee; 407/586-0000; **gaylordhotels.com**. The same complex contains Sunset Sam's Fish Camp, a more moderately priced seafood joint.

Flying In

Orlando International Airport is near the center of the city. While Orlando International is one of those sprawling affairs where trams take you out to remote terminals, it's fairly easy to make your way around — just be prepared for some very significant lines at check-in and security. (When they tell you to be at the airport at least two hours before your flight, they mean it here: It's not unusual to spend 30-45 minutes in the security lines in Orlando.) However, the main concourse of the airport resembles a large mall, so you'll have one last chance to stock up on Disney or Universal trinkets before your flight. Virtually every major and budget airline flies into Orlando International.

Despite being a large airport, there are relatively few car-rental agencies on site: only Alamo, Avis, Budget, Dollar, L & M, and National. If you rent with anyone else — like Hertz — you'll need to take a shuttle to an off-site facility. If you're traveling with the family and have a lot of luggage, bite the bullet and pay extra to rent from an on-site rental agency.

Orlando International Airport, Airport Blvd., Orlando; 407/825-2001; **orlandoairports.net**.

Orlando International is not the only airport in the Orlando area, however. Allegiant Air uses Orlando Sanford International Airport as an Orlando hub, and it's surprising how many cities are on the Allegiant Air route system with nonstop flights to Sanford (Greenville/Spartanburg, Sioux Falls, McAllen, to name just a few). Orlando Sanford International Airport is a smaller facility located in the northeast corner of Orlando. Alamo, Avis, Dollar, and Hertz all rent cars on site as well. Bring your cash, because you'll need to pay tolls to make your way anywhere from Sanford unless you're willing to take the back roads everywhere.

Orlando Sanford International Airport, 1200 Red Cleveland Blvd., Sanford; 407/585-4000; **orlandosanfordairport.com**.

→ atlanta braves

CHAMPION STADIUM

Capacity	9,500
Year Opened	1997
Dimensions	335L, 385LC, 400C, 385RC, 335R
Workouts Begin	9:30 a.m.
Address	700 S. Victory Lane, Lake Buena Vista, Disney World.

Lake Buena Vista is located in the southwest corner of Orlando. Take I-4 to Hwy. 192 West and follow signs to Magic Kingdom/Wide World of Sports, and take a right onto Victory Way. Directions at Disney World are clear and plentiful, but curiously there's no signage that points the direction to Champion Stadium. Instead, follow the signs to Wide World of Sports.

Champion Stadium

4

Osceola Pkwy.

Victory Way

W. Vine St.

192

417

0   0.5   1   KISSIMMEE

Mile

Baseball in the House of the Mouse

You can't accuse the Atlanta Braves of running a Mickey Mouse operation — even though the Braves spend March in the House of Mouse. The combination of Atlanta baseball fans and the family atmosphere of Disney World make for an irresistible spring-training experience.

The Braves train at Disney's Wide World of Sports and play their games at Champion Stadium (formerly known as Disney Field, the Ballpark at Disney's Wide World of Sports, and Cracker Jack Stadium). The new name doesn't necessarily refer to the Atlanta Braves — though of course the Braves front office would like you to think it does. Champion Stadium is one of the flashier venues for spring training, and it's also one of the largest: With 9,500 seats (80 percent between first and third base), only the largest Arizona ballparks and a few newer ballparks in Tampa can complete in terms of sheer size.

There is a very agreeable spaciousness to the ballpark, despite almost all the seating being concentrated in the two-deck grandstand (the only pure two-deck ballpark in the Grapefruit League, by the way). The lower level features two concourses — a small one at the back of the grandstand and a much larger one within the grandstand — while the upper level features a large concourse within the grandstand, four luxury boxes, and two open-air suites. The wider concourses make for some pleasant

The left-field berm provides a great view of the large Art Deco scoreboard.

milling around during the game, and there's an expanded area outside of the grandstand that can accommodate groups. (Alas, there's no concourse ringing the park; you'll miss out on the game action once you head to the concessions.)

Having most of the seats crammed into grandstand does have its pluses and minuses. On the one hand, we were sitting in the last row of the second deck (an open-air luxury suite was right behind us), and the view of the field was excellent. But these views came at a price: We were definitely crammed into narrower seats, and there was very little leg room between rows. The ballpark affords very little relief from the hot Florida sun: The second deck doesn't cover much of the first deck, while there's no roof at all shading the second deck. Also, there were no beverage holders attached to seats, so you pretty much have to hold onto your beverages for fear of someone kicking them over.

The design is in a Florida Spanish Mission design (you'll find similar design motifs scatted throughout the state) with some Art Deco touches, such as the large left-field scoreboard. The scoreboard is equipped with fireworks, some of which are fired after the singing of the National Anthem.

If you find the grandstand seating too confining — which you probably will, especially if you're there with a family — get to the game early and score some of the berm seating down the left-field line and across the outfield to the scoreboard. Except for a bare-earth walking area in the back, the berm slopes down toward the playing field. If you do plan on sitting on the berm, don't bother bringing a lawn chair, as the ground has too much of an angle for a chair. Instead, bring a large blanket and plop down in left-center field.

insider's tip

The branding of the Wide World of Sports complex could have changed by the time you read this. The plan is to dump the Wide World of Sports name and replace it with ESPN branding, but as of press time no formal plans have been announced. If you're looking for the ballpark and see references to ESPN but not to Wide World of Sports, you can assume the rebranding has taken place.

The ballpark sits within a larger sports complex in the southwestern corner of Disney World. Next door is the Milk House (an indoor arena used for AAU events), and close by there are tennis courts, a track-and-field complex, youth and adult baseball and softball fields (some of which are used by the Braves for morning workouts), and other various athletic fields. Between spring-training seasons the complex is used frequently for a variety of AAU and NAIA college events.

BALLPARK HISTORY

The Atlanta Braves moved their spring-training games to what was then known as Disney's Wide World of Sports in March 1997, shortly after the ballpark opened. The Orlando Rays (Class AA; Southern League) played at Champion Stadium between 2000 and 2003.

THE SPRING-TRAINING BALLPARK EXPERIENCE

Concessions

The concession stands feature standard fare: hot dogs, burgers, and fries. Nothing remarkable. Outside the first-base side of the concourse there's an open-air concession area with stands selling Philly cheese steaks, pizza, Slushies, and more. The offerings seem to change every year. You won't go hungry, of course, but there's enough variety to satisfy everyone in the family.

insider's tip

If you want to avoid the ballpark cuisine and would prefer a sit-down meal, the Wide World of Sports Cafe is next door. It's a good place to grab a beer as well — the prices are a little lower than you'll find in the ballpark.

insider's tip

The concourses can be quite crowded before the game as fans look for food and drinks. If your tickets are on the second floor, don't bother with the main-floor concessions; the concession stands on the second floor tend to be less crowded.

For the Kids

For being smack-dab in the Happiest Place in the Known Universe, there's little to entertain the kids: there's no children's play area or activities geared toward the young.

Parking

A paved parking lot is right outside the stadium; part of it is sold with a surcharge as priority parking, and part of it is free of charge as general parking. You'll need to arrive really early to score a paved parking spot. If you arrive closer to game time — as we inevitably do — you'll be stuck quite a ways from the stadium parking on a grassy field.

Autographs

The ballpark opens three hours before game time, and a ticket will get you access to the practice fields. (In past years practice started at 9:30 a.m.) Going to the practice field and flagging a player is your best bet in scoring an autograph, as the Braves are usually not very accessible before a game (although some will come to the edge of the right-field stands to sign before a game).

Champion Stadium sports the nicest interior concourses in the Grapefruit League.

If you wait after the game, watch for players leaving the ballpark via a walkway beyond the left-field wall; sometimes they'll stop and sign autographs there.

If You Go

Hotels

There are a plethora of hotel options within Disney World, and there's one huge advantage to staying in the park: The Disney transportation system runs to Champion Stadium. The resort closest to Champion Stadium is the Caribbean Beach Resort, which is classified by Disney as a moderately priced resort, which is a euphemism for $200 or so a night (plus taxes). A room at a lower-priced resort like the All-Star Sports Resort runs $150 a night (plus taxes, while a room at a high-end resort like the Grand Floridian can cost upwards of $440 a night. There's more information on area hotels in our Orlando chapter preceding this one. No hotel in the southwest corner of Orlando or Kissimmee is going to be too far away from Disney World and the ballpark, however.

What to Do Outside the Ballpark

Since you're coming to Florida to watch baseball, you'll be interested in the other training camps in the area. Spring-training venues within easy driving distance of Orlando include Kissimmee (Houston Astros), Viera (Washington Nationals), and Lakeland (Detroit Tigers). A further trip, but still doable, could involve a drive to Tampa Bay, where a plethora of teams train: Tampa (New York Yankees), Clearwater (Philadelphia Phillies), Bradenton (Pittsburgh Pirates), and Dunedin (Toronto Blue Jays).

Otherwise, the full joys of Orlando are available to you, as set out in the previous chapter covering the Magic Kingdom.

Flying In

The most convenient airport, obviously, will be Orlando International Airport. We cover this airport in our previous chapter on Orlando.

SPRING-TRAINING HISTORY

The Atlanta Braves have trained at the following sites since the team's entry in the National League as the Boston Beaneaters: Norfolk, Va. (1901); Thomasville, Ga. (1902-1904, 1907); Charleston, S.C. (1905); Jacksonville (1906); Augusta, Ga. (1908-1912); Athens, Ga. (1913); Macon, Ga. (1914-1915); Miami (1916-1918), Columbus, Ga. (1919-1920); Galveston, Texas (1921); St. Petersburg (1922-1937); Bradenton (1938-1940, 1948-1962); San Antonio (1941); Sanford, Fla. (1942); Wallingford, Ct. (1943-1944); Washington, D.C. (1945); Fort Lauderdale (1946-1947); West Palm Beach (1963-1997); Orlando (1998-present).

→ houston astros

OSCEOLA COUNTY STADIUM

Capacity	5,224
Year Opened	1984
Dimensions	325L, 405C, 325R
Surface	Grass
Local Airport	Orlando
Ticket Office	407/839-3900
Ballpark Address	1000 Bill Beck Blvd., Kissimmee.

From I-4, take Route 192 west off the Florida Turnpike or east off I-4. The ballpark is 1.5 miles west of the turnpike and two miles east of downtown Kissimmee.

Countdown in Kissimmee

Kissimmee stands in the shadows of Orlando and the Magic Kingdom. Similarly, the Houston Astros stand in the shadows of the Atlanta Braves — who train in the Magic Kingdom — in terms of attendance and mindshare during spring training. Check the *Orlando Sentinel* any time in March: The emphasis will be on the Braves, with any Astros coverage an afterthought.

Part of this reflects Kissimmee's social status in Orlando: There's a certain tackiness associated with the tourist offerings of the area when compared to Disney World and Sea World, though at the end of the day all are involved in the same search for the ever-elusive tourist dollar. And traditionally the Atlanta Braves have been a flagship team for baseball, though that status has lessened after some mediocre seasons and the loss of a national TBS broadcast deal.

The difference in organizations is reflected in spring-training facilities as well. The Braves train at a gorgeous facility in Disney World, while the Astros train at a less-glamorous locale at the end of a low-end tourist stretch in Kissimmee. And though two renovations in 2003 and 2007 to Osceola County Stadium did spiff up what had been an exceedingly ordinary ballpark, there's little evidence of baseball fever surrounding the Astros in spring training.

But if you're a baseball fan and happen to be in the Orlando area in March, Osceola County Stadium is definitely worth a visit. The ballpark is comfortable, the food selection is great, and the Astros are usually a competitive team. Just don't be expecting the glitz of Disney World or the scenery of Lakeland.

Osceola County Stadium has been the spring-training home of the Houston Astros since 1985, when the team shifted spring-training facilities from Cocoa. This was a shame, as the Astros had a perfect link to Cocoa. Cocoa Beach was the home to Major Anthony Nelson on *I Dream of Jeannie*, and as you all recall Major Nelson was…an astronaut!

insider's tip

For those who remember the Cocoa days, here's a bit of nostalgia: The former spring home of the Astros is still open and operating as CocoaExpo Sports Center. It's quite close to the Washington Nationals' spring-training home; we cover it in the Nats chapter.

The renovations to Osceola County Stadium and Complex, which carried a price tag of $18.4 million, increased the ballpark capacity to over 5,200 (5,225) with the addition of another 300 seats and the installation of armchair seating throughout the park. Other additions included a new press box, new concession stands, a new playground for children, and separate major and minor league clubhouses with state-of-the-art training facilities. Other new fan-friendly features include "Autograph Alley" and a party deck for private functions.

insider's tip

One byproduct of Osceola County Stadium being an older ballpark is a lack of covered seating. If sun is a concern for you, ask for reserved seating near the back of the main grandstand section: The roof isn't large, but it does offer some relief. (During the game you can seek shade in the concession concourse or in one of the covered picnic areas down each line.)

The improvements made Osceola County Stadium a more comfortable place without decreasing the intimacy level. (It's still the smallest ballpark in the Grapefruit League, even with the changes.) You'll need to leave the playing area to hit the concession stands located in the back of the grandstand, but the concession alley is fairly wide with multiple stands, so the traffic flow is never throttled.

No fancy videoboard here.

The locale still isn't great — there's nothing within walking distance and you'll feel like you're stuck in the middle of a cow pasture — but the added amenities will make you want to stick around all day.

insider's tip

The ballpark is located on Irlo Bronson Memorial Highway, also marked as Hwy. 192 and sometimes as Space Coast Highway, Vine Street, or Holopaw Road. This highway runs east-west through Kissimmee; virtually everything worth seeing in the city can be found in Hwy. 192, beginning in the east with the ballpark and ending in the west with Disney World. True, driving on Hwy. 192 can be a tremendous pain: It can be rather congested, the placement of tourist traps can be distracting for the kids, and the appearance of stop lights every half mile can slow you down. But staying on Hwy. 192 means you stand little chance of getting lost or inadvertently ending up on a toll road.

BALLPARK HISTORY

Osceola County Stadium has been the spring-training home of the Houston Astros since opening in 1985. The ballpark opened with an exhibition against the New York Yankees, won by the Astros 9-6.

Astros players enter the field from the left-field clubhouse.

THE SPRING-TRAINING
BALLPARK EXPERIENCE

Concessions

The food at Osceola County Stadium is pretty decent and very affordable if you're in the mood for ballpark fare. We've always found the upgrade to a jumbo dog to be worth the extra 50 cents, and the chicken tenders are a good buy. Other menu items include pizza, nachos, pop, candy, and other ballpark fare.

You'll also find a standard variety of beer — Bud, Bud Light, Miller Lite, Coors Light, or Michelob Ultra — on tap and in bottles.

You can even find lots of opposing players signing autographs at Osceola County Stadium.

Autographs

Osceola County Stadium is a prime spot for scoring an autograph, which makes it a favorite among baseball aficionados. Practice fields — but not the bleachers — are roped off, but you can show up to morning workouts and ask for a scribble as players enter and leave or try to lure them to the bleachers. Players sign them for fans lined up between the dugout and the foul poles before each game. The Astros come out of the left-field clubhouse and occupy the third-base dugout, so you'll want to stake out a good spot before the players arrive; the team sets up an Autograph Alley for easiest access to players and coaches.

Visiting teams train in the clubhouse down the right-field line and usually hang around there before the games. Because the crowds tend to be smaller at Astros spring-training games, it's a good place to score an autograph if your favorite players are visiting; they'll enter down the right-field line. You can also try to score an autograph as visiting players

Downtown Celebration is a short drive from the ballpark.

leave their clubhouse and head for their bus. Gates open two hours before each game.

For the Kids

The recent remodeling of Osceola County Stadium provided some tangible improvements for the under-10 set. First off, a fenced-in and rather impressive playground down the right-field line provides hours of amusement for those who don't really care who ends up as closer for the Astros. After the kids are worn out in the playground, they can hit the concession stands, which feature special kids' menus. Spring training is not always a kid-friendly time, but Osceola County Stadium is perhaps the best place for kids in all of spring training.

Parking

There's something galling about being forced to pay $9 for a spot on an unpaved field, especially when the ballpark is in the middle of open land, but this is the price you'll pay.

If You Go

What to Do in Kissimmee

Top of the list: more baseball. Spring-training venues that are within easy driving distance of Kissimmee include Orlando's Champion Stadium (Atlanta Braves), Lakeland's Joker Marchant Stadium (Detroit Tigers), and Viera's Space Coast Stadium (Washington Nationals). A further trip, but still doable, could involve Clearwater (Philadelphia Phillies), Tampa (New York Yankees), Bradenton (Pittsburgh Pirates), and Dunedin (Toronto Blue Jays).

Though located in the shadow of the giant mouse ears, Kissimmee has some legitimate attractions of its own. One of the more popular is Arabian Nights, where you are an honored guest at the wedding of a prince and a princess. You gather in the 1,200-person Black Stallion Arena — billed as the largest equestrian arena in the world — and then watch 50 horses performing as part of the ceremonies. It's not the dreadful dinner theater you can find scattered through Orlando. The food at Arabian Nights is decent, as well.

Arabian Nights, 6225 W. Irlo Bronson Memorial Hwy., Kissimmee; 800/553-6116. **arabian-nights.com**. *Adults, $56.60; children (3-11), $31.03.*

In a similar vein is Medieval Times. The premise is simple: You're the guests of honor at a jousting tournament, where knights gather to defend the honor of their kingdoms and seek the hand of a lovely princess. The games of skill include one-on-one jousts, javelin tosses, ring pierces, and more. As the games are held,

you're presented with a four-course meal — sans utensils, of course. The whole thing is held in a replica of a castle, complete with moat.

Medieval Times, 4510 W. Irlo Bronson Hwy., Kissimmee; 888/WE-JOUST; **medievaltimes.com**. *Adults, $56.95; children (3-11), $35.95.*

A slightly more modern take on dinner theater is Capone's Dinner and Show, where you're transported back to 1930s Chicago and surrounded by goofy mobsters and wacky flappers. Not really that outrageous given the excesses you find throughout Orlando, and the dinner show has won its fair share of awards from reviewers. Capone's Dinner and Show, 4740 W. Hwy. Irlo Bronson Hwy., Kissimmee; 800/220-8428; **alcapones.com**. *Adults, $59.99; children (4-12), $29.99.*

Where to Stay

There are several hotels within a mile of the ballpark, such as Stadium Inn and Suites (2039 E. Irlo Bronson Hwy., Kissimmee; 800/359-7234) and Quality Inn Heritage Park (2050 E. Irlo Bronson Hwy., Kissimmee; 407/846-4545; **choicehotels.com**), where the rooms run under $100 during spring training.

Do we recommend them? If you plan on basically living at the ballpark and don't care about where you stay, then we'd say yes. (If you can get in, that is; the Stadium Inn is sold out months in advance for spring training, especially on a weekend.) But be warned the area near the ballpark in Kissimmee can be a little rough; several years ago several Astros minor leaguers (including Morgan Ensberg) were robbed and tied up while hanging out in their spring-training hotel. So take a little care in picking out where you stay.

One alternative close to the ballpark that's appropriate for families is the Villas at Fortune Place (1201 Simpson Rd., Kissimmee; 407/348-0330; **dailymanagementresorts.com/Resort.aspx?resort=12**). These townhouses go for $100 or so and come standard with at least two bedrooms.

But there's really no reason to stay close to the ballpark unless you plan on taking all your meals at concession stands. There are plenty of great resorts and hotels with a Kissimmee address, but they are located in the western part of the city — close to Disney World. If you accept the inevitable traffic associated with the southwest corner of Orlando, you could stay anywhere and still have easy access to Astros games. Our previous chapter on Orlando covers the hotel scene in the area.

The Celebration Hotel.

RV Parks

Tropical Palms RV Resort (2650 Holiday Trail, Kissimmee; 800/647-2567; **rvonthego.com**) is located close to Old Town Kissimmee, a short drive from the ballpark. A little farther away is Kissimmee/Orlando KOA (2644 Happy Camper Place, Kissimmee; 407/396-2400; **koa.com/where/fl/09329/index.htm**); it's located closer to Disney World (and just off Hwy. 192 and I-4, a more convenient location for many), but is considered to be a more upscale (and expensive) facility.

Flying In

The closest airport is Orlando International Airport in the south-center of the city. While it's a bigger airport, it's fairly easy to make your way around, as a tram brings you from the gates to the central terminal. Just be warned that it's quite a hike from the gates to the terminals even with the tram.

You may also want to consider flying into Tampa and then driving to Orlando if the fare to Tampa is significantly cheaper. The drive is 79 miles and takes an hour and a half on I-4 — which has been upgraded in recent years and is now an easy and smooth drive — but if you can save $100 or so on your airfares, the drive will be worth it.

Spring-Training History

The Houston Colt .45s began their history with training camp in Apache Junction, Ariz., in 1962-1963. In 1964 spring training was shifted to Cocoa Beach, where the Astros trained until 1984. In 1985 the Astros moved to their current spring-training home in Kissimmee.

→ treasure coast

Finding Treasure on the Coast

Eastern Florida and the Treasure Coast are afterthoughts for many people attending spring training. But in many ways spring training at the cities on the Atlantic Ocean side of Florida — Viera, Port St. Lucie, Jupiter, and Fort Lauderdale — is more of a pure experience than you'll find in the hectic tourist towns of Tampa and Orlando.

For the purposes of this book we're treating eastern Florida as its own region. Technically, only Port St. Lucie and Jupiter are part of the Treasure Coast; Viera lies to the north and Fort Lauderdale to the south. But they are tied together in many ways. None of the four cities tend to be huge tourist destinations: They lack the flash of Orlando or heft of Tampa Bay, and fans attending games there tend to be mostly hardcore fans and locals. You don't get many casual fans. And in all four ballparks the emphasis is solely on baseball: Fans on the East Coast don't need no fancy suites. This is spring training at its most basic — and its best.

➔ baltimore orioles

FORT LAUDERDALE STADIUM

Capacity	8,340
Year Opened	1962
Dimensions	332L, 401C, 320R
Surface	Grass
Address	5301 NW 12th Av., Fort Lauderdale.

From I-95, take exit 32 (Commercial Boulevard) and travel west to N.W. 12th Avenue, also known as Orioles Boulevard, and make a right. Fort Lauderdale Stadium is the second stadium on your left-hand side.

Fort Lauderdale Stadium: Room for Improvement

Fort Lauderdale Stadium is not regarded as one of the gems of the Grape-fruit League, despite its status as the oldest ballpark still used for Grape-fruit League action: The restrooms are small, the concessions are limited, and the seats don't match. The Orioles have announced Spring Training 2009 will be their last in Fort Lauderdale, so don't invest in that Fort Lau-derdale condo if you're a Birds fan.

Not that many tears will be shed by Fort Lauderdale baseball fans: Fort Lauderdale Stadium is not old enough to be a classic stadium, and architecturally, it's not distinguished enough to be considered interesting enough to be worth saving should a new complex be built for the Orioles. (Heck, Fort Lauderdale Stadium and the Orioles didn't even warrant a mention in the most recent guide to Fort Lauderdale put out by Broward County.) Baseball hasn't proven to be the most exciting of pursuits in the greater Miami/Fort Lauderdale area for some time now, and once the Ori-oles leave we're guessing it will be a long, long time (if ever) before spring training returns to the area. And that seems to be just fine with everyone.

The Orioles have not been using Fort Lauderdale Stadium long enough to be identified with the ballpark. Fort Lauderdale Stadium was previously the spring-training of the New York Yankees, and many fans still associate the glory days of the Yankees in the 1960s with the relaxed atmosphere of

The O's are not a huge draw in Fort Lauderdale.

The press-box level features a single luxury box.

Fort Lauderdale. (In fact, the single suite was once the province of George Steinbrenner when the Yankees trained there.)

But despite some shortcomings, Fort Lauderdale Stadium is a fairly comfortable ballpark once you make your way to the grandstand. There's lots of legroom, and the seating is fairly close to the action. And given that there's been a minimum of changes to the ballpark over the last 40 years, you can experience spring training as it used to be.

insider's tip

Because of limited facilities next to the ballpark, the Orioles do not have both their major- and minor-league squads practice in the same area: The major leaguers practice in Ft. Lauderdale and the minor leaguers train in Sarasota at Twin Lakes Park (6700 Clark Road).

BALLPARK HISTORY

The facility previously served as the spring-training home of the New York Yankees until the team moved into its present home at Legends Field in 1996.

THE SPRING-TRAINING BALLPARK EXPERIENCE

Parking

There's a sea of parking next to the ballpark. Be prepared to pay $8 for the privilege.

Spring games at Fort Lauderdale Stadium are low-key affairs.

Concessions

Concessions are very limited because of the smaller size of the ballpark. You can bring in food, but be prepared to follow the MLB rules about what you can bring in (discussed earlier in this book).

Autographs

It's hard to score Orioles autographs at Fort Lauderdale Stadium: The parking lot adjacent to the clubhouse is closed to the public, so you're limited to attracting players to the stands. Gates open two hours before gametime, so you have a relatively small window of opportunity to score an autograph. Also, once spring-training games begin, Orioles workouts at Fort Lauderdale Stadium are closed to the public.

IF YOU GO

Where to Stay

There are many hotels within a mile of Fort Lauderdale Stadium, thanks to the location next to the airport, including chain hotels like Red Roof Inn and La Quinta.

As the ballpark is inland, you'll probably need to rent a car anyway, so any place within the greater Fort Lauderdale area will be convenient.

If you're planning on going to other training facilities in the area, you'll want to choose a centrally located hotel. Recommended for its location is the Radisson Suite Airport (1808 S. Australian Dr., West Palm Beach; 561/689-6888;

radisson.com). Or, if you want a little more excitement than Fort Lauderdale can provide, you're right on the doorstep of Miami: Stay somewhere on the waterfront and watch baseball during the day and beautiful people in North Beach at night. Given the layout of the Gold Coast area and the vast number of vacation facilities in the likes of Pompano Beach, Boynton Beach, and West Palm Beach, you shouldn't have a problem finding lodging in your price range.

What to Do Outside the Ballpark

Fort Lauderdale has a reputation as being the Venice of America, with more than 300 miles of navigable canals and waterways. It used to be known as a party town — especially during spring-break time — but it's been discovered by the horsy set, who all seem to own a boat and who love be out on the water every chance they get.

Many tourists find they can use water taxis to shuttle between hotels, restaurants, bars, and shopping areas. (Sadly, you can't take a water taxi to land-locked Fort Lauderdale Stadium.) Again, Fort Lauderdale's party reputation came about partly because the water taxis are especially good at shuttling people between bars. Shooter's Waterfront Café (3033 NE. 32nd Av., Fort Lauderdale; 954/566-2855; **shooterscafe.com**), The Parrot Lounge (911 Sunrise Lane, Fort Lauderdale; 954/563-1493; **parrotlounge.com**), and the downtown Riverwalk (**goriverwalk.com**) are known for being lively places, especially on weekends.

For families, there's the Museum of Discovery and Science (401 SW 2nd St., Fort Lauderdale; 954/467-6637; **mods.org**), and the Sawgrass Mills Mall (12801 W. Sunrise Blvd., Sunrise; 954/846-2300; **sawgrassmillsmall.com**). The Museum of Discovery and Science features over 200 interactive exhibits, including some dedicated to the marine wildlife of the area (sharks and coral reefs) and others devoted to aerospace. The mall features all the usual suspects set in an open-air format.

And, of course, you'll want to spend some time at the beach. If you're into a crowd, the beaches in Hollywood and downtown Fort Lauderdale may be a little too intense for you. For some peace and quiet head to Lloyd Beach in Dania; in addition to the beaches, the site is one of the state's most important nesting beaches for sea turtles.

Plus, it just wouldn't be a trip to Florida without a stop to a jai-alai fronton. The local jai-alai fronton is Dania Jai-Alai (301 E. Dania Beach Blvd., Dania; **dania-jai-alai.com**), which originally opened in 1953 as the second jai-alai fronton in the United States. The current 220,000-square-foot facility has seating for 5,600 and contains a sports bar, simulcast betting facility, poker tables, restaurants, banquet facilities, bars and snack bars. If you don't what jai-alai is, just think of it as an incredibly stylized handball game played with oversized gloves where the ball speed reaches 180 miles an hour and you're encouraged to bet on the outcome of matches.

Flying In

Fort Lauderdale is home to Fort Lauderdale Hollywood International Airport — technically, Fort Lauderdale Stadium is on airport land — and is served by all major airlines, including Delta, Continental, US Airways, JetBlue, Southwest, and American. You may also want to consider flying into Miami or Palm Beach and then driving to Fort Lauderdale if the fare to Miami is significantly cheaper. The drive from each is only 40 miles.

SPRING-TRAINING HISTORY

The Baltimore Orioles have trained at the following sites (including their years as the St. Louis Browns): St. Louis (1901); French Lick, Ind. (1902); Baton Rouge (1903); Corsicana, Texas (1904); Dallas (1905-1906); San Antonio (1907, 1919, 1937-1941); Shreveport (1908, 1918); Houston (1909-1910); Hot Springs, Ark. (1911); Montgomery, Ala. (1912); Waco (1913); St. Petersburg (1914); Houston (1915); Palestine, Texas (1916-1917); Taylor, Ala. (1920); Bogalusa, Ala. (1921); Mobile, Ala. (1922-1924); Tarpon Springs, Fla. (1925-1927); West Palm Beach (1928-1936); Deland, Fla. (1942); Cape Girardeau, Mo. (1943-1945); Anaheim (1946); Miami (1947); San Bernardino, Cal. (1948, 1953); Burbank, Cal. (1949-1952); Yuma, Az. (1954); Daytona Beach, Fla. (1955); Scottsdale (1956-1958); Miami (1959-1990); Sarasota (1989-1991); St. Petersburg (1992-1995); Fort Lauderdale (1996-present).

→ florida marlins / st. louis cardinals

ROGER DEAN STADIUM

Capacity	7,000 (6,000 seats, 1,000 berm seating)
Year Opened	1998
Dimensions	325L, 385LC, 400C, 375RC, 325R
Surface	Grass
Local Airport	Palm Beach
Dugout Locations	Cardinals on first-base side, Marlins on third-base side
Address	4751 Main Street, Jupiter

From I-95, exit at Donald Ross Road (exit 53) and travel east to Parkside Drive. Make a left and follow Parkside Drive to the Roger Dean parking lots, located on the right. There are plenty of signs pointing the way.

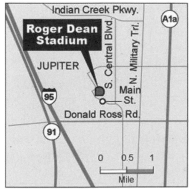

There's barely any elbow room for a Cardinals spring game, even on the berm.

Double Duty in Jupiter

The Florida Marlins share Roger Dean Stadium with the St. Louis Cardinals during the Grapefruit League spring-training season. Roger Dean Stadium is one of the newer stadiums in the Grapefruit League — the $28-million facility opened in February 1998 — and the total capacity is 7,000: 6,400 in box seats, bleachers and skyboxes, up to 300 on a party deck, and 300 in berm seating. There are six luxury suites as well.

It is one of the busiest ballparks in professional baseball: Besides hosting the Marlins and Cardinals in spring training the ballpark also hosts two Florida State League teams and a host of other events. The emphasis, understandably, isn't on luxury: It's on running a smooth operation that can be sustained year-round. (Yes, year-round: In December, for example, Roger Dean Stadium hosts the Wiffle Ball World Series.) Some might call it a little bland, having been built before the great explosion in spring-training facilities featuring wraparound concourses, tiki bars, and lots of party areas. At Roger Dean Stadium, there's no concourse ringing the inside of the ballpark: The concourse and concession area are located behind the grandstand. And there's really no theme associated with the ballpark; it's not done up in Spanish Mission style like many other Florida stadiums, for instance. Instead, Roger Dean Stadium is ringed with native oaks and palmetto trees in a very understated manner. Baseball is serious business at Roger Dean Stadium, and you don't need to be distracted by things like concession stands and concourses.

Originally Roger Dean Stadium was also the spring-training home of the Montreal Expos. However, when Jeffrey Loria sold the Expos and bought the Marlins, he retained the Florida rights and property that had belonged to the Expos, and he decided to move the Marlins' spring training to Jupiter while still paying on a spring-training lease at Space Coast Stadium in Melbourne. The word was that Loria wanted the team to train closer to his home in Palm Beach, but team officials insist that the swap was made in order to market the Marlins to Palm Beach County.

It is a spacious facility: The entire complex includes four major-league practice fields, eight minor-league practice fields, and three clubhouses (one for the Marlins, one for the Cardinals, one for the visiting team). Roger Dean Stadium was designed as part of a larger residential/retail development in eastern Florida. It was named for West Palm Beach car dealer Roger Dean, whose family bought the naming rights.

insider's tip

Tickets to Marlins games are easier to acquire than tickets to Cardinals games. Cards enthusiasts tend to be fanatical about their team from the beginning of spring training through the end of the season.

Be warned that Roger Dean can be one of the more expensive venues in the Grapefruit League, with the top ticket price reaching $26 in 2008. The price to any spring-training game at Roger Dean Stadium is the same no matter what team is playing, and that means you're paying as much to see the Marlins as you are the Cardinals. No offense to Marlins fans, but the Cardinals are by far the better spring-training draw, and it seems a little out of whack for tickets to be the same for both teams. Since the Cardinals draw well, you should really buy your tickets in advance, although those seeking cheap seats will

Concessions are tucked under the grandstand.

The Cardinals receive a little assistance from above.

be limited to $12 bleacher seats — the $12 berm and standing-room-only seats are available only on game days. (Yes, $12 for a berm seat is steep, even for spring training. Pity the Marlins fans who pay these prices because Cardinals fans are so zealous about their team.)

Some say a game at Roger Dean Stadium is one of the greatest experiences in spring training. It is a throwback to the days when the emphasis was on the game and not on the amenities. Of course, many say that's a false choice — in a place like Steinbrenner Field or City of Palms Park baseball comes first and foremost — despite what's going on at the party deck — but a game at Roger Dean Stadium is a relaxing event, to be sure.

BALLPARK HISTORY

The St. Louis Cardinals have trained at Roger Dean Stadium since it opened in 1998. The Montreal Expos trained there from 1998 through 2002, and in 2003 the Florida Marlins began training there.

THE SPRING-TRAINING BALLPARK EXPERIENCE

Concessions

You'll find the normal ballpark fare: hot dogs, hamburgers, soda, beer, etc. The signature concession offering is the Dean Dog, a 1/3-pound all-beef hot dog served on a special bun with grilled onions and peppers.

Parking

There are parking lots next to the ballpark, and there's also a ramp across the street if you prefer to park in the shade. You'll pay $9 for the privilege.

Autographs

Both teams will stop to sign autographs as they come to and off the field: The Cards are down the right-field line and the Marlins down the left

IF YOU GO

What to Do Outside the Ballpark

Jupiter is less than 20 miles from Palm Beach and even farther away from Miami, so you must be really, really into baseball in order to make a pilgrimage. Jupiter is in the midst of a planned Florida community, Abacoa, with all the good and bad that it entails. When the ballpark first opened, it was in the middle of nowhere. Since then, the surrounding development has expanded to the point where there are things to do should you decide to stay near the ballpark: You can find plenty of restaurants and movie theaters nearby, since what goes for a downtown Abacoa is located directly next to the ballpark.

Most of the attractions are located on Town Center Drive and Main Street, which feature a range of bars and restaurants. We're partial to Rooney's Pub, only because it's so weird and unexpected to have a bar named after longtime Pittsburgh Steelers owner Art Rooney, located blocks from the spring home of the Cardinals and the Marlins. No, we can't understand it, either, but Rooney's is a good place for a post-game tipple or two, preferably of the Irish sort. Rooney's Pub, 1153 Town Center Dr., Jupiter; 561/694-6610; **rooneyspub.com**.

We also enjoyed a post-game drink at J.J. Muggs Stadium Grill. It is what it is: a good neighborhood spot suitable for a drink and some bar food. J.J. Muggs Stadium Grill, 1203 Town Center Dr., Jupiter; 561/630-9669.

For more substantial meals, check out Costello's Pizzeria & Trattoria, where the emphasis is on New York-style pizza. Costello's Pizzeria & Trattoria, 1209 Main St., Suite 102, Jupiter; 561/776-5448.

Otherwise, there's not a lot to do in Jupiter, and what's there involves the sea. The Jupiter Inlet Lighthouse (Lighthouse Park, 500 Capt. Armour's Way, Beach Rd. and Hwy. 1, Jupiter; 561/747-8380; **lrhs.org/JIL.htm**) is the oldest structure in Palm Beach County, first lit on July 10, 1860. Designed by George Gordon Meade, a lieutenant at the Bureau of Topographical Engineers and later the general who defeated Robert E. Lee at Gettysburg, the lighthouse is still a working facility. It's open Wednesday-Saturday, 10-4 p.m., with a $7 admission charge.

Palm Beach is definitely worth a visit, if only to gawk at all the rich folks.

There are other spring-training venues within an easy driving distance. You could head 35 miles up the coast to Port St. Lucie (where the New York Mets train) or 65 miles down the coast to Fort Lauderdale (where the Baltimore Orioles train).

Dining

Between Jupiter and Palm Beach there are restaurant options for all tastes and price points. As you might expect, the emphasis in most restaurants is seafood, although steakhouses are also popular in the area. And even though the hoi polloi hang around the Palm Beach area in the spring, there are enough casual-dining establishments for the average spring-training fan.

Duffy's Sports Grill is a local chain of sports bars known for their burgers and chicken wings, with two locations in Jupiter. Jupiter West, 6791 W. Indiantown Rd., Jupiter; 561/741-8900. Jupiter East, 185 E. Indiantown Rd., Jupiter; 561/743-4405; **duffyssportsgrill.com**.

Keeping with the casual theme is the Too Bizarre Café and Wine Bar. Go for the baked brie and something from the extensive wine list. Too Bizarre Café and Wine Bar, 287 E. Indiantown Road, Fisherman's Wharf Plaza, Jupiter; 561/745-6262.

Where to Stay

Only one hotel is within a mile of the ballpark (and whether that's within walking distance depends on your definition, of course): Homewood Suites (4700 Donald Ross Rd., Palm Beach Gardens; 561/622-7799; **hilton.com**). There are plenty of hotels within a close driving distance of five miles or so; most are of the chain variety.

You can also look to Palm Beach and West Palm Beach for a hotel room as well. Those cities are, at the most, 20 miles from the ballpark and feature a huge selection of hotels at a wide variety of prices, ranging from the likes of The Breakers (One South County Rd., Palm Beach, 888/BREAKERS; **thebreakers.com**) at the high end to the more affordable chains, such as Hampton Inn or Residence Inn.

Clubhouses and team offices are located past left field.

RV Parks in the Area

There are no RV parks close to the ballpark; the closest is several miles away. In general, this is not RV territory.

Flying In

The closest airport is Palm Beach International Airport, which is about 25 miles away from the Jupiter area. Most major airlines fly into PBI, including American, AirTran, Continental, Delta, JetBlue, Southwest, Northwest, United, and US Airways.

You may also want to consider flying into Fort Lauderdale Airport or Miami International Airport and then driving to Jupiter if the fares are significantly cheaper. Miami International Airport is only 84 miles away from Roger Dean Stadium — and Fort Lauderdale Airport is even closer — so if you can save a few bucks for the price of a short drive, you should do so.

Spring-Training History: St. Louis Cardinals

The St. Louis Cardinals have held spring training in the following locations: St. Louis (1901-1902); Dallas (1903); Houston (1904); Marlin Springs, Texas (1905); Houston (1906-1908); Little Rock (1909-1910);

West Baden, Ind. (1911); Jackson, Miss. (1912); Columbus, Ga. (1913); St. Augustine, Fla. (1914); Hot Wells, Texas (1915-1917); San Antonio (1918); St. Louis (1919); Brownsville, Texas (1920); Orange, Texas (1921-1922); Bradenton (1923-1924); Stockton, Cal. (1925); San Antonio (1926); Avon Park, Fla. (1927-1929); Bradenton (1930-1936); Daytona Beach (1937); St. Petersburg (1938-1942); Cairo, Ill. (1943-1945); St. Petersburg (1946-1997); Jupiter (1998-present).

SPRING-TRAINING HISTORY: FLORIDA MARLINS

In 1993 the Florida Marlins first held spring training in Cocoa. The site was shifted to Jupiter's Space Coast Stadium in 1994, with the move to Roger Dean occurring in 2003.

→ new york mets

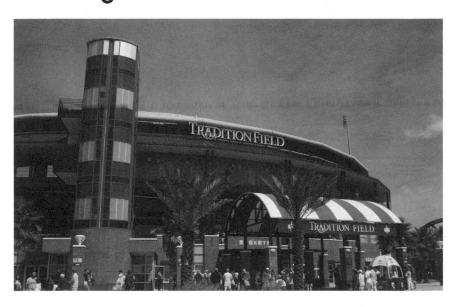

TRADITION FIELD

Capacity	7,800
Year Opened	1988
Dimensions	338L, 410C, 338R
Home Dugout Location	Third-base side
Phone	561/871-2115; 718/507-TIXX (in New York)
Local Airport	Palm Beach
Address	525 N.W. Peacock Boulevard, Port St. Lucie. From 1-95, take Exit 63-C (St. Lucie West Blvd.), east to Peacock Blvd, north to stadium. From U.S. #I: Take Prima Vista Blvd., west to Peacock Blvd., north to ballpark.

Building Traditions in Port St. Lucie

The trend in spring-training facilities is to locate new ballparks in the midst of megadevelopments that could be located anywhere. While these new ballparks have the amenities fans expect, they're generic in nature. Maybe we're a little too nostalgic, but we want the spring-training experience when we head to Florida: We want the palm trees, the alligators, the quaint ballparks located in out-of-the-way neighborhoods.

That's why Tradition Field is a breath of old school in the Grapefruit League. There are no developments within walking distance of the ballpark, just some municipal buildings next door, commercial buildings and warehouses nearby, and an RV resort up the street. No sports bars, no hotels, no entertainment complex, no trendy shops. Park on the right-field side of the ballpark and you'll wander across a sign warning you to stay away from the swampland because of the presence of alligators.

While we wouldn't exactly call the Tradition Field location bucolic — commercial development in Florida tends to sprawl, and there's definitely a lot of sprawl near the ballpark — you definitely know you're in Florida when you attend a Mets spring-training game.

Palm trees provide shade on the berm.

Tradition Field went from one of the dumpiest spring-training to one of the better ones in 2004, when the former Thomas J. White Stadium underwent a multimillion-dollar renovation that added more seating and clubhouse space, as well as some decorative elements that spiffed up the place.

insider's tip

As you approach the ballpark, take a minute to look at the monument across the street from the main entrance gates and underneath the American flag. The two pillars of steel come from the World Trade Center, salvaged after terrorists struck the New York City landmark on Sept. 11, 2001. It was donated to St. Lucie County by a local chapter of retired New York City firefighters and installed in March 2005.

It is a sobering reminder that even in this small Florida community Mets fans are never too far away from New York City.

Previously the ballpark was fairly generic in nature. A red-brick and blue-steel façade replaced the old concrete façade, while a picnic area and a tiki bar replaced some aluminum bleachers down the left-field line. In addition, the Mets installed a grass berm outside the right-field fence, perfect for lounging. It's still not an ideal ballpark: Access to the grandstand seating is through some fairly narrow walkways, and the concession areas still leave something to be desired. But the many changes over the years have made Tradition Field a very pleasant spring ballpark.

One plus: A large canopy ensures much of the grandstand seating is in the shade. Only the bleacher seating down the right-field line offers massive exposure to the sun, and the seats between the dugouts are shaded most of the game.

---

insider's tip

The cheapest seats in the house are in the outfield berm. If you're attending a game with a bunch of kids, that's the place to go: The kids can run around while you claim one of the new picnic tables. A few beers from the nearby concession stand won't hurt, either.

But be warned there are a few drawbacks to berm seating. You don't have access to the grandstand or its concessions if you have berm-seating tickets: The berm has a separate entrance and separate (limited) concessions. The berm can also be a sun field with limited shade, and during an afternoon game you'll spend a lot of time fighting the sun. So bring those sunglasses, caps, and sunscreen lotion.

Because of the large number of New Yorkers in the area, a Mets spring-training game seems like a Shea Stadium match gone tropical. Interestingly, the New Yorkers didn't live in Port St. Lucie before the Mets moved spring-training operations there in 1988, but the ballpark and the Mets' presence are cited as prime reasons why New Yorkers pushed the Port St. Lucie population by 28 percent since 1998.

The complex also houses the St. Lucie Mets of the Florida State League and the Mets' minor-league operations.

The ballpark originally was named for the late Thomas J. White, who founded St. Lucie West and worked to bring the Mets to the area. Naming rights were sold in 2004 to Core Communities, developer of the Tradition development near the ballpark.

BALLPARK HISTORY

The New York Mets have trained at Tradition Field since it opened in 1988.

THE SPRING-TRAINING BALLPARK EXPERIENCE

Concessions

While it's not exactly like being in the Big Apple, the concessions at the ballpark will ease the homesickness somewhat.

Normally you don't think of a knish as a ballpark food, but it's offered at Tradition Field. And it's a traditional knish: mashed potato wrapped in dough and then baked. For $3, the huge knish certainly was filling, and on a cool spring day it was comfort food to the max. More comfort food can be found down the third-base line, where a local bagel shop offers bagel and deli sandwiches made with Boar's Head meats.

If you're looking for New York takes on traditional ballpark foods, Nathan's hot dogs are served throughout the ballpark, as are hot pretzels, sausages, cheesesteaks, and Carvel ice cream. The beer selections are more Florida than New York City: Yuengling, Rolling Rock, and Bass, among others. Popular among Mets fans are the buckets of ice and six Buds, Michelob Ultras or Bud Lights selling for $25. The tiki bar and a bar in back of the grandstand offer more exotic beer choices, like Land Shark Beer, as well as mixed drinks and frozen concoctions.

The obligatory Tiki bar.

Almost all concessions are located in back of the grandstand, although some items are sold in the left-field tiki-bar area. You will miss the action when you head out for that knish, so plan accordingly.

Autographs

There are no formal places for autographs at the ballparks; fans gather next to the dugout in hopes of snaring a wayward Met. You can also try hanging around the clubhouses before and after the games.

Parking

Parking is $5 and located adjacent to the ballpark. Arrive early: With only two entrances to the parking lot, things can back up close to game time. You could scout for some free parking on the adjacent streets, but this isn't a very pedestrian-friendly area, so beware.

The workout facilities are beyond the left-field wall.

Minor League Complex

The minor-league complex is located directly north of Tradition Field, while the main practice field is located directly west of the ballpark. The minor-league complex features a separate entrance and parking area, which you can access via Peacock Boulevard.

IF YOU GO

What to Do Outside the Ballpark

Port St. Lucie is basically a manufactured community: Port St. Lucie Boulevard and Highway 1 are the main drags, but there's nothing like a downtown per se, and no obvious place to hang out before or after the game.

So you'll need to find and make your own entertainment. Like many other Florida communities, golf plays an important role in Port St. Lucie. What makes Port St. Lucie different is the sanctioning of the PGA: The PGA runs a club and learning center in Port St. Lucie and has established a museum there as well, all under the auspices of the PGA Village.

The PGA Golf Club (1916 Perfect Dr., Port St. Lucie; 800/609-9067; **pgavillage.com**) features three championship courses: The Ryder Course, designed by Tom Fazio, features rolling hills and a lot of water hazards; the Wanamaker Course, also designed by Fazio, has a classic Florida feel;

and the Dye Course (designed by Pete Dye) has a links-style layout. Many of the hotels have an agreement with the golf club for room/links specials. If your game is not quite up to a championship-course level, some time at the PGA Learning Center — which features a driving range and a number of practice holes for work on the short game — is in order.

For inspiration, try a trip to the free PGA Historical Center (8568 Commerce Centre Dr., Port St. Lucie; 772/370-5410; **pgavillage.com**) is in order. Focused on the long history of the PGA, which was formed in 1916, the PGA Historical Center contains memorabilia like Donald Ross's work desk. It's open 10-4 daily before Easter, and 10-4 weekends thereafter.

The PGA doesn't have a monopoly on golf in Port St. Lucie, though. Alas, most of the courses are attached to housing/retirement communities and not open to the public. There's only one municipal 18-hole course run by the city, and only a few public courses, such as the notable Fairwinds Course in nearby Fort Pierce.

After the Game

There are the usual chain and fast-food restaurants in the area, including several on Peacock Boulevard approaching the ballpark, so you won't go hungry. For instance, there's a Friendly's at 230 Northwest Peacock Boulevard. Most New Yorkers know what a Friendly's is. For those who don't, Friendly's is a kid-friendly sitdown restaurant featuring ice cream, burgers, and other family-oriented fare. You can also expect more restaurant offerings at a new development at the corner of St. Lucie West Boulevard and Peacock Boulevard.

At the game you'll notice young folks — mostly younger women — in the stands selling beer and other concessions. They're wearing Duffy's T-shirts. Duffy's is a local chain of sports bars offering good food, a decent variety of beer, and an abundance of big-screen TVs showing sporting events of all sorts. (If you happen to be at spring training during March Madness, Duffy's is the perfect hangout. Chances are good you'll find your favorite team's game on one of the many TVs.) The Duffy's closest to the ballpark is also the largest in the chain: Superplay USA (1600 N.W. Courtyard Circle, Port St. Lucie; 772/408-5800; **superplayusa.com**) features 48 lanes of bowling, a video arcade, batting cages, laser tag, an indoor 9-hole miniature golf course and the Duffy's menu. Perfect for rowdy kids and tired parents.

If your more immediate goal is good food and sporting events on the big screen, we'd recommend you head south to the Stuart Duffy's, located in the heart of the historic downtown area. Florida is in a transitional state these days: The ways of old-time Florida — the kind we associate with the traditional spring-training vibe — are rapidly disappearing under the weight of a gazillion strip malls and retirement complexes. Stuart is a throwback to old-school Florida, with a vibrant downtown on the waterfront. The downtown Duffy's features a patio (with flat-screen TVs; no escaping sports here), a traditional sports-bar décor and a friendly staff. The prices are right, too: Thanks to a $2 beer special we walked out stuffed with a barbecue burger and Killian's for under $10. Take some time to walk around downtown Stuart. There are plenty of watering holes, but the real attraction is the chance to soak up some real Florida atmosphere. Everything in Port St. Lucie is new; there's the patina of authenticity in Stuart. The same goes for nearby Fort Pierce and Jensen Beach: If you're planning a multiday trip, some time spent poking around the old downtowns of the Treasure Coast is time well-spent.

Duffy's, 1 S.W. Osceola Blvd., Stuart; 772/221-4899; **duffyssportsgrill.com**. *To get there from Port St. Lucie, head south on Hwy. 1 (also referred to as Federal Highway) to downtown Stuart. The route can be a little challenging, but it is well-marked. As you head south on Hwy. 1, keep in mind the exit to downtown Stuart is on the left.*

Where to Stay
The only lodging within real walking distance of the ballpark (and then it's a stretch) is Castle Pines Golf Villas (575 N.W. Mercantile Place, Port Saint Lucie; 772) 336-3333; **castlepinesgolfvillas.com**). Golf is a big pastime in Port St. Lucie — as you've already seen in this chapter — and the Castle Pines Golf Villas offers 54 holes of golf and a variety of accommodations, ranging from guest rooms to three-bedroom townhouses. Prices begin at $92 nightly for a room.

Also within walking distance is the Perfect Drive Golf Villas at PGA Village (525 N.W. Lake Whitney Place, Port St. Lucie; 772/873-0515; **perfectdriveatpgavillage.com**). Here you'll find guest rooms as well as one- or two-bedroom villas. They also offer spring-training packages that include plenty of free golf.

insider's tip
There is limited public golf in the immediate Port St. Lucie area. Your best bet for combining golf with a Mets spring-training trip is to stay at a hotel either on a course or affiliated with one.

South of the ballpark on Peacock Boulevard are several chain hotels, including the Hampton Inn and Suites (155 S.W. Peacock Blvd., Port St. Lucie; 772/878-5900; **hamptoninn.com**), Mainstay Suites (8501 Champions Way, Port St. Lucie; 772/460-8882; **www.choicehotels.com**) and Springhill Suites (2000 N.W. Courtyard Circle, Port St. Lucie; 772/871-2929; **marriott.com**). All three feature one-bedroom suites as well as regular hotel rooms.

insider's tip

Unless you're an utter cheapskate and want to avoid the very reasonable parking fee at Tradition Field, there's really no good reason to stay next to the ballpark (unless the idea of combining golf with your stay appeals to you). During our last spring visit we had a wonderful stay at the Hilton Garden Inn PGA Village (8540 Commerce Centre Dr.; Port St. Lucie, 772-871-6850; **hilton.com**). It's a newer property and very accessible to the PGA Village facilities. Though the traffic in Port St. Lucie and surrounding areas can be a pain, there are a lot of hotel options within a 30-mile drive; if the sea is your thing, there are plenty of waterfront properties in Port St. Lucie, Jensen Beach, and Stuart.

RV fans should note the presence of the high-end St. Lucie West Motorcoach Resort just down Peacock Boulevard from the ballpark (St. Lucie West Motorcoach Resort, Outdoor Resorts of America, 800 N.W. Peacock Blvd., Port St. Lucie; 772/336-1135; **outdoor-resorts.com/stlucie**). It's billed as a motorcoach-only resort (limited to Class A RVs), and a quick glimpse inside the gates showed some lovely landscaping and clean facilities. It features its own 9-hole par-3 course, lighted tennis courts, and high-end amenities like cable TV and WiFi, but it is a little spendy at $70/night.

Farther away is the Port St. Lucie RV Resort (3703 S.E. Jennings Rd., Port St. Lucie; 772/337-3340; **portstluciervresort.com**), but it carries a daily price of under $50.

Flying In

The closest airport (40 miles away) to Port St. Lucie is Palm Beach International Airport. Most major airlines fly into PBI, including Air Canada, American, AirTran, Continental, Delta, JetBlue, Southwest, Northwest, United, Spirit, Sun County, and US Airways.

An alternative is Melbourne International Airport, located less than 60 miles north of Port St. Lucie. It's a small airport, and the only major airline flying in is Delta.

If you're planning on visiting several spring-training sites, you may want to fly into Orlando and then drive down to Port St. Lucie. Most of the 125 miles between Orlando and Vero Beach is on I-95 and the Bee Line or, alternately, the Florida Turnpike.

SPRING-TRAINING HISTORY

The New York Mets have had only two spring-training venues in team history: St. Petersburg's Al Lang Field (1962-1987) and Port St. Lucie (1988-present).

→ washington nationals

SPACE COAST STADIUM

Capacity	8,100
Year Opened	1994
Dimensions	340L, 404C, 340R
Surface	Grass
Local Airport	Melbourne or Orlando
Address	5800 Stadium Parkway, Melbourne.

From the north, take I-95 to Exit 195 (Fiske Boulevard, Rockledge), take a left on Fiske Boulevard and follow it around to Space Coast Stadium. From the south, take I-95 to Exit 191 (Wickham Road), take a left on Wickham Road and follow it until Lake Andrew Drive. Take a right on Lake Andrew Drive and follow it to Stadium Parkway. Take a right on Stadium Parkway. Space Coast Stadium will be on your left. (There are plenty of signs pointing the way to the ballpark.).

121

A National Space Plan

The Washington Nationals haven't been a spring-training hit in Viera, which is a shame: Space Coast Stadium is one of the cooler ballparks in the Grapefruit League. There's no mistaking it as you approach from the north or the south. Looming over the Florida landscape, the stadium looks like a spaceship that's landing in the middle of nowhere. It sits above the flat Florida landscape, shining brightly with its red, white, and blue exterior.

Given Viera's proximity to the Johnson Space Center (just 13 miles away) and the traditional home of the U.S. space program in Cocoa Beach, the theme at Space Coast Stadium is, of course, space exploration. Foul poles commemorate the Challenger and Columbia shuttle disasters, but other reminders of the space program are now gone, such as the model of the Discovery shuttle and the space-themed concessions.

Those features were eliminated as part of ballpark renovations undertaken at the behest of the Nationals. The exterior of the ballpark was painted red, white, and blue — the team colors — and the teal seats highlighting the ballpark's origins as a Florida Marlins training facility were replaced by traditional blue seats. The hand-operated scoreboard is gone as well, replaced by a spiffier electronic display. This is very much now the home of the Nationals.

The seating is new at Space Coast Stadium.

At first glance you'd assume that this ballpark is in the middle of nowhere. Not quite: Despite appearances, the ballpark is only three miles from I-95 and about an hour from Orlando via the Bee Line Expressway. The ballpark is also about 10 miles from Cocoa Beach, which features a slew of hotels along the waterfront and near the freeway. If you're headed to spring training, a trip to Space Coast Stadium isn't a chore at all; you could easily take in two games by combining a visit to Space Coast Stadium with another game at Champion Stadium (the spring training home of the Atlanta Braves) or Osceola County Stadium (the spring-training home of the Houston Astros), or you could head down the coast via I-95 and take in a New York Mets game in Port St. Lucie.

But the ballpark won't be in the middle of nowhere for much long, as the nearby Viera development continues to grow at a brisk pace (during a recent visit it was slow going heading north of the ballpark to the freeway, as construction vehicles clogged the roads) and other major retail expansion occurs (several big-box retailers recently signed agreements to build new stores south of the ballpark along the freeway) throughout the Space Coast, thanks to its location between Orlando and Cocoa.

insider's tip

If you go to spring-training games, try to sit on the first-base side of the grandstand: Your view will be good and you'll avoid staring in the sun. Avoid the right-field bleachers in the day: You'll be hot and staring into the sun. The most shaded seats — and thus the most desirable ones, if you want some relief from the sun — are in the back of the sections to the left and right of the main grandstand, under the canopies.

Space Coast Stadium isn't a very flashy venue: The seating is basic, the amenities are good but not great, and the location isn't outstanding. But it's comfortable, and given that the Nationals rarely sell out a game, it's a good bet you can pick up a good seat on an impulse.

insider's tip

The Nationals train at the Carl Barger complex right next to the ballpark. You can wander back and catch a minor-league game. You should also check if a "B" is being played if you get to the complex early.

COCOA EXPO

Old-timers will remember the years the Houston Astros trained in Cocoa: The tie-ins between the Astros and the space program were simply too much too great to ignore, and it was fitting that America's space-age team was training on the Space Coast. During those days it was called Astrotown, and the team played at Cocoa Stadium.

BALLPARK HISTORY

Space Coast Stadium was built in 1994 to be the spring-training home of the Florida Marlins. When Jeffrey Loria bought the Marlins and sold the Montreal Expos to Major League Baseball, part of the agreement was that the Marlins would shift spring-training headquarters to Jupiter, while the Expos would move spring training from Jupiter to Melbourne. When the Nationals were sold to the Lerner family, they remade the ballpark to serve the image of the team.

THE SPRING-TRAINING BALLPARK EXPERIENCE

Concessions

You'll find standard ballpark fare at the concession stands located behind the grandstand: hot dogs, burgers, pizza, soda, and beer. In addition, there is taco salad served in a baseball helmet, while a sausage grill includes Italian sausages smothered in onions and peppers, bratwurst, cheddarwurst, and Cajun sausages.

A beer deck beyond the left-field home-run fence is a comfortable place to buy a picnic-table ticket and settle in with a cold one or two.

Parking

For being built out in the middle of nowhere, you'd think that someone would have thought to put in adequate and accessible parking. Not so. The parking is $6, and much of it is on unpaved fields a fair hoof from the ballpark. You can't park along the highway and walk in, unfortunately.

That Cocoa ballpark is still is use, and it's worth a side trip if you're interested in seeing an old spring-training venue. Cocoa Expo Sports Center is used mostly for baseball and soccer youth tournaments, with the occasional lacrosse and marching-band competition thrown in. The ballpark stands as it did when the Florida Marlins trained there in 1993, the first year of the team's existence and the last year the complex was used for pro baseball. The seating is gone, but the rails, dugouts, and press box remains.

Cocoa Expo Sports Center, 500 Friday Rd., Cocoa; cocoaexpo.com. From I-95, take Hwy. 520 eastbound. Turn right when you see the complex; the ballpark is in plain sight.

Autographs

Your best bet is luring playing to the edge of the stands. There's no organized autograph line for the players or coaches.

IF YOU GO

Cruising the Space Coast

The Space Coast of Florida (Titusville, Cocoa Beach, Melbourne, and Palm Bay) may not be as touristy as Orlando, but there are some definite things to do if you're in town for spring training. The one mandatory stop for out-of-towners is the Kennedy Space Center, where NASA launches and lands space shuttles. While access to launches isn't as casual as it was before 9/11, you can still sign up for a limited-access pass to the launch through NASA or view the launch from outside Kennedy Space Center grounds.

The adjoining Kennedy Space Center Visitor Complex features a full-scale replica of the Space Shuttle Explorer as well as exhibits honoring the history of the space program. You'll also go through a simulated Apollo 8 mission, complete with special effects.

You can get to the Kennedy Space Center directly from I-95 (follow the omnipresent signs). If you're coming out from Orlando, hop on the Bee Line Expressway and head east until you hit the signs for the Kennedy Space Center. Kennedy Space Center, 321/449-4444; **kennedyspacecenter.com**. *Admission: $40.28, adults; $29.68, children (3-11). Additional fees apply for guided tours and historical exhibits.*

Space Coast Stadium in the old days, when the Expos trained there.

Nearby is Port Canaveral, where several cruise lines — Disney, Carnival, Royal Caribbean and Holland America, among others — set sail for exotic destinations in the Caribbean, Bahamas, and Central America. But most folks don't know about the three parks within Port Canaveral: Jetty Park, Ports End Park, and Freddie Patrick Park. All three feature fishing and camping. The pier at Jetty Park is also well regarded as a great place to watch a space-shuttle launch.

After seeing a gazillion billboards for Ron Jon, you'll assume it's this huge shrine to surfing. While a drive into Cocoa Beach is worth a trip — and be sure to hum the theme from *I Dream of Jeannie* while you imagine where Major Nelson lived — you'll probably be a little disappointed in the 52,000-square-foot store, where the main product seems to be Ron Jon t-shirts. Yes, there are surfboard rentals and kayak rentals at the facility, but the main emphasis is on Ron Jon merchandise. (Although it is kinda cool that Ron Jon stays open 24 hours: You never know when you'll need a Ron Jon muscle shirt at 3 a.m.) Don't say you weren't warned. Ron Jon Surf Shop, 4151 N. Atlantic Av., Cocoa Beach; 321/799-8888; **ronjons.com**.

March is harvest season for the citrus growers in Florida, and that means the local packing houses are bursting with action. Family-owned and -managed Harvey's is one of the largest on the Space Coast, and there are three processing plants between Viera and Cocoa. Yes, there is plenty of orange juice for sampling — it's squeezed right there at the plant — and you can ship some back home as well. Harvey's, 3700 U.S. 1, Rockledge; 321/636-6072; **harveysgroves.com**.

You're not exactly in the middle of nowhere when you attend spring training in Viera, but your entertainment options are severely limited. Former Brevard County Manatees GM Buck Rogers shared with us his choices for what to do while attending Nationals spring-training games.

For Families: Beef O'Brady's Sports Pub. Located in East Viera, approximately one mile east of Space Coast Stadium (as the crow flies), Beef O'Brady's caters to families. If you're into sports, Beef's — as it's affectionately called — is the place. Satellite TVs, great food, inexpensive...get the pressed Cuban sandwich with cole slaw. Beef O'Brady's, 5410 Murrell Rd., Suite 101, Viera; 321/633-4030; **beefobradys.com**.

For drinking/relaxing: The Avenue Viera mall. Located just south of the ballpark, the mall features everything from an Applebee's and Chili's to a food court, upscale retail, and movie theaters. Forget everything you know about malls, this isn't your typical mall; built in concentric circles with parking between the circles, it's a new design that caters to shoppers, diners, who want to go out but not in! It'll be loaded with things to do for those who like to relax. The Avenue Viera, I-95 and Wickham Road, Viera; **shoptheavenue.com**.

Where the players hang: Carabba's. After a daytime spring-training game, head south of the stadium two miles until you hit Wickham Road, and then head east for approximately 1.5 miles. Carabba's Italian Restaurant is on the left in SunTree. Get the Italian sausage or the meat ravioli.

Night life: The beach. Head beach side and bring a designated driver, because the action is everywhere you want to be, and cops don't accept "I only had two beers" as an excuse. Between the college spring breakers and bikers (Daytona Beach's Bike Week is in March, and we receive overflow hotel patrons), there's something (and somebody) for everybody. Play it like Vegas: What happens in Melbourne stays in Melbourne.

Where to Stay

The hotels in the area tend to be spread out, and as they are often full in March (mostly unrelated to spring training), some planning is required. Baymont Inn Melbourne (7200 George T. Edwards Dr., Melbourne; 321/242-9400; **baymontinn.com**) is less than two miles from the ballpark, but there's not a huge advantage to staying there, as you'll need a car to get around anyway. There is also a cluster of hotels near Melbourne International Airport fairly close to the ballpark.

Our recommendation: Stay in Cocoa Beach, which is less than 10 miles from the ballpark. Cocoa Beach is right on the coast, and many of the hotels are right on the beach, so you can combine some tan time with baseball time. (And even if these hotels aren't on the coast, they will usually feature good swimming facilities.) All the major chains are represented in Cocoa Beach, including Holiday Inn Express Hotel & Suites, Super 8, Best Western, Ramada Inn, Hampton Inn, Hilton Cocoa Beach Oceanfront, Doubletree Cocoa Beach Oceanfront, and Radisson.

Flying In

The closest airport is Melbourne International Airport, located 12 miles away from the complex. It's not exactly a busy airport: Delta flies six times a day between Atlanta and Melbourne.

Most folks will want to fly into Orlando International Airport. While it's a bigger airport, it's fairly easy to make your way around, as a tram brings you from the gates to the central terminal. Just be warned that it's quite a hike from the gates to the terminals even with the tram.

SPRING-TRAINING HISTORY

Washington Nationals/Montreal Expos have held spring training in the following locations: West Palm Beach (1968-1972); Daytona Beach (1973-1980); West Palm Beach (1981-1997); Melbourne (1998-2002); Jupiter (2003-present).

→ tampa bay / st. petersburg

Tampa Bay: The Heart of the Grapefruit League

The Tampa/St. Pete area was one of the first in the nation to wholeheartedly embrace spring training: From Tarpon Springs in the north to Sarasota in the south, Tampa Bay has played host to dozens of teams during March since the late teens. For Tampa Bay, spring training was an extension of what the region did well — promote unique tourism — in a backwoods kind of way. Spring-training news in the 1920s and 1930s was equal parts baseball and kitsch, a time when legendary sportswriter Damon Runyon would spend more time chronicling the actions of a newly acquired alligator than the home-run exploits of Babe Ruth — much to the chagrin of Ruth.

Today's Tampa/St. Pete area bears little resemblance to the sleepy area originally host spring training for virtually every older franchise in baseball at some point, and most of the ballparks — save Bradenton's McKechnie Field — are considerably more polished and professional than the rickety, wooden ballparks once housing teams looking for the latest spring phenom. Six teams train in the region: New York Yankees (Tampa), Toronto (Dunedin), Philadelphia (Clearwater), Detroit (Lakeland), Pittsburgh (Bradenton), and Cincinnati (in Sarasota, at least through 2009).

For today's baseball fans, Tampa Bay is still spring-training nirvana. Because of the high concentration of teams in the area (and many more in central Florida and the region), you could take in a game a day and merely scratch the surface of spring training Tampa Bay style.

Of course, one cannot live on hot dogs and Class A-bound rookies for long, and at some point you'll need to venture past the ballpark and your hotel room and take in the local sights. As a major metropolitan area, Tampa/St. Peter has a lot to offer.

First, an explanation of the geography of the area. Tampa Bay is really a set of cities, with Tampa to the northeast and St. Petersburg to the southwest. Tampa and St. Pete are the largest in the area and contain the vast majority of attractions. Clearwater and Dunedin are in the northwest quadrant of the Bay and comprise a fast-growing area, while Bradenton and Sarasota are to the south and at times feel like they're worlds away

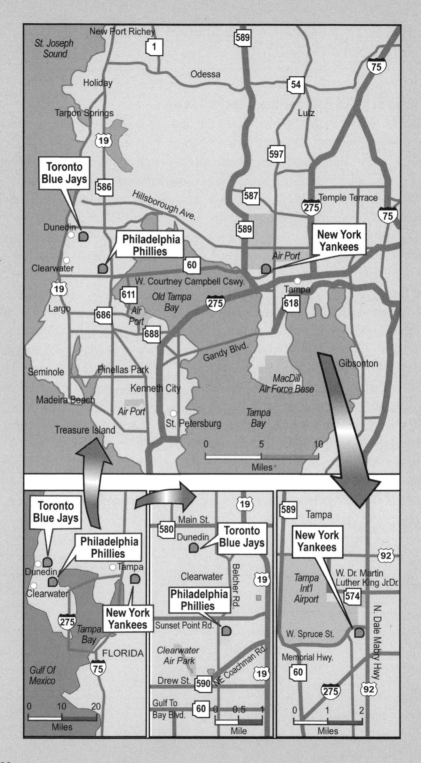

The bayfront in St. Petersburg.

from the rest of the Bay. Lakeland, while not truly part of the Tampa-St. Pete metro area, is close enough to make for a short drive to and from the big city, though it certainly stands on its own as a separate entity.

Though it can feel a tad sprawling at times, it's relatively easy to get around Tampa Bay: None of the ballparks are too far away from the main freeways (I-4, I-275) or the Courtney Campbell Causeway, so you should feel comfortable staying anywhere in the area and be able to easily make it to your ballpark of choice, as long as you avoid rush-hour traffic.

Tampa Attractions

Tampa/St. Pete has turned into a business center for Florida and the southern United States, and it lacks some of the more colorful roadside attractions found in the likes of Orlando. Perhaps that's why spring training has always been popular in the area: There's little competition for the attention of fans in March, no House of Mouse on the horizon, no trained whales or dreary tourist attractions.

Still, there's plenty for the family to do during February and March. If you're bringing the kids to spring training, take them to Busch Gardens, located eight miles north of downtown Tampa. Busch Gardens is a theme park built around a zoo, various rides, and an adjacent water park. It's a large place, so plan on spending a full day there — or, better yet, drop off the wife and kids and head to a game while they take in the delights of Busch Gardens). Busch Gardens Tampa Bay, corner of Busch Boulevard and 40th Street, Tampa; 888/800-5447; **buschgardens.com**. *Adults, $67.95; children (3-9), $57.95; Internet discounts available.*

If you want to see African animals in a little more affordable milieu, there's the Lowry Park Zoo in Tampa. Actually, the zoo features animals of all sorts, ranging from local flamingos, panthers, and alligators to Indian rhinoceros, Komodo dragons, and Angolan Colobus monkeys. Lowry Park Zoo, 1101 W. Sligh Av., Tampa; 813/935-8552; **lowryparkzoo.com**. *Adults, $18.95; seniors, $17.95; children (3-11), $14.95.*

The Florida Aquarium is one of the leading attractions in Tampa and the perfect place to see the wide ecological variety of Florida in a single visit. The aquarium isn't one large tank, but rather a series of habitats organized by theme: wetlands, bays and beaches, coral reef, and more. This allows you to see a greater variety of wildlife in a wide range of habitats; freshwater and saltwater wildlife is featured as well as mammals and amphibians that live in a wetland environment, such as otters and turtles. Among the wildlife on display are American alligators, turtles, sharks, stingrays, snook, octopus, sea horses, goliath grouper, and otters. Kids will also enjoy the Explore-A-Shore outdoor play area, featuring a two-story pirate ship and water jet sprays. For an additional fee you can tour the Bay on a catamaran and look for some of the 400 bottlenose dolphins inhabiting the area. Florida Aquarium, 701 Channelside Drive, downtown Tampa; 813/273-4000; **flaquarium.org**. *Adults, $17.95; seniors (60+), $14.95; children (3-11), $12.95.*

Those more in a mood to party will want to head to Ybor City, Tampa's Latin Quarter. Once home to numerous cigar factories, Ybor City is now a shopping and entertainment oasis. Located on 7th Avenue East between 15th and 20th streets, Ybor City's larger buildings can be seen from the freeway and the area is well-marked on the freeway, while a streetcar runs every 15-20 minutes from downtown Tampa.

The center of the Ybor City Historic District is (appropriately enough) Centro Ybor, bounded by 7th and 8th avenues and 16th and 17th streets. It's a good place to begin your visit, and although the chains have moved into the area — Marble Slab Creamery, Victoria's Secret, and Starbucks all have local outposts — there's definitely enough local color to go around when you combine Florida weird with the laidback Ybor City vibe in hotspots like Tampa Bay Brewing or Adobe Gila's, There are three main activities in Centro Ybor — drinking, cigar smoking, and movie watching

— and we'd recommend the first two. The cigar craze has peaked in most of the world, but in Tampa it's still a prime pursuit, and you can find plenty of folks — women included — puffing away on a stogie and hanging out at one of the dozen or so cigar vendors and restaurants/bars, including Stogie Castillo's. A good place to start is Ybor City State Museum (1818 9th Av.; 813/247-6323; **ybormuseum.org**), which details the history of cigar manufacturing in the area. And yes, you can still buy hand-rolled cigars in Ybor City: there are at least six such vendors in the district. Centro Ybor Visitor Information Center, 1600 E. 8th Av., Tampa; 877/9-FIESTA; **ybor.org**.

Also worth a trip is downtown St. Petersburg, where the BayWalk Center and the Pier are worth a visit. The Pier is located on the waterfront and features a five-story inverted pyramid with giant tubes bubbling with fish and creatures from the sea, complete with a second-floor aquarium filled with native and tropical fish and sharks. You'll also find educational exhibits from the Great Explorations Museum, with the historic H.M.S. Bounty docked pierside. Upstairs is one of the more notable restaurants in the Tampa Bay area: Columbia's, a family institution serving Cuban fare. You'll need a reservation, but a sunset view of downtown is worth the wait.

BayWalk is an upscale shopping and dining area. The whole family will enjoy TooJay's Gourmet Deli, where your inner New Yorker can be soothed with some lox or a huge pastrami sandwich. The Pier is located at the end of Second Avenue N.E. on the downtown St. Petersburg waterfront; St. Petersburg; 727/821-6443; **stpete-pier.com**. BayWalk Center, 125 2nd Av. N., St. Petersburg; 727/895-9277; **yourbaywalk.com**.

For the truly surreal, there's the Salvador Dali Museum in St. Pete. Get it? Surreal? Good. Probably not something the kids would enjoy, but it's something the adults may find interesting. Salvador Dali Museum, 1000 3rd St. S., St. Petersburg; 727/823-3767; **salvadordalimuseum.org**.

And, of course, there are the beaches. Truth is, it's a little chilly to be swimming in the ocean in March, but that shouldn't stop you from taking a walk on one of the many public beaches in Tampa Bay. One popular destination is Clearwater Beach, which isn't actually a beach: It's an island outside of Clearwater. It has the prototypical white beaches along with some amenities (cabanas and umbrellas for rent), along with concessions and a slew of restaurants. We use this merely as an example and discuss it more in our Dunedin chapter; it's hard to go wrong with any beach on the Gulf side of the Tampa Bay area. Clearwater Beach, 100 Coronado Dr., Clearwater Beach; 727/447-7600.

Al Lang Field.

Sadly, one of the great baseball attractions in downtown St. Petersburg is no more. Al Lang Field was the home of spring training in St. Pete from 1916 through spring 2008, when the Tampa Bay Rays ended the run with one final March at the quaint waterfront ballpark. Though a 1977 "renovation" largely replaced the charm of an old wooden ballpark with a concrete monstrosity, Al Lang Field was a must-visit for generations of spring-training aficionados. As of this writing the specific future of Al Lang Field isn't known; it will certainly be torn down. One of the best things about wandering around the area is the presence of historic plaques celebrating the history of spring training in the area. We suspect these plaques will be removed once Al Lang Field is torn down, but a call to the local Chamber of Commerce (727/821-4069) wouldn't be out of line if you're a history buff and want to see them one last time.

Tampa Bay Hotels

Hotels in Tampa tend to be concentrated near the airport, in downtown, and along the waterfront on the north side of the Bay, off the Courtney Campbell Causeway (which connects Tampa and Clearwater). They also tend to be popping up close to some spring-training headquarters; for instance, there are several newer hotels close to the Phillies' spring-training headquarters in Clearwater.

We'll cover specific hotel recommendations on the team pages. Though we include Sarasota and Lakeland in this overview chapter, they're large and separate enough to warrant further coverage in the Reds and Tigers team pages, respectively. By and large, the distance between spring-training facilities in Tampa is small enough so that you don't need to be worried about staying too far from the action; staying close to the action is always a good idea, but if you can save a few bucks by staying farther away, why not?

If you plan on visiting multiple venues in the Tampa Bay area, a central location would make sense unless you plan on jumping from hotel to hotel. In Tampa, there are two centrally located hotel clusters: the airport area and the Rocky Point Island area. We're not going to list all of the airport hotels, for they are legion and corporate in their facelessness. One exception: The InterContinental Hotel Tampa (4860 W. Kennedy Blvd., Tampa; 866/915-1557; **intercontampa.com**) is a recently renovated upper-scale hotel convenient to both the Yankees and Phillies training camps.

Rocky Point Island has a little more character, as most of the hotels are on the waterfront and there are many restaurants nearby. Rocky Point Island is bisected by the Courtney Campbell Causeway, which connects Tampa and Clearwater, and is located on the north side of Tampa Bay. Fans attending spring training in any of the area training sites — Dunedin, Clearwater, Tampa, Sarasota, and Bradenton — will find Rocky Point Island to be convenient headquarters.

Hotels on Rocky Point Island include:
- → Hampton Inn, 3035 N. Rocky Point Dr., Tampa; 813/289-6262; **hamptoninn.com**.
- → Holiday Inn Express Rocky Point Island, 3025 N. Rocky Point Dr., Tampa; 813/287-8585; **holiday-inn.com**.
- → Doubletreee Guest Suites, 3050 N. Rocky Point Dr. W., Tampa; 813/888-8800; **hilton.com**.
- → Radisson Bay Harbor, 7700 Courtney Campbell Causeway, Tampa; 813/281-8900; **radisson.com**.
- → Chase Suite Hotel, 3075 N. Rocky Point Dr., Tampa; 877/433-9644, 813/281-5677; **woodfinsuitehotels.com**.
- → Sailport Resort, 2506 N. Rocky Point Dr., Tampa; 800/255-9599, 813/281-9599; **sailport.com**.

Tampa Bay Restaurants

Spring-training traditionalists tend to flock around the same restaurants every year; it's part of the ritual, and we cover many of these places in the team chapters. Tampa Bay is a pretty good restaurant area, and while we won't cover every notable dining establishment in the area here, we will touch on some places we think are worthy of special attention. (We will also cover notable restaurants near each of the spring-training ballparks.)

Bern's Steak House is a Tampa institution for red-meat eaters. Yes, the decor is somewhat alarming — the word bordello comes to mind — but the steaks are among the finest in the world. The 18-page menu is a work of art, featuring long and loving descriptions of the various offerings. Begin your meal with one of the three steaks tartar (or, for a change of pace, go for the chateaubriand carpaccio) and then follow with a main course of steak. (Yes, chicken and fish are on the menu , and we're sure they're great, but why bother at such a noteworthy steakhouse?) Order a side veggie raised on Bern's organic farm. Top it off with a fine Armagnac in the Harry Waugh Dessert Room. The place is an institution; enjoy and don't worry about the bill. Bern's Steak House, 128 S. Howard Av., Tampa; 813/251-2421; **bernssteakhouse.com**.

There many other good steakhouses in the Tampa area besides Bern's — Charley's, Shula's, Ruth's Chris, The Palm — but locals recommend Fleming's, located a little over a mile from Steinbrenner Field. Again, this is a traditional steakhouse, pure and simple, with an emphasis on service. Some may dislike the place because it's part of a chain, as Fleming's is the high-end offering from Outback Steakhouse. But this is the hometown Fleming's, and obviously the one where most attention is paid. Fleming's Prime Steakhouse, 4322 W. Boy Scout Blvd., Tampa; (813) 874-WINE (9463); **flemingssteakhouse.com**.

Football fans will remember Lee Roy Selmon, the first Tampa Bay Buccaneer inducted into the Pro Football Hall of Fame. Of course, he has a local restaurant, which is convenient to Steinbrenner Field. The emphasis at Lee Roy Selmon's is comfort food with Oklahoma roots: ribs, steaks, mashed potatoes, etc. Lee Roy Selmon's, 4302 W. Boy Scout Blvd., Tampa; 813/871-3287; **leeroyselmons.com**.

Ferg's Sports Bar & Grill is a huge downtown St. Pete sports bar; the converted garage features a slew of outdoor decks and some pretty decent food. Ferg's Sports Bar & Grill, 1320 Central Av., St. Petersburg; 727/822-4562; **fergsonline.com**.

The Press Box is the prototypical sports bar, with 23 TV screens scattered throughout the premises. This is the place to go if you want to check out some NCAA basketball tournament action in a March visit. The Press Box, 222 S. Dale Mabry Hwy., Tampa; 813/876-3528; **pressboxsports.com**.

The Bay Street area of International Plaza is close to the Yankees' training facilities and features a wide range of (mostly chain) restaurants appropriate for the whole family, including The Cheesecake Factory, Capitol Grille, Champps, TooJay's Gourmet Deli, Bar Louie, and Blue Martini. It can be quite the zoo, as the open-air layout and many outdoor seating areas creates a very festive atmosphere, but it's a top-notch gathering area. The mall features a slew of upscale shops. Again, it's close to Steinbrenner Field and relatively convenient for those attending Phillies spring training as well. International Plaza/Bay Street, 2223 N. West Shore Blvd., Tampa; 813/342-3790; **shopinternationalplaza.com**.

Tampa Golf

Tampa is not necessarily known as a golfing nirvana. As a matter of fact, Tampa has a reputation of lacking first-class golf courses open to the public, especially freestanding courses that aren't surrounded by housing. While this reputation has changed somewhat in the last ten years, golfers who want to combine a round with a spring-training game may need to do a little work in terms of driving and scheduling to secure a tee time at a good facility. Here are a few course suggestions to get you going, but be prepared to deal with many water hazards no matter where you play.

World Woods, located an hour north of Tampa in Brooksville, is generally regarded as the finest course in the area. With 36 holes and a nine-hole short course, World Woods comprises two courses (Pine Barrens and Rolling Oaks) designed by Tom Fazio, with Pine Barrens the more challenging (and scenic) of the two. They both play at the same distance from the championship tees — just under 7,000 yards — but they are different in design, with Pine Barrens featuring several dramatic signature holes (including one where ladders are needed to access parts of the fairway) and Rolling Oaks sporting a more traditional and mainstream design. The 4th and 15th holes at Pine Barrens are considered to be two of the most outstanding holes in the state. World Woods, 17590 Ponce De Leon Blvd., Brooksville; 352/796-5500, ext. 4; **worldwoods.com**. *To get there from Tampa, take the Suncoast Parkway (589) north, a toll road, to the end, and then go right (east) on Hwy. 98 for a half-mile. Reservations (guaranteed with a credit card) can be made up to 90 days in advance.*

University of Tampa baseball field at night.

If you're interested in lodgings near the Phillies' or Blue Jays' camps in Clearwater or Dunedin, respectively, consider a stay at the Innisbrook Golf Resort, located just up Hwy. 19 in Palm Harbor (close to Tarpon Springs). The PGA Chrysler Championship is played at the resort's Copperhead Golf Course, but if your game is not up to the PGA level you can always take in one of three (Island, Highland North, Highland South) other courses on the resort. It's a place to take the whole family, with a pool and spa featuring two water slides and a cascading waterfall. Guests at the resort have priority when reserving tee times. Innisbrook Resort and Golf Club, 36750 U.S. Hwy. 19 N., Palm Harbor; 800/456-2000; **innisbrookgolfresort.com**.

The TPC of Tampa Bay was designed by Bobby Weed and is a fairly open, flat course (when designing it, Weed actually removed about half the trees present to create a more spacious layout), though definitely on the longer side with plenty of banks for television purposes. TPC of Tampa Bay, 5300 W. Lutz Lake Fern Rd., Lutz; 813/949-0090; **tpctampabay.com**.

The Eagles Golf Club features two 18-hole courses: The Lakes (where there's water on virtually every hole) and The Forest, which features a more rolling design edged by dense forests. The Eagles Golf Club of Tampa Bay, 16101 Nine Eagles Dr., Odessa; 877/446-5388; **eaglesgolf.com.**

Bardmoor Golf and Tennis Club has hosted PGA and LPGA events in the past and has won awards for "Tampa Bay's Favorite Public Golf Course" from the St. Petersburg Times. Bardmoor Golf and Tennis Club, 8001 Cumberland Rd., Largo; 727/392-1234, ext. 209; **bardmoorgolf.com**.

Finally, there's Mangrove Bay, a 72-hole championship-level course maintained by the city of St. Petersburg. You'll need to work a little to snare a tee time, as reservations are taken only up to seven days in advance. Mangrove Bay, 875 62nd Av. NE., St. Petersburg; 727/803-7800; **stpete.org/golf/mangrove.htm**.

OTHER SPORTS

The St. Pete Times Forum, located in downtown Tampa, is home to the NHL's Tampa Bay Lightning and the AFL's Tampa Bay Storm. Both teams are surprisingly popular: although the Lightning initially worked hard to find an identity past an appeal to expatriate northerners, hockey is now established in the Bay after the emergence of starts like Vincent Lecavalier and a 2004 Stanley Cup championship. Arena football, too, is surprisingly popular, as fans love the flash of the indoor game. Both teams have regular-season games scheduled in February and March. St. Pete Times Forum, 401 Channelside Dr., Tampa; 813/301-6500; **sptimesforum.com**.

College baseball is popular in the area, and a baseball purist will want to check out a game at the University of Tampa or the University of South Florida, who often play night games as a nice accompaniment to an after-

Red McEwen Field.

noon major-league game. USF is located northwest of downtown Tampa, and the team plays at Red McEwen Field, a small ballpark housing the Tampa Yankees for the first two years of that team's existence. Built in 1967, Red McEwen Field features plenty of exposed bleacher seats and a nice covered picnic area down the left-field line. But we won't kid you: The facilities are Spartan, to say the least, and the real appeal to a game at Red McEwen Field is Big East and USF baseball (both of which are usually decent), not the comfy surroundings. *Red McEwen Field is located at the corner of Bull Run and Elm Dr. on the USF campus. Follow the signs to the Sun Dome; the ballpark is next door. Parking adjacent to the ballpark.*

The University of Tampa is located right off downtown Tampa at one of the most picturesque campuses anywhere. University of Tampa Baseball Field is a small ballpark, but the Spartans program is solid, with plenty of NCAA tourney appearances in recent years and some top rankings along the way. Both Lou Piniella and Tino Martinez played here as well. A strong schedule means you're likely to see some good baseball from both teams, and the ballpark is pretty nice by D-II standards, with exposed bleacher seating close to the action. Downtown Tampa makes a nice backdrop during a night game. *The University of Tampa Baseball Field is located at the corner of Cass Street and North Boulevard, at the northwest*

Plant Hall, the former Tampa Bay Hotel.

corner of the University of Tampa campus off downtown Tampa. Parking adjacent to the ballpark.

insider's tip

If you attend a University of Tampa game, give yourself time to walk around the campus. The main building on campus was once the grand Tampa Bay Hotel, and pictures from that era can be found throughout the building and the Henry Plant Museum. The Tampa Bay Hotel was built to impress: The minarets atop the towers would have been seen from a good distance (especially for those visitors arriving by boat), and the huge porches were ideal for lounging. Plant Hall is the large building.

A short walk from Plant Hall is the John H. Sykes College of Business building. In front is a historic marker celebrating the site of what some say is Babe Ruth's longest home run, a 587-foot shot coming when the Babe was a babe with the Boston Red Sox. Given the accuracy of records from that era, we're not going to go out on a limb and definitively argue the historic veracity of such a claim. But it is interesting to see the marker and imagine the spring-training atmosphere when Plant Field was a training site and the Tampa Bay Hotel team headquarters. A more genteel time, to be sure.

Flying In

Considering the size of the Tampa Bay area, there are a plethora of airports in the area.

The largest is Tampa International Airport, located near both the center of town and Steinbrenner Field, the spring home of the New York Yankees. (Sit on the left side of a plane approaching from the north and you'll have a view of the ballpark as you land.) Virtually every major and minor airline flies into Tampa International Airport. It is a larger airport: All of the gates are in remote buildings, requiring a tram ride to and from the main terminal. Tampa International Airport, 5503 W. Spruce St., Tampa, Florida 33607; 813/870-8700; **tampaairport.com**.

Smaller is St. Petersburg-Clearwater International Airport, located on the west side of the bay. This airport specializes in low-fare carriers in the United States and Canada (which makes it popular for those Canadian fans heading to Dunedin): Allegiant Air and US 3000 are the largest airlines flying in, while Sunwing Airlines flies directly from Toronto. It's also small enough where the car-rental agencies (Avis, Enterprise, Hertz, National, and Alamo) are truly on site. St. Petersburg-Clearwater International Airport, 14700 Terminal Blvd., Clearwater; 727/453-7800; **flyt2pie.com**.

To the south is Sarasota Bradenton International Airport, located in Sarasota. All the major airlines fly here — AirTran, Northwest, American, Air Canada, JetBlue, Continental, US Airways, and Delta — though not necessarily on a daily basis. If you're a Pirates or Reds fan and planning on spending most of your time in the southern Bay area, this convenient airport is worth a look. Sarasota Bradenton International Airport, 6000 Airport Circle, Sarasota; 941/359-2770; **srq-airport.com**.

insider's tip

If you want to save a few bucks on airfare to spring training, be prepared to be flexible. There's so much variance among airline prices these days that you could easily find a much cheaper fare from your city to St. Pete or Sarasota rather than Tampa International; in these cases you'll need to make sure that a lower fare is worth the inconvenience of a longer drive.

The same thing goes for Orlando. There's no hard-and-fast rule about which airport tends to be cheaper. If you have the time, compare fares from both: Orlando is about 75 minutes from Tampa on Interstate Highway 4 (even less if you're staying near Disney World or Kissimmee), and it's very convenient to fly into Orlando even if you're staying in Tampa when there's a significant price difference in airfares. A makeover of I-4 in recent years makes it a smooth drive. Besides, you're on vacation: Relax and take in the scenic Florida countryside.

→ cincinnati reds

ED SMITH STADIUM

Capacity	7,500
Year Opened	1989
Dimensions	340L, 375LC, 400C, 375RC, 340R
Surface	Grass
Local Airport	Tampa
Address	2700 12th Street (12th Street and Tuttle Avenue), Sarasota.

Coming from the north on I-75, exit at University Parkway; go west on University to Tuttle; turn left and head south on Tuttle; stadium is located on the right at the intersection of 12th and Tuttle. There is adequate signage to the stadium.

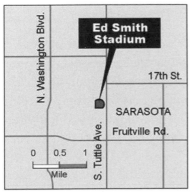

Sarasota: Cheeseburgers and Circuses

This is the end of the road for Ed Smith Stadium as the spring home of the Cincinnati Reds, who are slated for a move to Goodyear, Arizona in 2010 to share a new complex with the Cleveland Indians. You know, we're not going to wail over the loss of Ed Smith Stadium as a training facility. The ballpark really isn't that nice, and the Reds have never done anything to put their imprint on the place.

Still, it will probably be worth a trip to Ed Smith Stadium for one last hurrah, if only to say goodbye to the place.

And a Reds spring game has its peculiar charms — it certainly is an intimate affair. First off, you're never really far from any action at Ed Smith: There's little foul territory, so the first few rows are very close to the action. The whole complex occupies a relatively small footprint in Sarasota, and as admission to practice fields is free of charge, it's an easy day to take in a morning practice and then saunter over to the ballpark for a 1 p.m. game. The ballpark seats 7,500: 6,500 in armchair seats and 1,000 in the bleachers.

But it's not as though Ed Smith is this sparkling facility: It's functional, but hardly quaint or picturesque. The Reds have scaled back on anything making the facility homey or noteworthy (dropping all its signature food items over the years), and in the end Ed Smith Stadium is a fairly vanilla facility that sometimes shows its age, lacking an outfield seating berm and more armchair seats.

insider's tip

Workouts are usually scheduled at 9 a.m. daily at Ed Smith Stadium and the adjacent Sarasota Sports Complex.

The Cincinnati Reds are a relatively new arrival to Sarasota and Ed Smith Stadium, after having moved from Plant City in 1998. Ed Smith Stadium opened in March 1989 as the spring-training home of the Chicago White Sox, who shifted their spring-training home to Tucson Electric Park in Arizona. Ed Smith Stadium and the surrounding spring-training complex includes four-and-a-half practice fields and 35,000 square feet of clubhouses and office space.

The future of Ed Smith Stadium is cloudy as this book goes to press. The place sits on a formal disposal site — no one quite knows what's buried in the drums found sticking out of the ground when the dugouts were renovated in recent years — and without the Reds it's likely the place will either be torn down or scaled back to an amateur facility. Normally we'd decry the loss of another ballpark, but some just aren't worth saving — and Ed Smith Stadium fits into that category. The Cincinnati Reds will embark on a new chapter for spring training in 2010, and the end of the Ed Smith era will not bring many tears to fans or players.

BALLPARK HISTORY

Ed Smith Stadium opened in 1989 as the spring-training home of the Chicago White Sox. When the ChiSox moved spring operations to Arizona, the Reds moved to Ed Smith Stadium from Plant City in 1998.

Major-league teams have trained in Sarasota since 1924. The New York Giants, Boston Red Sox, and Chicago White Sox played there in past spring training camps.

THE SPRING-TRAINING BALLPARK EXPERIENCE

Concessions

At one point the food at Ed Smith Stadium was a cut above the average ballpark cuisine, but over the years signature items like Marge's Cheeseburgers (named for former Reds owner Marge Schott) were dropped from

A panoramic view of the playing field.

the offerings. Today the only really great food item is a Big Red Smokey, cooked the way they are in Cincinnati.

Autographs

Get to the ballpark early: Autograph areas are set up near home plate, but the areas are cleared 30 minutes before game time. Otherwise, Reds players will come up to the edge of the playing field if the urge hits them. As the training fields are open to the public, a smart Reds fan will head over there to score an autograph of an up-and-comer in the Reds farm system and hold onto it.

Parking

There's plenty of parking onsite for $7 per car. You can also try to score a free spot in the surrounding neighborhood.

IF YOU GO

Where to Stay

There's really nothing within walking distance of Ed Smith Stadium: Since the ballpark is less than two miles away from Sarasota-Bradenton Airport, any of the airport hotels — Comfort Inn, Howard Johnson, Hampton Inn — will do you fine. And there's a wide variety of accommoda-

A sun field, to be sure.

tions throughout the city, from the Ritz-Carlton (1111 Ritz-Carlton Dr., Sarasota; 941/309-2000; **ritzcarlton.com**) on the high end to a wide variety of perfectly acceptable chains on the low end. But you could very easily stay in Tampa or St. Pete and head down to Sarasota for the day.

What to Do

Sarasota is only 65 miles outside of Tampa-St. Pete and close to Bradenton, so you're in the midst of spring-training nirvana: Venues within easy driving distance of Sarasota include Lakeland (Detroit Tigers), Tampa (New York Yankees), Clearwater (Philadelphia Phillies), Bradenton (Pittsburgh Pirates), and Dunedin (Toronto Blue Jays). In addition, the Baltimore Orioles' minor leaguers practice at Twin Lakes Park (6700 Clark Road, Sarasota). You can expect your trip to spring training to be filled with lots of baseball in the Tampa/St. Pete area.

Outside of baseball spring training, Sarasota is best known as the former winter home of the Ringling Bros. and Barnum & Bailey Circus and one of its founders, John Ringling. Ringling and his brothers grew up in Baraboo, Wis., and began their own small circus in 1870, charging a penny per performance. They were successful, and by 1907 they were in position to buy the Barnum & Bailey Circus, creating a circus giant. In 1927 Ringling moved the circus's winter headquarters down to Sarasota and set up his personal winter base as well. Despite his roots in the circus — solidly lower- and middle-class entertainment — Ringling saw himself as a patron of the arts and spent the millions generated by his circus on a collection of European masterworks and a palatial Sarasota winter estate. Overspent, actually: During the Great Depression, Ringling lost control of the circus to creditors, although his nephew John Ringling North continued to run the circus until 1967. Since then the circus has gone through a series of owners. It also downscaled over the years and moved away from a tent show to an area spectacle, eliminating the need for colorful wagons and parades to announce the presence of the circus in town.

Upon Ringling's death, his estate passed through to the state of Florida, which set up the Ringling Museum of Art. It encompasses three distinct facilities:

→ The Ringling Museum of Art, which features Ringlings' outstanding collection of 17th-century Baroque paintings, including pieces by Rubens, Van Dyck, and Velazquez. The museum is housed in the largest building on the estate.

→ The Ringling Circus Museum, which features surprisingly little memorabilia from what was arguably the most famous and noteworthy circus in America. (In his bequest leaving the estate to Florida, Ringling did not include any circus memorabilia and clearly wanted his legacy to be his extensive art collection.) Kids expecting to be wowed with death-defying feats and marvelous circus acts may be a little disappointed.

→ Cà d'Zan Mansion, the palatial winter home of John and Mable Ringling. The Venetian Gothic mansion was designed to be reminiscent of two of Mable Ringling's favorite hotels and overlooks Sarasota Bay. The residence, with 32 rooms and 15 baths, is an opulent mix of Barcelona terra cotta, English veined marble, and Flemish tapestries. The house can be accessed only through a scheduled tour.

Ringling Museum of Art, 5401 Bay Shore Rd., Sarasota; 941/359-5700; **ringling.org**. *Adults, $19; seniors, $16; students/children 6-17, $6; children under 6, free.*

For those who don't want to mess with art during spring training, there's a Sarasota museum worth a visit: the Sarasota Classic Car Museum, located (conveniently) across the street from the Ringling Museum. The collection features over 100 automobiles representing all 100 years of car history, including John Lennon's Mercedes Roadster, Paul McCartney's Mini Cooper, the original Batmobile, and one of the only five Cadillac station wagons ever made. Sarasota Classic Car Museum, 5500 N. Tamiami Tr., Sarasota; 941/355-6228; **sarasotacarmuseum.org**. *Adults, $8.50; seniors, $7.65; juniors (13-17), $5.75; children (6-12), $4; under 6, free.*

For those from a land-locked clime, a visit to the aquarium is a must during a Florida visit. In Sarasota, the appropriate visit would be the Mote Marine Laboratory, which combines a research mission with public exhibits on marine life, including a shark tank and a touch tank where both kids and grownups can handle mollusks, crabs, and rays. Mote Marine Laboratory, 1600 Ken Thompson Parkway, Sarasota; 941/388-4441; **mote.org**. *Adults, $17; seniors, $16; children (4-12), $12.*

The Sarasota Jungle Gardens began life as an impenetrable swamp and then was developed in the 1930s as a tropical paradise. To do so, its owners imported a slew of tropical trees, plants, and flowers from around the world. (You probably couldn't get away with such an extensive import of non-native foliage today.) Many of these plants and trees are still thriving: You can wander through the grounds and find exotic species like the Australian Nut Tree, a Bunya Bunya Tree, Banana Trees, and a Peruvian Apple Cactus. Individual habitats feature birds of prey, reptiles, and birds of the rainforest. Sarasota Jungle Gardens, 3701 Bay Shore Rd., Sarasota; 941/355-5305; **sarasotajunglegardens.com**. *Adults, $14; seniors, $13; children (3-12), $10.*

And, of course, you can just wander around the countryside: Sarasota County boasts 35 miles of beaches and six barrier islands. Siesta Key combines scenic beaches, fine dining, and family activities into one destination. Siesta Beach is a classic white beach, made up of 99 percent pure quartz, while Turner Beach is well-regarded by shell collectors.

Sarasota Restaurants

It's not hard to escape the circus vibe in Sarasota, where an artsy atmosphere translates into a laid-back nightlife. Indeed, one of the things we'll miss most when the Reds move is the chance to hit the many good restaurants and bars in the area.

No matter where you go for dinner, a great night begins with a trip to the Ritz-Carlton Beach Club (1234 Benjamin Franklin Dr., Sarasota; 888/363-6237; **www.rcmcsarasota.com**) and its famous Tiki Bar for a Green Flash Cocktail. Yes, it's excessively sweet and gaudy — rum, Midori, and pineapple are highlighted with flashing ice cubes — but really, so is most of what's great about the gulf coast of Florida.

Marina Jack, on the waterfront, features several restaurants and lounges specializing in (what else?) seafood. A salt-water aquarium will entertain the kids, while the adults will enjoy the late-night atmosphere of the Deep Six Lounge. Marina Jack, 2 Marina Plaza, Sarasota; 941/365-4232; **marinajacks.com**.

For something more upscale, Peruvian ceviche is the highlight menu item at the Selva Grill (1345 Main St., Sarasota; 941/362-4427; **selvagrill.com**). Ceviche—freshly prepared seafood—is the perfect item for a seaside restaurant, and the Selva Grill is renowned for its many nightly selections.

More appropriate for the whole family is Troyer's Dutch Heritage Restaurant, a family-style Amish restaurant specializing in stick-to-your-ribs meals of roast beef, ham, and mashed potatoes. Yes, it's a little odd to find an Amish restaurant on the Gulf Coast of Florida, but then again there are many oddities in Florida. 3713 Bahia Vista, Sarasota; 941/955-8007; **troyersdutchheritage.com**.

Finally, one more seafood restaurant of note: the Crab & Fin, which features fish and caviar from around the world. It's also worth a drive because of its location: St. Armands Circle, located on the island of Lido Key. St. Armands Circle was originally planned by John Ringling as a world-class tourist destination, and although he died before the project was launched, St. Armands Circle has developed into an attractive mix of upscale restaurants, shops, and hotels. True, it is touristy — Tommy Bahama has an outpost here — but you are a tourist during spring-training season, after all. Crab & Finn, 420 St. Armands Circle, Sarasota; 941/388-3964; **crabfinrestaurant.com**.

Flying In
Sarasota-Bradenton Airport (**srq-airport.com**) is the closest airport to the ballpark and the most convenient. It's a small airport served by AirTrain, Delta, JetBlue, US Airways, and American Eagle.

The largest airport closest to Sarasota is Tampa International Airport and the most convenient. It's not the biggest airport in the world and is easy to navigate. All the major airlines fly into Tampa.

SPRING-TRAINING HISTORY

The Cincinnati Reds have trained in the following locations: Cincinnati (1901-1902); Augusta, Ga. (1903); Dallas (1904); Jacksonville (1905); San Antonio (1906); Marlin Springs, Texas (1907); St. Augustine (1908); Atlanta (1909); Hot Springs, Ark. (1910-1911); Columbus, Ga. (1912); Mobile, Ala. (1913); Alexandria, La. (1914-1915); Shreveport (1916-1917); Montgomery, Ala. (1918); Waxahachie, Texas (1919); Miami (1920); Cisco, Texas (1921); Mineral Wells, Texas (1922); Orlando (1923-1930); Tampa (1931-1942); Bloomington, Ind. (1943-1945); Tampa (1946-1987); Plant City, Fla. (1988-1997); and Sarasota (1998-2009).

→ detroit tigers

JOKER MARCHANT STADIUM

Capacity	8,500
Year Opened	1966; renovated in 2003
Dimensions	340L, 420C, 340R
Surface	Grass
Local Airport	Orlando or Tampa
Home Dugout	Third base
Address	Al Kaline Dr., 2301 Lakeland Hills Blvd., Lakeland Take exit 33 off I-4 onto Hwy. 33 South. Tiger Town and the ballpark are approximately 2 miles on the left. There is signage pointing out two parking areas next to the stadium.

The Traditions of Tiger Town

Tiger Town is the last great traditional spring-training site now that the Los Angeles Dodgers have abandoned Dodgertown. The Tigers have been training in Lakeland since 1934 (taking a break for the war years, of course) and playing in Joker Marchant Stadium since 1966. In those many years Tiger Town has evolved into a complete training complex that includes the ballpark, other training fields, dorm, training facilities, and team clubhouses.

Do not miss an opportunity to attend a spring game at Joker Marchant, even if you're not a Tigers fan. The handy location between Tampa and Orlando makes it an easily accessible destination for many spring-training fans, and the historic venue is definitely worthy of a visit.

Tiger Town is also one of the more historically interesting sites in the Grapefruit League. It was built on the site of a World War II flight school, the Lodwick School. Between 1940 and 1945 more than 8,000 cadets, including British Royal Air Force cadets, attended the Lodwick School of Aeronautics and more than 6,000 graduated. Some of the remnants of that school still exist, including several hangars that have been renovated and used for various purposes. (Sadly, the most recent renovations to Tiger Town included the removal of a runway beyond the outfield wall.)

In keeping with the site's history the ballpark décor changed before spring training 2007. Detroit's Class A affiliate received a name change to the Lakeland Flying Tigers and adopted an aviation motif throughout the ballpark. As a result concession stands are called canteens (among other things), and there's a lot of camouflage in the concourse.

Thanks to a 2003–2004 renovation, Joker Marchant is again one of the most pleasant venues in spring training. The $11-million renovation, designed by HKS, brought about new faux red-tile roofs that create lofty shaded, covered concourses and bright stucco towers, arches, columns, and walls that anchor the exterior. Tigers fans might remember the garish

The left-field berm features a play area for the kids.

orange seats in the grandstand; the new Joker Marchant features ballpark-green individual armchair seats with cup holders, with three new rows along the backstop, bringing fans within 50 feet of home plate.

A new vertical backstop screen replaced the old canopy screen, while the seating bowl was angled toward the infield and extended down the right field line 94 feet, bringing fans closer to the action.

The concourses provide much-needed shelter from rain and the sun and features new and renovated restrooms, re-themed concessions, and improved signage. Ornamental fencing and natural wood trellises accent the perimeter and entry gates to create an open plaza.

The outfield area has been upgraded with a 16-foot-high, above-grade grass seating berm and trellised patio lined with mature palms, while the batter's eye hides a new maintenance building. The bullpens were relocated to the outfield area in full view of the stands and dugouts.

As a condition of the renovations, a new lease keeps the Tigers in Lakeland until 2019.

No matter where you sit, bring the sunscreen. Only the last 10 rows of the grandstand — those sitting in front of the suite level — sees any shade at all, while anything beyond the dugouts is in a sun field. It's even worse in the outfield berm area, where you'll be staring into the sun for much of a typical afternoon game. You'll also be fighting the sun in the left-field

Avoid the far bleachers if you can.

bleachers, which are a little unusual; this section is large and pitched at more of an angle than the rest of the ballpark. We don't recommend you sit out there unless you have no other options.

Which is a distinct possibility. Detroit fans tend to be pretty loyal to their Tigers, even when times were bad in recent years. The capacity of Joker Marchant is now around 9,000 (8,000 seats, with room for 1,000 or so out on the berm), and attendance is pretty steady: Crowds of 5,000 or more are fairly common. It's still a good place to visit if your favorite team is in town, but don't be surprised if you're a Red Sox or Yankees fan and the game is sold out.

The addition of six new furnished suites, themed after Tiger all-time greats Ty Cobb, Charlie Gehringer, Hank Greenberg, Willie Horton, Al Kaline, and Hal Newhouser, provide a comfortable perch to watch the game. Flanking the suites on either side of the press box and suites are two open-air covered patio lounges, four new restrooms, and a food service catering pantry.

Tigers spring-training games are fairly low-key events, thank goodness. About the only between-innings excitement comes when the grounds crew interrupt their infield grooming to dance along with what has become the National Anthem of Baseball, the Village People's YMCA.

The best thing about a Tigers spring-training game, however, is the laid-back atmosphere and easy accessibility to players and staff. If you go, watch for Tigers President David Dombrowski sitting behind home plate — he'll be the guy with the stopwatch, checking out his pitching staff.

BALLPARK HISTORY

Joker Marchant Stadium was built in 1966 for $360,000 and named after the city's popular parks and rec director, Marcus Thigpen "Joker" Marchant (MAR-chant).

THE SPRING-TRAINING BALLPARK EXPERIENCE

Concessions

For the most part, you can find the normal ballpark fare at the ballpark: hot dogs, peanuts, soda, pizza, beer, ice cream, etc. We had one of the most unique foot-long hot dogs ever at Joker Marchant Stadium: The dog was a foot-long, served in a normal-sized bun. Kinda awkward.

The pizza, of course, is Little Caesars: Tigers owner Mike Illitch made his money by launching the Little Caesars pizza chain. Of much better quality are the smoked turkey legs, the barbeque pork sandwiches, the Italian sausage, and the occasional strawberry short cake. Why strawberry

The concessions now carry a military theme.

short cake? The region around Lakeland, especially Plant City, is known for its early-season strawberry crops. At Joker Marchant, the strawberries are also served with Dairy Queen soft-serve ice cream. Wandering vendors offer the strawberry delicacies. They're also available at a booth down the third-base line, which also serves Edy's ice cream.

insider's tip

Most of the beer served at Joker Marchant Stadium is of the standard corporate type. For something to remind you of home, a portable beer stand down the left-field line offers a variety of microbrews, including some from Michigan-based Bell's.

Autographs

The Tiger Town complex encompasses four practice fields in a cloverleaf layout, Joker Marchant Stadium, and Kaline Field, a small diamond located past the Marchant Stadium left-field corner. Before the start of spring

HENLEY FIELD

The 800-seat Henley Field, the former spring-training home of the Tigers, still exists and was used by the Lakeland Tigers for the 2002 season while Joker Marchant underwent renovations. It is of a classic Spanish Mediterranean de-

sign; echoes of it can be seen in the Joker Marchant renovations. The Cleveland Indians used Henley Field for spring training from 1924 to 1927, and the Tigers used it for spring training between 1934 and 1966. Florida Southern University now calls Henley Field home.

How the Detroit Tigers ended up in Lakeland and Henley Field is an interesting story. As we noted, the Cleveland Indians trained here for four years, a tenure that gave Lakeland its Cleveland Heights area. (Cleveland Heights is located in the southern part of the city; the Cleveland Heights Golf Course — located on Cleveland Heights Boulevard, of course — is another reminder.) But the training all practices take place on the four cloverleaf fields and Kaline Field. A roped-off path runs between the practice fields and the clubhouse, and that's the place to snare players once they leave practice, which traditionally has begun at 10:30 a.m.

Once games start, the minor leaguers take over the cloverleaf fields, with the major-league squad decamping to Kaline Field or Marchant Stadium. On game days or before practice the place to snare an autograph is "Autograph Alley," down the right-field line, near the team offices and home clubhouse. Players mill around Autograph Alley and chat with fans in addition to signing autographs. Autograph Alley is manned from the opening of the gates two hours before game time to about 20 minutes before the actual start of the game.

If you arrive early enough, you can hang around the parking lot and irritate players as they arrive. You can also hang around the parking lot and try to attract their attention as they leave.

Indians didn't last in Lakeland, and the city filled the void the next several years by attracting minor-league squads, including the Reading Keystones, the Newark Bears, and the Columbus Senators, for spring training. (Not that Henley Field was not being used: It also served as the home of the Lakeland High School baseball and football teams.) In 1934, the Tigers came to town after city fathers guaranteed a $1,000 gate share, but the local Chamber of Commerce's reluctance (or inability) to pay it almost forced the Tigers to find a new training camp, but in late October 1934 the Tigers announced they'd be back — and the team has been there ever since, save a three-year period when all MLB teams trained close to home during wartime.

One big reason the Tigers kept coming back was because of longtime team executive Jim Campbell, who lived in Lakeland during the offseason. And it didn't hurt that Lakeland was located in a dry county: Campbell and other team officials felt the lack of alcohol (and its accompanying sins, like women and gambling) would help the team.

Henley Field is roughly 1.5 miles south of Joker Marchant Stadium. Head south on Lakeland Hills Boulevard. Turn right on Parkview Place, and then turn left at Florida Avenue. The ballpark will be on your left. There's a small parking lot on the north side of the ballpark, with more parking on surrounding streets.

Parking

Parking is $7 on adjacent lots. Get to the ballpark early: because there's only one main entrance to the ballpark parking lot and traffic gets congested on Lakeland Hills Boulevard.

insider's tip

Here's a super-secret back way into the Joker Marchant Stadium parking areas especially handy if you're coming from the south. There's an overflow entrance on the south side of the parking lots. To access it, go east on Bella Vista Street and hang a left (north) on Gilmore Avenue.

IF YOU GO

What to Do Outside the Ballpark

In recent years Lakeland has made *Money Magazine*'s "Best Place to Live in America," coming in tenth in 1998. Lakeland is regarded as representing the best of Florida: Its economy has benefited from the technology-company growth in both Tampa and Orlando, and it's also benefited from the rise of tourism in both cities. It does live up to the name: There are 38 lakes within the city limits.

This is citrus country, but today's economy is considerably more varied. Though many of the 170,000 people in the area either work in the citrus industry or go into Tampa for a job, more work at companies like grocery-store-chain Publix, which is headquartered in Lakeland. As the area has thrived, so has downtown Lakeland, which has experienced a renaissance of sorts in the last decade. You can find some decent nightlife in downtown Lakeland. Worth a visit are Molly McHugh's Irish Pub (111 S. Kentucky Av.), which regularly features live music; the 210 City Club (210 E. Pine St.), which features a sleek décor, a long list of martinis, and club music; and Mitchell's Coffee House (235 N. Kentucky Av.), which features live music on weekends.

Downtown is also home to a historic district, home to many restored buildings dating back to the early 1900s. It's a typical Florida smaller-town downtown in terms of architecture, and one gets the sneaky suspicion that the designers of Celebration, Disney's designed community near Disney World, basically stole the layout and feel of Lakeland and re-created it: There's a small lake and a scenic old hotel, the Terrace, on one end of downtown, and a slew of lakefronts with antique stores. Much of the downtown was renovated in recent years, to good effect.

Artsy types will delight in Lakeland. Worth a drive is the campus of Florida Southern College (111 Lake Hollingsworth Drive; **www.flsouthern.edu**), where nine buildings (dubbed "Child of the Sun") comprise the largest grouping of Frank Lloyd Wright-designed buildings in the world. Built between 1941 and 1948, the initial buildings were constructed by students and supervised personally by Wright. You can go to the campus student center and pick up a brochure detailing the history of the buildings before you embark on a tour.

The ballpark is ringed with palm trees.

One final recommendation: golf. Within a 50-mile radius of Lakeland there are more than 60 golf courses and over 500 holes of private and semiprivate golf courses. Within the city limits Eaglebrooke (1300 Eaglebrooke Blvd., Lakeland; 863/701-0101) has been awarded four stars by *Gold Digest*. One of the best public golf courses in the state is located in nearby Haines City: **Southern Dunes Golf Club** (2888 Southern Dunes Blvd., Haines City; 866/TEE-BONE), a longer (7,227 yards) course with the reputation of being a very difficult play.

Lakeland is also centrally located and makes a good base for spring training, as the city is located on I-4, the main interstate running between Tampa and Orlando. There are six spring-training camps within an easy drive: Pittsburgh Pirates (Bradenton), Toronto Blue Jays (Dunedin), Atlanta Braves and Houston Astros (Orlando/Kissimmee), New York Yankees (Tampa), and Philadelphia Phillies (Clearwater).

Where to Stay

Book early. The town fills up on weekends when the Tigers are in town, and a decent hotel room can be scarce. The best time to go is mid-week, in the middle of March.

There is no hotel within walking distance of Joker Marchant Stadium. There are plenty within a short (under two-mile) drive, including:

→ Holiday Inn (North) Lakeland Hotel, the spring-training home of the Tigers; 3260 N. Hwy. 98, Lakeland; 863/688-8080; **holiday-inn.com**. Be warned rooms here are extremely hard to snare, but it will be a place where you are almost sure to see a player. The hotel management certainly worked the Tigers brand when snaring the team's contract: The hotel bar is now known as the Tigers Dugout and decked out with Detroit memorabilia.

→ Howard Johnson Executive Center, 3311 Hwy. 98 N., Lakeland; 863/688-7972; **hojo.com**.

→ Comfort Inn and Suites, Lakeland, 3520 N. Hwy. 98, Lakeland; 863/859-0100; **choicehotels.com**.

→ Super 8 Lakeland, 601 E. Memorial Blvd., Lakeland; 863/683-5961; **super8.com**.

→ Sleep Inn, 4321 Lakeland Park Dr., Lakeland; 863) 577-1170; **sleepinn.com**.

→ Crestwood Suites, 4360 Lakeland Park Dr., Lakeland; 863/904-2050; **crestwoodsuites.com** (a place we'd recommend, especially for families).

→ La Quinta Inn, 1024 Crevasse St., Lakeland; 863/859-2866; **laquinta.com**.

Because you'll be driving to the ballpark anyway, don't feel compelled to stay near Joker Marchant Stadium. Lakeland isn't quite the sleepy little Florida town it was a decade ago, and the resulting growth has led to an abundance of hotels, including chains of all sorts, in the area. (During our last visit we stayed in a Hilton Garden Inn close to the airport, on the other side of town from the ballpark. It was no big deal to drive to and from the Tigers games, and there were plenty of things to do in the immediate area.) Most of the newer chain hotels are located off the freeways on the outskirts of town, while the inner part of the city features older places like the Scottish Inn, which are still popular with longtime spring-training attendees.

If you want a more authentic Florida experience — but one of the spendiest in town — check out The Terrace Hotel in downtown Lakeland. First opening in 1924, The Terrace features 73 guest rooms, a lovely little verandah, and a spectacular dining room, the Terrace Grill. Make sure you get a room overlooking Lake Mirror. (The Terrace Hotel, 329 E. Main St., Lakeland; 863/688-0800; **terracehotel.com**.)

RV Parks

The Lakeland RV Resort is located three miles north of Joker Marchant Stadium, conveniently just off Lakeland Hills Boulevard. Part of the Carefree chain of RV resorts, the Lakeland RV Resort has 230 full hook-up sites, a heated pool, and high-speed Internet access. (Lakeland RV Resort, 900 Old Combee Rd., Lakeland; 863/687-6146; **carefreervresorts.com**.)

Where to Eat

Lakeland really isn't considered the fine-dining capital of Florida, but there are a number of good restaurants in the area. You can stick close to the freeway and eat at one of the many chain restaurants, but you can also venture into town for a good meal.

Best known is Mario's (1833 Edgewood Drive E., Lakeland; 863/688-9616; **meetmeatmarios.com**), specializing in Northern Italian cuisine. Sparky Anderson was a regular when he managed the Tigers. Take it for what it is: There's usually a reason these guys are baseball players and not restaurant critics.

Also recommended by the locals are:

→ Peebles Bar-B-Que (503 Dixie Highway, Auburndale; 863/967-3085): Florida barbeque tends to be on the tame side, but this joint is the exception. Peebles is open only on Thursdays, Fridays and Saturdays. 11 a.m.-9 p.m. (We'd suggest swinging by, ordering out, and having a tailgate party before the game.) And bring cash or a check — no credit cards accepted.

→ Reececliff (940 S. Florida Av., Lakeland; 863/686-6661) is a classic Florida diner, featuring burgers, fish sandwiches, and the ubiquitous sweet tea.

→ Kelly's Diner (2825 Winter Lake Rd. [SR 540], Lakeland; 863/868-5311) offers Southern specialties like biscuits and gravy for breakfast and fried chicken, meat loaf, and hot beef for lunch. It's housed in a typical Florida bungalow and outfitted like a 1950s diner.

→ Sam Seltzer's Steakhouse (4820 S. Florida Av., Lakeland; 863/701-9414; **samseltzers.com**) is known for its prime rib.

→ If you need a reminder of home, bd's Mongolian Grill has a Lakeland outpost at 1474 Town Center Dr.

→ Between downtown Lakeland and south of Joker Marchant Stadium is Ale Gator's (1313 E. Memorial Blvd., Lakeland; 863-616-9200), a Hooters-like bar and restaurant overlooking Lake Parker. Sit out on the patio and enjoy a nice Florida evening.

Flying In

The closest airport to Lakeland is in Tampa. It's a bigger airport that is serviced by all the major airlines. The Orlando airport, which is farther away and much bigger, can be daunting, so if fares are equal you'll definitely want to fly into Tampa.

SPRING-TRAINING HISTORY

The Detroit Tigers have trained in Lakeland since 1934. Other spring-training homes of the Tigers: Detroit (1901); Ypsilanti, Mich. (1902); Shreveport (1903-1904); Augusta, Ga. (1905-1907); Hot Springs, Ark. (1908); San Antonio (1909-1910); Monroe, La. (1911-1912); Gulfport, Miss. (1913-1915); Waxahachie, Texas (1916-1918); Macon, Ga. (1919-1920); San Antonio (1921); Augusta, Ga. (1922-1926); San Antonio (1927-1928); Phoenix (1929); Tampa (1930); Sacramento (1931); Palo Alto, Cal. (1932); San Antonio (1933); Lakeland (1934-1942); Evansville (1943-1945); and Lakeland (1946-present).

→ new york yankees

STEINBRENNER FIELD

Capacity	10,200
Year Opened	1996
Dimensions	318L, 399LC, 408C, 385RC, 314R
Surface	Grass
Local Airport	Tampa
Address	1 Steinbrenner Dr., Tampa (corner of Dale Mabry Highway and Martin Luther King Blvd.)

Take I-275 to North Dale Mabry (U.S. Hwy. 92), exit 41B (old 23). Proceed north approximately three miles. Steinbrenner Field will be on your left, across from Raymond James Stadium. Follow the signs for parking, as you'll park on the opposite side of Dale Mabry from the ballpark.

Yankee Legends in Tampa

Steinbrenner Field is one of the most popular venues in the Grapefruit League: It's the largest, it's usually crammed with Yankees fans, and it feels much different than most of the ballparks in the Grapefruit League, coming close to feeling like a major-league ballpark. Part of that was intentional in the design. It's basically a miniature Yankee Stadium, as the outfield fences are the same dimensions as those in Yankee Stadium, the decorative elements ringing the grandstand are exactly like those found at the original and new Yankee Stadium, the wind screens down each line spell out YANKEES (just in case you've forgotten where you are), and a miniature Monument Park honoring former Yankee greats is located behind the grandstand.

To say that Steinbrenner Field isn't the classiest facility in the Grapefruit League would be an understatement. There's really not *too* much of anything. There are just enough suites to entice the moneyed (and many of the 12 luxury suites are leased by local firms, not expatriate New Yorkers), and just enough high-end seating in the first few rows of action to please big-buck fans. And the addition of right-field picnic tables and bar seating in right field may be more expensive than almost all the grandstand seating, but it's not outrageous ($30 in 2007). It is a ballpark built for Yankees fans.

The new group tables in right field.

It was one of the last large ballparks built for spring training lacking a concourse level ringing the entire playing field. At Steinbrenner Field, most fans are expected to stay in their seats and watch the action, not walk around and view the action from many different levels. (That's not totally true anymore: With the addition of a party deck and bar in the right-field corner, the ability to move around the ballpark while watching the game was greatly enhanced.) The grandstand has two levels and comprises most of the seating in the sta-

There's no doubt as to who plays at Steinbrenner Field.

dium, while there are 12 luxury suites relatively far away from the action.

In fact, there are no bleacher seats or general-admission seating at all in Steinbrenner Field, as all the seats are reserved armchair seating. Box seats and field seats have padding.

The newest seats in the ballpark are in right field, and they're beauts. In a textbook example of how to expand a ballpark, the right-field party area was expanded to a full bar with table and rail seating. The metal tables seat between four and eight and are in the shape of home plate. The high-top bar stools sit in front of bar rails right in back of the home-run fence. For the casual fan who wants to hang out with a group as much as they're concerned about who the backup catcher will be, the tables are a godsend; the barstools are great for smaller groups as well. The bad thing is that fans in these seats will be fighting the sun for the first three innings or so of a night game (the setting sun will be right in their eyes); for an afternoon game it won't matter.

The Yankees also set up a practice field next to the monument area outside the park. With their own concession stands, bleachers, and rest-rooms, the scaled-down practice field is a wonderful place to watch a practice before the actual games start, a good place to get close to the players.

If you're a Yankees fan, Steinbrenner Field is nirvana, a shrine to Yankeedom. If you're not a Yankees fan, you may not be quite enthused. It's a very businesslike park, lacking all the informality that makes spring training such a wonderful experience for both fans and players. Want an autograph? Fuggedaboudit. The Yankees train in a remote area and then enter the ballpark without stopping to greet the fans. There's no berm in the outfield, so you couldn't get close to Hidecki Matsui if you wanted. The concessions are located on a concourse behind the grandstand, and while they are very extensive, they feel like they're in a different world than the actual ballgame. It's also worth noting that Steinbrenner Field sports the biggest souvenir store in the Grapefruit League.

insider's tip

George Steinbrenner, the Yankees braintrust, and selected guests can be found at spring-training games in Suite 1. It's the one farthest to the left as you're facing the suite level from the playing field.

Steinbrenner Field is centrally located in Tampa. It's located only three miles from the airport and directly across from Raymond James Stadium (home of the NFL's Tampa Bay Buccaneers). Chances are good you'll see it from the airplane during your approach if you fly into Tampa.

BALLPARK HISTORY

Steinbrenner Field has been the spring-training home of the New York Yankees since it opened. At the beginning of the 2008 regular season it was renamed Steinbrenner Field in honor of Yankees owner and area resident George Steinbrenner; before that it was known as Legends Field, and many local residents still refer to it by that name. (You may even see a street sign or two referring to it as Legends Field as well.)

Before the move to Tampa, the Yankees trained at Fort Lauderdale Stadium, currently the spring-training home of the Baltimore Orioles.

THE SPRING-TRAINING BALLPARK EXPERIENCE

Concessions

There is no end to the concessions at Steinbrenner Field; it is a mall food court disguised as a ballpark. The concessions run on both sides the entire distance of the outer concourse ringing the grandstand, with the inner stands offering mainstream ballpark fare (hot dogs, beer, popcorn, peanuts, hamburgers, beer, soda, etc.) and the outer stands offering local delicacies.

The Yankees do a good job of bringing in local firms to work their own concession stands, upping the variety of what's available.

Autographs

When you enter the training complex from the parking lot, you'll see the Yankees on a fenced-in practice field on your left. You'll be quite a distance from the players, so don't bother trying to score an autograph from that angle, though you can get closer if you head for ground level and enter the field via a gate behind home plate. The Yankees warm up on this practice field. In the past it used to be hard to snare an autograph, but in recent years the team obviously put more emphasis on telling players to warm up to fans. At practices it's common to find players — stars and scrubs alike — easily accessible and happy to sign autographs. Spring training tends to be reunion time for the Yankees as well, and you'll find former greats like Reggie Jackson and Whitey Ford just hanging out as well. Go ahead; they're happy to talk with average fans, and they're even polite to the professional autograph hunters.

The main entry for most into the ballpark.

HUGGINS-STENGEL FIELD

Despite the Yankees' long tradition of training in the Tampa Bay area, there are very few monuments to that history.

One monument of sorts resides in a residential neighborhood in St. Petersburg. At first glance there's not much to Huggins-Stengel Field. Out past center field there's a bucolic lake line you find scattered throughout Florida, with a modest building sitting down the first-base line.

That lake is Crescent Lake, and it marks the location of what was known for many decades as Crescent Lake Park, the longtime spring home of the New York Yankees. There's nothing from the Babe Ruth era remaining, and except for two monuments honoring Miller Huggins and Casey Stengel — for whom the current field is named — there would be no indication this was the place

Parking

Wear your walking shoes to the ballpark. Parking costs $8 (it seems to rise every spring) and is a fair distance from the ballpark. You must walk on an overpass over a six-lane highway (Dale Mabry) from the parking lot to the ballpark. From the overpass, you can enter on a second-floor level — located on the right-field corner of the ballpark — or go down the stairs to a main entrance near the souvenir shop.

IF YOU GO

What to Do Outside the Ballpark

Steinbrenner Field is in the middle of Tampa, so the information in our Tampa chapter particularly applies to Yankees fans.

In addition to the general Tampa activities, there are some other noteworthy attractions and restaurants within a short distance of the ballpark that will give you a true flavor of Tampa. Dale Mabry Highway is an interesting stretch of road: Between a retail cluster at I-275 and the ballpark is a vast wasteland of strip clubs, gas stations, and fast-food joints. Not a place to hang out with the kids.

Near Steinbrenner Field is La Teresita, a down-home neighborhood Cuban joint with some great food: Cuban sandwiches, shredded beef, and fried plantains. You can get the food to go (which would make for some interesting tailgating at the Steinbrenner Field parking lot) or sidle up to the counter. La Teresita, 3246 W. Columbus Dr., Tampa; 813/879-4909; **lateresitarestaurant.com**.

where Ruth, Gehrig, and DiMaggio trained. (The building, however, was used as a clubhouse during the later Yankee days there.)

By 1931 the field was known as Huggins Field, and in 1963 the current name was adopted. Besides the Yankees, the Mets, Orioles, and Cardinals all trained at Huggins-Stengel Field.

As did the expansion Tampa Bay Devil Rays. Take a look around the field and check out the limited amenities. You're basically talking about a diamond, some chain-link fence, and a small clubhouse. Compare that to the training complexes of today, and you'll have a great appreciation of how much spring training has changed in only a decade.

If that's too adventurous for you, less than a mile away from the ballpark is the newest Florida outpost of the Champps chain of sports bars. Yes, it's a chain, but the food at Champps is pretty decent, there's always some sort of game on a multitude of televisions, and the location is convenient. In the same complex is Too Jay's, a popular Florida deli chain. The food should appeal to any New Yawker: The portions may not be quite as grotesque as those found at the Carnegie Deli, but the pastrami and corned beef both are excellent, and the Dr. Brown's is nice and cold. There are also a variety of other restaurants in the general area, located adjacent to the International Mall. 2223 N. West Shore (off Boy Scout, behind the Shops of Baystreet), Tampa. Champps, 813/353-0200; **champps.com**. Too Jay's, 813/348-4101; **toojays.com**.

It seems mandatory that every Florida city has a seafood restaurant named Crabby Bill's or Captain Bell's or Grumpy Gus's. (OK, just kidding on the last one.) In Tampa, a spring-training tradition is Crabby Bill's at the Radisson Bay Harbor Hotel, which has served as a team hotel for the Yankees in the past. At Crabby Bill's, the emphasis is on seafood and the views from the beach bar. If Crabby Bill's is not to your liking, there are several other local and chain restaurants in the general vicinity. Crabby Bill's, 7700 Courtney Campbell Causeway, Tampa; 813/281-8900; **crabbybills.com**.

Where to Stay
Given that most Yankees fans are rather fanatical in nature, many readers of this book will want to stay as close to the ballpark as possible. (One

imagines they would sleep in their cars outside the ballpark if they could.) There are three hotels within easy walking distance of the ballpark:

→ Holiday Inn Express Hotel & Suites, 4750 N. Dale Mabry, Tampa; 813/877-6061; **hiexpresstampa.com**.

→ Comfort Inn Airport at Raymond James Stadium, 4732 N. Dale Mabry, Tampa; 813/874-6700; **tampacomfortinn.com**.

→ Tampa Stadium (Hillsborough) Microtel Inn & Suites, 5405 N. Church Av., Tampa; 813/739-2244; **microtelinn.com**.

→ Tampa Days Inn Airport/Stadium, 2522 N. Dale Mabry, Tampa; 813/998-2090; **daysinn.com**.

Of these, the Holiday Inn Express is probably the nicest; it was recently rennovated.

Steinbrenner Field is less than three miles from the airport, so any of the many airport hotels would work out. In addition, there are a slew of hotels located halfway between the hotel and the airport, advertising themselves as "airport stadium" hotels — like the Hilton Tampa Airport Westshore and the Howard Johnson Airport Stadium Hotel. You won't be able to walk to Steinbrenner Field from these hotels, but their proximity will come in handy if you're staying for multiple games.

Though farther away from the ballpark, the Rocky Point Island area of Tampa houses many popular hotels. We cover them in the Tampa intro.

Spring-Training History

The New York Yankees have held spring training in the following locations: Baltimore (1901); Savannah, Ga. (1902); Atlanta (1903-1904); Montgomery, Ala. (1905); Birmingham, Ala. (1906); Atlanta (1907-1908); Macon, Ga. (1909); Athens, Ga. (1910-1911); Atlanta (1912); Hamilton, Bermuda (1913); Houston (1914); Savannah, Ga. (1915); Macon, Ga. (1916-1918); Jacksonville (1919-1920); Shreveport (1921); New Orleans (1922-1923); St. Petersburg (1924-1942); Asbury Park, N.J. (1943); Atlantic City (1944-1945); St. Petersburg (1946-1950); Phoenix (1951); St. Petersburg (1952-1961); Ft. Lauderdale (1962-1995); and Tampa (1996-present).

→ philadelphia phillies

BRIGHT HOUSE NETWORKS FIELD

Capacity	8,500 (7,000 fixed seats, 1,500 berm seating)
Year Opened	2004
Dimensions	329L, 408C, 330R
Surface	Grass
Local Airport	Tampa
Address	601 N. Old Coachman Road, Clearwater.

Take Hwy. 19 north of St. Petersburg to Drew Street, where you'll head west until you get to Greenwood Avenue. At Old Coachman Road hang a right; the ballpark is ahead on your right.

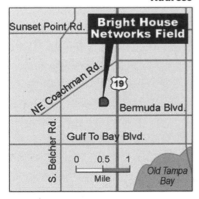

Newer is Better in Clearwater

If there is a gold standard among Grapefruit League ballparks, it is Clearwater's Bright House Networks Field. It is the standard by which older ballparks are evaluated and new ballparks are planned. It's not the biggest or the most historic, but on virtually every level it's the nicest, and it works very well on a functional level: You never, ever feel crushed or crowded, even when you're queuing up for parking or an entrance to the ballpark. We really can't think of a better time at a spring-training game than to spend the afternoon at Bright House Networks Field.

When the Phillies were planning Bright House Networks Field before 2004, they knew they had a task in coming up with a replacement to what was a very fine facility, Jack Russell Stadium. Yes, Jack Russell was a neighborhood park with a rich tradition and a renowned Tiki Bar. But at the end of the day, Bright House Networks Field far surpasses Jack Russell Stadium. Bright House Networks Field, if anything, is more intimate despite being a larger facility: The front-row seats are five feet closer to the action than those at Jack Russell (which makes batters happy: The foul territory here is postage-stamp-sized), and outfield berm seating puts fans right on the edge of the action — practically close enough to touch Ryan Howard.

Best of all, the Phillies kept the best of Jack Russell. The Tiki Bar is out in left field and is bigger and better than ever: It's a great place to grab one of the bar stools and down a margarita or three while soaking in the warmth after a cold and wet Philly winter. Groups can socialize and catch some action in the reserved picnic tables down the third-base line. And families can let the kids run loose while throwing down blankets in the outfield berm.

JACK RUSSELL STADIUM

Even though Bright House Networks Field is a great facility, we can't help but experience a little twinge of sadness when we think about the team's former spring home, Jack Russell Stadium. Opening in 1955, Jack Russell Stadium was a true neighborhood ballpark, a low-slung facility with true box seats and plenty of shade. True, it was small — capacity was just under 7,000, and the clubhouse and office space were cramped — but it was homey, and no matter how bad the Phillies were the fans flocked down to Clearwater to cheer on their boys.

But it adds a slew of amenities never even considered for Jack Russell: an outfield berm perfect for lounging in the sun, luxury boxes for the hoi polloi, and a huge video screen sponsored by Hooters.

The location of Bright House Networks Field is more convenient for fans and the team. The ballpark was built next to the Phillies' existing minor-league training facilities, so things are centralized for the team and for fans wandering the practice fields before games. While Jack Russell was in the middle of a residential neighborhood with limited parking, Bright House Networks Field is right next to Clearwater's main

Close to the action on the large berm.

drag (Highway 19) and considerably easier to get to, even when the Phillies anticipate a sellout (which happens often in spring training). Ample parking in the area also makes things easier for fans.

There are two entrances to the ballpark (one down each line), but most fans will enter from the west side to a third-base entrance because of parking considerations. The ballpark itself features a Spanish Mediterranean motif popular in Florida. A concourse rings the entire ballpark, while a

Today, Jack Russell Stadium is no more: It was torn down in 2007 after several attempts were made to find an alternative use. The things that made it charming — the small footprint, the neighborhood location — ultimately worked against it when it came to youth tournaments or other uses. You can't say Clearwater officials didn't do everything they could to save the old place, but at the end of the day it wasn't enough.

second deck features luxury boxes, club seats (with wait service), and group areas.

insider's tip

When shopping for tickets, keep in mind that there are very few bad seats in the park. All are angled toward the pitchers' mound — even those down the first-base line — while a picnic area down the third-base line allows you and a set of friends to reserve your own picnic table for an entire game. Given the popularity of the Phillies in spring training, you may not have much of a selection when it comes time to reserving your seats: You'll want to sit to the left of home plate in order to take advantage of any shade from the hot Florida sun. And if all you want to do is sit at the Tiki Bar and sip fruity drinks, buy a berm-seating ticket and arrive early at the ballpark.

BALLPARK HISTORY

The Philadelphia Phillies have been training in Clearwater since 1947 and at Jack Russell Stadium from 1955 through 2003. The team opened Bright House Networks Field in Spring Training 2004.

THE SPRING-TRAINING
BALLPARK EXPERIENCE

Concessions

It wouldn't be a Phillies spring-training game if a Philly cheesesteak sandwich wasn't on the menu. The concession stand directly behind home plate features Philly cheesesteaks served on authentic Amoroso rolls.

The Tiki Bar: Still a classic.

Otherwise, the four main concession stands scattered throughout the concourse feature your average ballpark fare. Of special note is the dedicated beer concession stand down the third-base line: it features the widest variety of beers, including Yuengling. Yuengling represents a marriage of sorts between Pennsylvania and Florida: tThe Yuengling Brewing's roots date back to 1829 when the Yuengling family established a brewery in Pottsville, Penn., but a 1999 acquisition of a former Stroh's brewery in Tampa gave Yuengling a toehold in Florida, and the beer is now marketed as a local beer.

And yes, there are drink holders at every seat, so load up on the food and drink.

Autographs

The Phillies enter the field from the left-field tunnel, so your best chance of scoring an autograph is before the beginning of the game as they arrive. (Similarly, visiting players enter the playing field from a tunnel down the right-field line.) If you arrive early enough, you can try to attract the attention of a player as they enter or leave the practice fields directly of the ballpark; players park between the ballpark and the practice fields as well.

For the Kids

A special kids' area in the left-field corner of the ballpark should keep the young ones busy for hours. A supervised playground area lets them burn off a lot of steam, while a concession stand devoted to kid-specific treats will boost them up. You'll still be able to see the action while keeping the kids in sight.

Parking

There are two parking lots to the south and to the west of the ballpark. The lot to the west is small and fills up quickly; the lot to the south is larger. As you head west on Drew Street, the south lot will be the one to your right, and you should park there if possible. If that lot is full, head west and follow the signs. Most fans will be directed to the DiMaggio recreation complex, which isn't far from the ballpark. Parking is $7.

insider's tip
At the beginning of spring training, the Phillies practice at the next-door Carpenter Complex. They usually begin at 10 a.m.

IF YOU GO

What to Do Outside the Ballpark

Clearwater is less than 20 miles outside of Tampa-St. Petersburg and less than five miles from Dunedin, so you're in the midst of spring-training nirvana: Spring-training venues that are within easy driving distance of Clearwater include Lakeland (Detroit Tigers), Tampa (New York Yankees), Dunedin (Toronto Blue Jays), and Bradenton (Pittsburgh Pirates).

You can expect your trip to spring training to be filled with lots of baseball in the Tampa area.

The thing to do in Clearwater is really nothing: Head to one of the many beaches and soak up some sun. We already mentioned Clearwater Beach as a prime activity in our earlier chapter on Tampa attractions. One popular local attraction is Pier 60 Park, located at Causeway and Gulf Blvd. Pier 60 Park is a white-sand beach that runs north for 1.3 miles and features shops, restaurants, a bait shop, beach concessions, and nightly entertainment.

Be warned: You won't be the only one heading to Clearwater Beach. After all, March is spring break for a lot of people uninterested in base-ball, and they love the sun and the sand enough to flock to Clearwater in search of cheap beer and good food. You can find both at one of the four Frenchy's in the area. They specialize in serving lots of beer and fresh grouper sandwiches. Our favorite is Frenchy's Rockaway Grill (7 Rockaway St., Clearwater Beach; 727/446-4844; **frenchysonline.com**), as you can sit on the deck and enjoy outdoor dining on the waterfront. For something more traditional, Heilman's Beachcomber (447 Mandalay Av., Clearwater; 727/442-4144; **heilmansbeachcomber.com**) is old-time Florida at its best. The Palm Pavil-ion (10 Bay Esplanade, Clearwater; 727/446-2642) is owned and run by Phillies fan Ken Hamilton, so his outdoor deck is a must-visit for anyone traveling down from Philadelphia. And Villa Gallace (109 Gulf Blvd., Indian Rocks Beach; 727/596-0200; **villagallace.com**), a high-brow Italian restaurant, has been a traditional favorite of Phillies players and front-office personnel.

Oh, the beaches. There are a lot of them in the area, with over 26 miles of beaches running up and down the key. We're not going to tell you the best beach for your particular desires, but a place we love visiting because of the slower pace is Indian Rocks Beach. If you go, be prepared to make a day of it: Gulf Boulevard, the main drag, is crowded and slow.

insider's tip

Highway 19, which runs next to the ballpark to the west, is a hellacious stretch of highway even on the best of days: It's busy and cluttered with frequent stoplights. On the other hand, Old Coachman Road, which runs next to the ballpark to the east, is two lanes and never very busy. Consult your map and then head over there for some clear driving.

The Phillies may have moved spring training from Jack Russell Stadium, but one March tradition remains: Lenny's Restaurant (21220 U.S. Highway 19 N., Clearwater; 727/799-0402). Phillies players have been coming to Lenny's since it opened in 1980, and the fans soon followed, cramming the restaurant on game days. And when the Phillies moved last spring into Bright House Networks Field, Lenny's was the big winner: The new ballpark is actually closer to Lenny's than Jack Russell was.

Lenny's caters to Phillies fans: In March the staff hangs Phillies pennants and other team memorabilia. The restaurant more than doubles its number of customers in March and adds more staff and special dishes designed to appeal to Pennsylvania customers, such as scrapple (a fried pork delicacy). The place is crammed with red-clad fans before a home game, so arrive early.

Where to Stay

Clearwater is in the western part of the Tampa Bay region, north of St. Pete and west of Tampa. You could stay anywhere within the Tampa Bay area (as we explained in our previous chapter on Tampa Bay) and be within a reasonable drive of the ballpark.

However, Clearwater is a suburb on the rise, with lots of new development hotels in the area surrounding the ballpark, and it would not be difficult to snare an affordable hotel room near the ballpark. Many are within walking distance of the ballpark, although the lack of sidewalks and the busy traffic flow on Hwy. 19 make this a problematic method of arriving at the ballpark.

Within a mile of the ballpark are:

→ Hampton Inn Clearwater, 21030 Hwy. 19 N., Clearwater; 727/797-8173; **hamptoninn.com**.

→ Radisson Hotel Clearwater Central, 20967 Hwy. 19 N., Clearwater; 727/799-1181; **radisson.com**.

→ Econo Lodge Central, 21252 Hwy. 19 N., Clearwater; 727/799-1569; **econolodge.com**.

→ La Quinta, 21338 Hwy. 19 N., Clearwater; 727/799-1565; **lq.com**.

These are fairly low-rent hotels. If a luxury gig is more your style, don't bother staying close to the ballpark; instead, check out the Belleview Biltmore (25 Belleview Blvd., Clearwater; 800/237-8947; **belleviewbiltmore.com**).

In addition, the hotels on the Campbell Causeway listed in our section opener on Tampa are also convenient to the ballpark: You can take the Causeway to Hwy. 19 or Old Coachman Road, head north to the next stoplight (Drew Street), and you're right at the ballpark.

Flying In

The closest airport to Clearwater is St. Petersburg-Clearwater International Airport, located on the west side of the bay. This airport specializes in low-fare carriers in the United States and Canada; Allegiant Air, for instance, flies directly there from the Allentown airport. It's also small enough where the car-rental agencies (Avis, Enterprise, Hertz, National, and Alamo) are truly on site.

In case you can't get a flight into St. Pete-Clearwater, you'll want to check out Tampa International Airport. All the major airlines fly into Tampa.

SPRING-TRAINING HISTORY

The Philadelphia Phillies have held spring training in the following locations: Philadelphia (1901); Washington, N.C. (1902); Richmond, Va. (1903); Savannah, Ga. (1904); Augusta, Ga. (1905); Savannah, Ga. (1906-1908); Southern Pines, N.C. (1909-1910); Birmingham, Ala. (1911); Hot Springs, Ark. (1912); Southern Pines, N.C. (1913); Wilmington, N.C. (1914); St. Petersburg (1915-1918); Charlotte (1919); Birmingham, Ala. (1920); Gainesville (1921); Leesburg, Fla. (1922-1924); Bradenton (1925-1927); Winter Haven (1928-1937); Biloxi, Miss. (1938); New Braunfels, Texas (1939); Miami Beach (1940-1942); Hershey, Penn. (1943); Wilmington, Del. (1944-1945); Miami Beach (1946); and Clearwater (1947-present).

→ pittsburgh pirates

McKechnie Field

Capacity	6,562
Year Opened	1923; last renovated in 1993
Dimensions	335L, 375LC, 400C, 375RC, 335R
Surface	Grass
Local Airport	Sarasota or Tampa
Address	1611 9th Street W. (17th Avenue West & 9th Street West), Bradenton.

From St. Petersburg, go south on Hwy. 41, make a right turn onto 17th Avenue West and continue to McKechnie Field.

McKechnie Field: A Spring-Training Classic

It is authentically old, without the faux sheen of retro features so prevalent in ballparks these days. Built in 1923 for the St. Louis Cardinals and known by many oldtimers as the former spring home of the Atlanta Braves franchise, McKechnie Field is basically the same ballpark where Roberto Clemente gracefully patrolled the outfield, where Willie Stargell engaged the fans, and where Henry Aaron awed onlookers with his sheer power and determination. It's not the gaudiest of ballparks, and the Pittsburgh Pirates aren't exactly crammed with superstars these days, but spring-training aficionados know McKechnie Field is a throwback to the way spring training used to be: an intimate affair played in a neighborhood ballpark.

True, it's not totally the same as it was when Clemente and Aaron took the field. A 1993 renovation added a larger press box and some amenities, while lights were installed before the start of spring training in 2008. Neither really changed the character of the place. Regulars — both vendors and fans — fill the grandstand: Beer vendor Kevin Beauregard is known for inciting the crowd to action on a slow afternoon, while most of the ushers seem to know all the regulars on a first-name basis.

McKechnie Field is located about 30 minutes south of St. Petersburg in the sleepy community of Bradenton, off downtown Bradenton in a residential area. There's limited parking next to the ballpark, or you can park in one of the many private lots within a few blocks of the ballpark.

The overall comfort level in McKechnie is very high. Seating is divided into three basic areas. The three grandstands are mostly shaded (a press box sits above the center grandstand, while canopies shade the other two): In early March it can be a little chilly at a game when a cool breeze wafts into the grandstands. The bleachers, on the other hand, are uncovered. The one drawback to McKechnie: The seats are a little on the cozy side and of a slightly unusual design. Those of us featuring above-average girth will feel a little cramped. (For those who find the plastic seats to be a little on the hard side, the Bradenton Pirates Boosters Club will happily rent you a seat cushion for $1.)

The Pirates have been training in Bradenton and playing games at McKechnie Park for 34 years. Though there has been baseball played at McKechnie Field since 1923, it's actually one of the newer stadiums in Florida spring training in some ways, as the facility was rebuilt in 1993. It's built in a Florida Spanish Mission style, with white stucco on the main grandstand. The design is like most spring-training facilities: There are box seats on the field side of a wide concourse and bleacher seats on the other side of the concourse. The Pirates sell box seats, reserved bleachers, and general-admission seats; the reserved bleachers seats are shaded, which is an important consideration for all games.

insider's tip

Though spring-training operations have been professionalized in recent years, the Pirates still stay close to their roots by working with the "Bradenton Pirates Boosters," who man the concession stands and the front-gate turnstiles. They're also responsible for putting up flags beyond the outfield fence near the batters' eye commemorating historic landmarks in Pittsburgh Pirates history: The black flags commemorate National League titles, the gold flags represent World Series championships, and the white flags honor divisional champions.

In 2008, things changed forever at McKechnie Field when lights were installed. Now, lights at a spring-training ballpark aren't always essential: Most teams play a handful (at most) of night games each spring. For many years the Pirates were the only team lacking lights for spring training, an omission that didn't seem all that remarkable, really. But we now have lights at McKechnie Field, and the Pirates held night games during Spring Training 2008, just like everyone else.

No other teams play in McKechnie Field the rest of the year. And the Pirates don't actually train at McKechnie Field, at least not at the begin-

Perhaps the most unique press box in the Grapefruit League.

ning of spring training. When pitchers and catchers report, the team trains at Pirate City, located about five miles away from McKechnie Field at 1701 27th St. E. (Roberto Clemente Memorial Drive), with morning workouts beginning at 9:30 a.m. daily. When spring-training games begin, the Pirates shift morning workouts to McKechnie Field, while the minor-leaguers continue to work out at Pirate City.

Pirate City is a prototypical spring-training facility, with five playing fields and a two-level dorm. The fields are named for some legends in Pirate baseball history — the Waner brothers, Pie Traynor, Honus Wagner — while the infield facility is named after Bill Mazeroski. If you really want to get close to a player, this is the place to do it. You can watch the games on the practice fields; they feature small wooden bleachers and the odd picnic table. Also, it's here that the "B" games are held, usually at 10 a.m., as well as minor-league matchups, which usually begin at 1 p.m. And there's plenty of free parking.

THE SPRING-TRAINING BALLPARK EXPERIENCE

Concessions

The aforementioned Beauregard sells beer and peanuts in the stands, but most fans will want to head to the back of the grandstand for a series of

Concessions are located under the grandstand.

food booths. When it comes to variety, some of the best dining in the Grapefruit League is at McKechnie. All the concessions are located under the grandstand, and there are an amazing variety of offerings, including local favorite Demetrios pizza. Highly recommended is the foot-long hot dog: It's meaty, beaty, big, and delicious. Other foods on the spring-training menu are hamburgers, pizza, Greek salads, fruit smoothies, ice-cream sundaes, and Subway sandwiches. The beer selection is fairly average. Worth seeking out is a Mexican food booth selling Negro Modelo and Pacifico beers.

Autographs

Players sign autographs before games at an Autograph Alley down the right-field line. You can also try luring a player to the edge of the seating area before a game. Another good place for autographs, though, is Pirate City: Fans have a lot of access to players there, and a more casual atmosphere means more autograph opportunities.

Parking

There is limited parking next to the ballpark. You'll be able to find some street parking within walking distance of the ballpark, and many locals rent out parking-lot spots for under $10 within two blocks of the ballpark.

IF YOU GO

What to Do Outside the Ballpark

Bradenton is only 65 miles outside of Tampa-St. Pete and close to Sarasota, so you're in the midst of spring-training nirvana: Spring-training venues that are within easy driving distance of Bradenton include Lakeland (Detroit Tigers), Tampa (New York Yankees), Clearwater (Philadelphia Phillies), Dunedin (Toronto Blue Jays), and Sarasota (Cincinnati Reds). You can expect your trip to spring training to be filled with lots of baseball in the area.

If you arrive at the ballpark early enough, you'll want to eat at Popi's Place, known for its Belgian waffles. Team officials and announcers have been seen at Popi's before home games. Really, a stop here is mandatory if you're a serious Bucs fan. Popi's Place, 818 17th Av. W., Bradenton; 941/746-7078.

Bradenton is still a sleepy citrus town — home to the main Tropicana orange-juice plant — so there are not many attractions near the ballpark. Those looking to soak up some sun should head to Longboat Key and Anna Maria Island, both of which are known for their sandy beaches and relaxed atmospheres. Bradenton is also known for its manatees: The South Florida Museum is home to Snooty and Mo, two West Indian Manatees that swim and play in the museum's specially designed 60,000-gallon aquarium. South Florida Museum, 201 10th St. W., Bradenton; 941/746-4131; **southfloridamuseum.org**.

Pirate City is located next to Mixon Fruit Farm, which is the quintessential Florida orange farm, featuring a large orange grove and a wide variety of citrus products. As you know, a day without orange juice is a day without sunshine, and combining a visit to Pirate City with a side trip to Mixon makes for a great morning. Mixon Fruit Farm, 2712 26th Av. E., Bradenton; 941/748-5829, 800/608-2525; **mixon.com**.

Where to Stay
Bradenton is in the southern portion of Tampa Bay, so you could stay anywhere in the Bay and have easy access to the ballpark.

If you do decide to stay in Bradenton, there are three hotels within a few miles of the ballpark:
- → Rodeway Inn, 2303 1st St. E., Bradenton; 941/747-6465; **choicehotels.com**.
- → Holiday Inn Bradenton-Riverfront, 100 Riverfront Dr. W., Bradenton; 941/747-3727; **holiday-inn.com**.
- → Bradenton-Days Inn, 3506 1st St. W., Bradenton; 941/746-1141; **daysinn.com**.

Flying In
The closest airport to Bradenton is Sarasota Bradenton International Airport. Most major airlines fly here — AirTran, Delta, Northwest, US Airways, Air Canada, JetBlue, and American Eagle — though not necessarily on a daily basis, so your schedule may not allow for a flight there.

The largest airport in the region is Tampa International Airport, located on the north side of the bay opposite Bradenton. Most will find it more convenient to fly into this much larger airport.

SPRING-TRAINING HISTORY

The Pirates have been training in Bradenton and playing games at McKechnie Park since 1969; before that the Pirates trained in Ft. Myers from 1955 to 1968. Other spring-training homes of the Pirates over the years: Selma, Ala. (1900); Thomasville, Ga. (1900); Hot Springs, Ark. (1901-14; 1920-1923); Dawson Springs, Ky. (1915-17); Jacksonville, Fl. (1918); Birmingham, Ala. (1919); Paso Robles, Cal. (1924-34); San Bernardino, Cal. (1935; 1937-1942; 1946; 1949-52); San Antonio (1936); Muncie, Ind. (1943-45); Miami Beach, Fla. (1947); Hollywood, Cal. (1948); Havana, Cuba (1953); and Fort Pierce, Fla. (1954). The Bradenton Growers of the Florida State League played at McKechnie Field in the 1923, 1924 and 1926 seasons.

→toronto blue jays

DUNEDIN STADIUM

Capacity	6,106
Year Opened	1990
Dimensions	335L, 380LC, 400C, 363RC, 325R
Surface	Grass
Local Airport	Tampa
Address	311 Douglas Av., Dunedin

Take Hwy. 19 north from St. Petersburg, take Sunset Point Road (Route 588) west for two miles, and then head north on Douglas Avenue for a half mile.

BBQ at the Ballpark

You don't need to be a Toronto Blue Jays fan to appreciate a spring-training game at Dunedin Stadium. It's a place where fan/player interaction is at a premium, where a game is just a game and not just some huge marketing event. If you're looking for a flashy time filled with huge crowds, tiki bars, and fans lined up wall to wall, then Dunedin Stadium is not for you.

Indeed, one of our favorite spring-training experiences is parking in downtown Dunedin, grabbing a late breakfast, and then walking down the Pinellas Trail to the ballpark early enough to score some autographs, watching a laid-back spring match, and then heading back to downtown Dunedin for Happy Hour. There's no such thing as a bad spring-training experience, but some experiences are better than others.

The ballpark is always crowded but never uncomfortable, filled mostly with Canadians escaping the Great White North for the warmer climes of Florida. There's cold Labatt Blue on tap, which is always a plus. (Expect a longer line for the Canadian delicacy: There are relatively few beer taps for a ballpark of this size.) And Dunedin is one of the hidden gems in the Tampa-St. Pete area, a refreshing respite from the hustle and bustle along the bay.

Just be warned that Dunedin Stadium is really set up for families, not spring-training rowdies. The grassy berm attracts families chasing down their smaller children, while groups set up shop in the picnic areas. The atmosphere at Dunedin Stadium is probably the most casual in the Grapefruit League. Blue Jays have been known to chat with fans between innings — an act that's become a no-no in the increasingly formalized spring training. And many of the fans in the stands are regulars: There's a large Canadian contingent retuning annually to Dunedin, like the swallows to Capistrano.

If you plan on attending several games, you may want to look into buying a season ticket. The Blue Jays host an on-field post-game barbeque for season-ticket holders, the only team to do so.

insider's tip

The Blue Jays are one of the few teams left that train in one location and play their games in another. When spring training opens, the team can be found at the Cecil B. Englebert Complex (1700 Solon Av.), in Dunedin. At the beginning of March, the team then shifts major-league practices to Dunedin Stadium. Traditionally, workouts begin at 9 a.m.

Overall, Dunedin Stadium is not the most comfortable of venues. First, there's absolutely no covered seating in the ballpark, so remember the sunscreen. Second, the ballpark was built in the days before fan comfort became a prime consideration for ballpark designers, so the seats are small and crammed together. The seating area is bisected by a walkway. Box seats are on the field side of the walkway, while bleachers are on the other side.

Most longtime spring training fans remember the Blue Jays training first at Grant Park and then at Dunedin Stadium. This is the second time around for the Dunedin Stadium name: It was known as Knology Park between 2004 and 2008, as a local cable-TV provider bought the naming rights to the ballpark.

Considering the Toronto Blue Jays have now been around for 25 years, it's fairly remarkable that the team has had only one spring-training site in team history. The Blue Jays began life on March 11, 1977, when the team beat the New York Mets 3-1. At that time the Blue Jays played in 3,417-seat Grant Field, which was one of the oldest stadiums used in the Grapefruit League, dating back to 1930.

However, Grant Park didn't keep up with the many new spring-training facilities that were popping up in Florida in the 1980s, and by 1989 the Blue Jays were working on a plan to replace Grant Field with a new stadium and spring-training facility. As a result, the city of Dunedin invested $2.4 million into a new stadium at the site of the old stadium, and Dunedin Stadium became the new spring-training home of the Toronto Blue Jays in 1990. In 2002 Dunedin spent $12 million on a new spring-training complex for the Blue Jays, which include new training facilities, offices, new hitting cages, and five full fields at the Cecil P. Englebert Recreational Complex.

insider's tip

Take a close look at the warning track. Mixed in are crushed seashells, an homage to local beaches.

THE SPRING-TRAINING BALLPARK EXPERIENCE

Concessions

The concessions at Dunedin Stadium are straightforward: The two main concession stands offer the likes of hot dogs, grilled-chicken sandwiches, hamburgers, nachos, BBQ-pork sandwiches and more. (Alas, no true Ca-

Former closer Billy Wagner has them lining up in the pregame autograph area. Photo by Jim Robins.

nadian smokies, only American-style brats.) Look around for the grouper sandwiches — they're worth a wait in line. Most Blue Jays fans will opt for a Blue, but others will want to check out the Corona or the other corporate brews on tap or in bottles.

Parking

The 100 onsite parking spaces are reserved for season-ticket holders. Otherwise, you'll need to park in the surrounding area at a spendy $10 per car. You can find cheaper lots within a few blocks of the ballpark, however. Watch the signs, as you will get harassed if you park in a space or lot reserved for local residents. This lack of available parking is one reason we park downtown and walk the several blocks to the ballpark via the Pinellas Trail. The fact that the trail goes directly through a bucolic residential area is a nice bonus; the respite from the hustle and bustle of the greater Tampa Bay area is refreshing.

Autographs

Among the best spots for autographs is the open area down the left-field line, where the players go to and from the clubhouse. In addition, players from both teams come to the edge of the stands to sign autographs before a game as well, with visiting players next to the third-base dugout and Blue

Jays players next to the first-base dugout and in the bullpen down the right-field line. We're not talking about scrubs here; during our last visit we chatted with Twins closer Joe Nathan as he happily signed balls for a crowd of adoring kids.

IF YOU GO

What to Do Outside the Ballpark

Dunedin is actually one of the oldest cities in Florida and for a time was a major seaport in the area. Today, the area is better known for its beaches and its proximity to Tampa/St. Petersburg. If you're craving some rays, you should check out Caladesi Island, which has been called one of the top 10 beaches in the United States. Also worth checking out is Honeymoon Island, which was settled in the 1930s as a honeymoon resort and is now a state park.

Dunedin Stadium is a mile or so south of downtown Dunedin, which features small shops and restaurants. Chances are you're going to be thirsty before or after the game, and there are a few joints in downtown Dunedin that are worth a visit. The folks in Dunedin apparently appreciate a snort now and again, because downtown is crawling with bars.

In fact, one of our favorite spring-training experiences is to park in downtown Dunedin, have a nice brunch at one of the many dining establishments, and then walk down the Pinellas Trail south to the ballpark. It's only a mile, and it saves you from the crowds fighting over the few parking spots outside the ballpark. (On weekends you can park downtown without worrying about a time limit in the conveniently located parking lot.) Our personal favorite for brunch on the weekend is Café Alfresco, located right on the Pinellas Trail where it intersects Main Street in downtown Dunedin. We're fans of the Crab Cakes Benedict, but pastries and espresso drinks are also on the menu. Sit on the covered patio if it's a nice day. Café Alfresco, 344 Main St., Dunedin; 727/736-4299; **cafealfrescoonline.com**.

After the game, we drop by the Iris Restaurant (234 Douglas Av., Dunedin; 727/734-0779; **irisfamilyrestaurant.com**) for a piece of goober (peanut-butter) pie.

And save room for a specialty cocktail at another downtown establishment. For instance, Kelly's Chic-a-Boom Room features "martoonis," which apparently is a cross between a martini and a cartoon. Your teeth will ache after sipping a "Barry White," which contains Stoli Razberi, Godiva white chocolate liqueur, and Chambord; these are martinis for people who don't like the taste of real liquor. But the ambiance is cool, there frequently is live music on the docket, the wine list is superb, and a wide range of beers is on tap. It's all part of the Kelly's complex, which features a good restaurant and a nightclub. Kelly's, 319-325 Main St.; Dunedin; 727/736-0206; **kellyschicaboom.com**.

Beer lovers will appreciate Dunedin Brewery, which brews a wide variety of beers on site. Recommended: the Piper Pale Ale, the Highland Games Ale and the Leonard Croons Old Mean Stout, although they all may not be on tap when you visit, as not all the selections are available year-round. There's also a limited food menu and live music on the weekends. Bonus: The brewpub is within walking distance of the ballpark, on the same street — Douglas Avenue. Dunedin Brewery, 937 Douglas Av., Dunedin; 727/736-0606; **dunedinbrewery.com**.

Flanagan's Irish Pub is exactly what you'd expect: a faux Irish pub featuring Irish beers (Guinness, Harp, and Smithwick's) and Irish foods like fish and chips, bangers and mashed, and corned beef and cabbage. Flanagan's Irish Pub, 465 Main St., Dunedin; 727/736-4994; **flanagansirishpub.net**.

Casa Tina Mexican Grill features authentic Mexican foods like moles and vegetarian dishes. Casa Tina's Mexican Grill, 369 Main St., Dunedin; 727/734-9226; **casatinas.com**.

For those who like their food and drinks more traditional in nature, Norton's Sports Bar is a testosterone haven, featuring 18 televisions (all featuring some manner of sporting event) and seven video games, including multiple Golden Tee's with big screens. Maybe it's a guy thing, and maybe it's a little perverse-to-do thing while on spring break in Florida, but we love playing video golf on vacation. Norton's Sports Bar; 1824 Main St., Dunedin; 727/734-2053; **nortonsbar.com**.

Where to Stay

Dunedin is in the northwest corner of the Tampa Bay region and adjacent to Clearwater. We cover the hotel scene in the Tampa Bay region in our previous chapter covering Tampa Bay, but if you're a diehard Blue Jays fan and want to stay as close to the ballpark as possible (or on the Gulf Coast, overlooking the water), there are a few hotels worth noting.

The Best Western Yacht Harbor Inn (150 Marina Place, Dunedin; 727/733-4121; **bestwestern.com**) is at Dunedin's Marina Plaza and overlooks St. Joseph's Sound. It's an old two-story motel-style establishment, but it's been recently refurbished, and you can't beat the location: Besides being on the waterfront it's also the hotel closest to the ballpark — you can walk through downtown Dunedin on your way to a game.

The Pinellas trail leads from downtown Dunedin to the ballpark.

Also located less than a mile from the ballpark are the Holiday Inn Express and Suites (975 Broadway St., Dunedin; 727/450-1200; **holiday-inn.com**) and Comfort Suites (1941 Edgewater Dr., Clearwater; 727/489-5000; **comfortinn.com**).

RV Parks in the Area

It's not really within walking distance, but the Dunedin Beach RV Resort is located on the Pinellas Trail and close to area beaches. Bring a bike and take the trail to the ballpark. Dunedin Beach RV Resort, 2920 Alt 19. N., Dunedin; 727/784-3719.

Flying In

The closest airport to Dunedin is St. Petersburg-Clearwater International Airport, located on the west side of the bay. This airport specializes in low-fare carriers in the United States and Canada (which makes it popular for those Canadian fans heading to Dunedin): Sunwing Airlines, for example, flies direct from Toronto. It's also small enough where the car-rental agencies (Avis, Enterprise, Hertz, National, and Alamo) are truly on site.

In case you can't get a flight into St. Pete-Clearwater, you'll want to check out Tampa International Airport. All the major airlines fly into Tampa; Air Canada flies daily from Toronto.

SPRING-TRAINING HISTORY

The Toronto Blue Jays have been training at this site since 1977, first at Grant Field and then at Dunedin Stadium.

arizona and the cactus league

If the Grapefruit League represents tradition and stability, the Cactus League represents the Wild West. It's probably no surprise that the Cactus League can directly trace its roots to one of the original baseball rebels, Bill Veeck — the outlaw owner who sent a midget to bat, shot off fireworks after homers, and generally rankled his fellow MLB owners.

When Arizona interests lured the New York Giants and the Indians West in 1947, spring training was a different beast in terms of economics and schedules. Teams had trained out West many times before World War II — most notably the Chicago Cubs, who first trained in Santa Monica in 1905 and then trained on California's Catalina Island between 1922-1942 — and the economics were simple: Owners would get some small Florida community to subsidize spring training, teams would spend a few weeks training (or drying out, in some cases), and then the teams would hit the road, barnstorming their way home.

But as baseball became a big business, so did spring training. Owners were working every angle in search of more revenues, and spring training became one obvious target: With players basically working for free (salaries didn't kick in until the season started), spring training was a way to generate revenue without a lot of overhead. Barnstorming gradually gave way to longer stints at training camp; instead of going to where the fans were by barnstorming, baseball teams got the fans to come to them in a much less expensive fashion.

The Cactus League became a reality in 1947 when Horace Stoneham's New York Giants and Bill Veeck's Cleveland Indians took up residence in Phoenix and Tucson, respectively. That Veeck ended up in Tucson wasn't a surprise — he loved the Southwest and at the time owned a ranch near Tucson — and Stoneham was a natural for Phoenix, as he developed business interests in the area. Stoneham went Veeck one further by developing a luxury development in conjunction with spring training, a route that several team owners took over the years (and are still taking; more than one owner has floated the idea of combining a ballpark with a big-buck development).

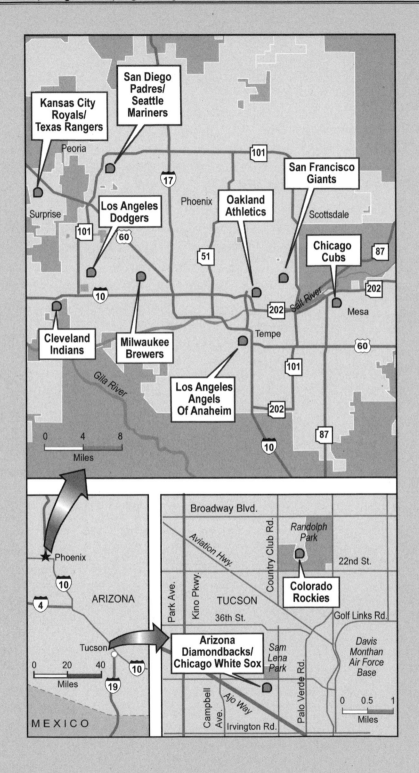

More and more teams were attracted to Arizona after Veeck and Stoneham's arrival. Most were lured with economic incentives: Communities were all too willing to build facilities for teams, who benefited from a growing fan base (i.e., transplanted retirees) and a growing economy. (Some, however, were accidental: When the Seattle Pilots were moved to Milwaukee in 1970, team officials decided to keep the team's training base in Arizona anyway.) And over the years teams shifted between Arizona and Florida: The Indians, Astros, Rangers, Royals, and Orioles have all trained in both states.

Baseball's move toward the West also hastened the growth of the Cactus League: With the move of the Los Angeles Dodgers to a Glendale training facility, all eight Western MLB teams now train in Arizona. If you're running the Seattle Mariners or the San Diego Padres, you want to make it as easy as possible for your fans and the media to attend spring training.

Today, the Cactus League is a lively institution in Phoenix and Tucson, with the most ever teams training in Phoenix with the arrival of Cleveland and the Dodgers in 2009 and the Cincinnati Reds in 2010, giving Arizona 14 teams in 2009 and 15 in 2010. True, there are some clouds on the horizon for Tucson, as the three teams training there look at shifting operations north to Phoenix. We're not going to get into whether that's a good idea. Let's just say that any day in March with baseball and a warm breeze is definitely a day worth living, no matter if you're in Phoenix or Tucson.

→ phoenix

Phoenix: The Heart of the Cactus League

With nine teams training in the region, Phoenix is the psychic center of the Grapefruit League. Located in the Valley of the Sun, Phoenix combines the spirit of the Wild West with a bustling economy and a diverse population to create one of the largest metropolitan areas in the country.

Understanding diversity (and we don't mean that in a politically correct way) is the key to understanding the Phoenix area. Spend any time in the area and you realize that there's no "one" Phoenix; instead, Phoenix is made up of interconnected communities, and part of the fun is exploring the many facets of the Phoenix area.

The greater Phoenix area is made up of the following areas:

→ **Downtown Phoenix** used to be a ghost town after hours, but it's now the city's sports and entertainment center. Even though no team plays at Bank One Ballpark — the home of the Arizona Diamondbacks — until the end of spring training, you'll still find baseball fans hanging around downtown sports bars like Cooper's Town (which we'll discuss later).

→ The **Camelback Corridor** is a repository of serious money in the Valley. Many corporations call this area home, while much of the high-end shopping in the region can be found there as well.

→ **Scottsdale** is the upscale part of town, but downtown Scottsdale is also home to a section celebrating the Wild West and Phoenix's place in the settling of the West.

→ **Tempe** is home to Arizona State University, considered one of the best party colleges in the country. ASU co-eds are among the most attractive in the world, and they hang out on or near Mill Avenue in Tempe. (We'll discuss Tempe in more depth in the Los Angeles Angels of Anaheim chapter.)

→ **Mesa** is largely a residential area to the west of Tempe. (We'll discuss Mesa in more depth in the Chicago Cubs chapter.)

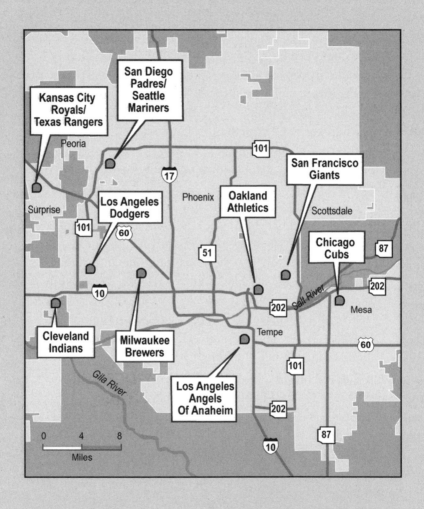

→ The northwestern and western suburbs have evolved into their own little spring-training worlds, with six teams training in four facilities. At times **Surprise**, **Goodyear**, **Glendale**, and **Peoria** really don't feel like part of the Valley of the Sun, as they're made up mainly of housing developments that seemingly sprawl forever.

Navigating the Valley of the Sun

Despite its sprawling nature, the Valley of the Sun is surprisingly easy to navigate. Once you master your location relative to the freeways or to one of the major streets in the region, you stand a much better chance of not getting lost in a new area.

Why? Because the entire region is built in a grid system extending to the outer regions of the area. Freeways and bypasses intersect the grid at convenient points, making Phoenix easy and convenient to navigate.

Two major freeways service the area: I-10 and I-17. I-10 enters the region from the west (where it's known as the Papago Freeway), runs through the center of Phoenix, and then heads south to Tempe and Tucson. This is the one freeway you'll spend some time driving, as it's the best way to reach the western and northwestern suburbs. I-17 (Black Canyon Freeway) comes in from the north and loops south of downtown before merging with I-10 (the merged stretch is called the Maricopa Freeway) near Sky Harbor International Airport.

Hwy. 60 (Grand Avenue) runs through the northwest quadrant of the region from downtown Phoenix all the way past Surprise. When you look at maps, you'll be tempted to take Hwy. 60 from the center of town to Peoria and Surprise. Don't. Hwy. 60 is filled with stop lights and traffic and is rarely worth the fuss. Instead, use Hwy. 101 as a shortcut. Hwy. 101 loops around the north side of town and is a true freeway. To go to Peoria from downtown, the quickest way is not the most direct way — Hwy. 60 — but rather taking Hwy. 10 to Hwy. 101 and then heading north. Hwy. 101 is also the fastest way to reach the Maryvale neighborhood, Peoria, and Surprise.

insider's tip

You won't see Maryvale on the map. Technically, Maryvale is a Phoenix neighborhood, located in the southwestern part of Phoenix.

Once in the city, there are some major streets that will get you any-where: Washington Street, Buckeye Road, Van Buren Street, McDowell Road, Thomas Road, Indian School Road, and Camelback Road are all major east-west streets running through Phoenix and the entire area.

insider's tip

You can easily figure out the approximate location of an address. All addresses begin at Central Avenue (which runs north-south through downtown) and Washington Street (which runs east-west through downtown). Streets are on the east side of town, while avenues are on the west side of town. Camelback Street is 50 blocks north of Washington Street, so you can usually determine where you are relative to Camelback and Washington.

Arriving in Phoenix

Sky Harbor International Airport is the major airport in the region. It is also one of the most confusing airports in the United States, thanks to a poor design that splits the airport into three unconnected terminals. If you're planning on meeting buddies in the Phoenix airport, don't plan on merely meeting by the luggage-claim or car-rental areas — because there are three terminals, there are three car-rental areas.

And you will want to rent a car unless you plan on spending all your time directly next to a ballpark. We'll say it again: Phoenix sprawls, and no one walks. Public transit is good if you want to get around the center city but is completely lacking for those making their way to spring-training

Sunshine and a place to stand: Who needs more?

facilities. To make your way around in Phoenix, a car is essential. Parking is almost always free and plentiful.

Sky Harbor International Airport, 3400 E. Sky Harbor Blvd., Phoenix; 602/273-3300; **phxskyharbor.com**.

insider's tip

Even though the Valley sprawls, the spring-training sites are conveniently located in relation to the airport. To reach Scottsdale from the airport, take Hwy. 202 (the Red Mountain Freeway) to Hwy. 101. To reach downtown Phoenix, take I-10 west. To reach Surprise or Peoria, take I-10 west to Hwy. 101 north. To reach Glendale or Goodyear, take I-10 west. To reach Tempe or Mesa, take I-10 or Hwy. 60 (the Superstition Freeway).

A smaller airport, Phoenix-Mesa Gateway, features flights from Allegiant Airlines. Smaller markets are served by Allegiant, and given the presence of the Cubbies, it's a little surprising not to see any Allegiant flights from O'Hare or Midway. However, Cubs fans in Peoria or Rockford are in luck. Alamo, Enterprise, and Hertz have facilities there. Phoenix-Mesa Gateway Airport, 6033 S. Sossaman Rd., Mesa; **phxmesagateway.com**.

Phoenix Attractions

With so many spring-training facilities in a concentrated area, you'll be able to hit at one game daily during your stay (or two if the scheduling gods are smiling upon you). You'll spend much of your time at the ballpark, but you will probably want a few more diversions during the course of your stay. There's something for everyone in Phoenix; we'll list some of the more popular indoor and outdoor attractions here. (The many attractions of Scottsdale are listed later in this chapter.) Here we'll pass along some family-friendly activities suitable for the entire family.

Camelback Mountain, located in the northeast part of town, is a popular destination for hikers and nature lovers. There are four trails — two for inexperienced hikers, running less than an eighth of a mile, and two for very experienced hikers, reaching 1.5 miles. You can find parking for the various trails at East McDonald Drive and Tatum Boulevard. A warning: Even on the shorter trails you run some risk of dehydration and sunburn, so bring water and sunscreen.

The Desert Botanical Garden is 50 acres of trails and exhibits covering the ecosystem of the Sonoran desert. It's home to 139 endangered species of plants, as well as the most cacti you've seen in your life. Desert Botanical

Garden, 1201 N. Galvin Pkwy., Phoenix; 480/941-1225; **dbg.org**. *Adults, $10; seniors, $9; children (13-18), $5; children (3-12), $4.*

Also a great hiking spot is Papago Park, located in the eastern part of town near Phoenix Municipal Stadium, the spring home of the Oakland Athletics. For those just wanting get outside there are some nice level trails through the desert brush. For those wanting a challenge there's rock-climbing trails.

Located near both the Desert Botanical Garden and Papago Park is the Phoenix Zoo, a great place to take the kids. The layout is organized by theme — there are separate trails with Africa, Tropics, and Arizona themes, along with a Children's Trail — with over 1,300 animals on display, and traversing the whole place should take about three hours. Phoenix Zoo, 455 N. Galvin Pkwy., Phoenix; 602.273.1341; **phoenixzoo.org**. *Adults, $16; seniors, $11; children, $7.*

Architecture buffs will be fascinated by Taliesin West, Frank Lloyd Wright's winter home, and the Biltmore, inspired by Wright's architecture style. Located in Scottsdale, Taliesin West takes its inspiration from the Arizona landscape: Like all Wright buildings, the scale is intimate and low to the ground, while almost all of the materials were locally sourced. Taliesin West, 12621 Frank Lloyd Wright Blvd., Scottsdale; 480/860-2700; **franklloydwright.org**.

The Arizona Biltmore Resort may be the most unique hotel in Phoenix. Located in the Camelback Corridor, the Arizona Biltmore was designed by Albert Chase McArthur, a former student of Frank Lloyd Wright, who served as the consulting architect. The Wright influence is obvious: The hotel is constructed of precast concrete blocks (a building material favored by Wright) in a unique geometric pattern. The blocks were designed by local artist Emry Kopta in a distinctive "Biltmore Block" pattern. Gum magnate William Wrigley Jr. was an early investor in the project and by 1930 owned the entire place, but curiously he never combined it with his other great passion, the Chicago Cubs, who instead trained for many of the Wrigley years on Catalina Island. During the 1930s and 1940s it was the place to winter in Phoenix. Irving Berlin wrote "White Christmas" while lounging poolside at the Biltmore. Stop by even if you're not staying there; the lobby is an oasis and a nice place for a post-game cocktail. Arizona Biltmore, 2400 E. Missouri Av., Phoenix; 800/950-0086; **arizonabiltmore.com**.

Speaking of the Camelback Corridor, a pleasant evening can be spent at the Biltmore Fashion Park. All the major trendy stores are represented in the open-air mall, but our preference is to do dinner at Sam's

College games, like this one at Packard Stadium, are a great alternative to a pro game.

Café or Steamers Genuine Seafood, poke around at the Borders Book-store or Apple Store, and then stop for a treat at Häagen-Dazs or the Para-dise Bakery. Biltmore Fashion Park, 24th St. and Camelback Rd., Phoenix; 602/955-8400; **shopbiltmore.com**.

Recommended Phoenix Restaurants
There is an amazing diversity of restaurants in the Valley of the Sun. The region helped make Southwestern cuisine one of the most innovative food movements of the last 15 years, and today you can find world-class res-taurants throughout the region. You can also find a wide range of sports bars and restaurants, too, if your tastes don't run to haute cuisine. In this section, we'll give you a little of each. We also will list recommended res-taurants close to each of the spring-training ballparks.

Cooper's Town is a mandatory stop during Cactus League spring train-ing, even if no team is near Chase Field, the regular-season home of the Arizona Diamondbacks. Cooper's Town, located two blocks from Chase Field, was created by baseball fanatic and rocker Alice Cooper, who set-tled in Phoenix after his shock-rock days and was looking for a new chal-lenge. The result was Cooper's Town, an entertainment complex featuring a restaurant and outdoor stage sometimes featuring live music.

The themes are sports and rock and roll (think of a Hard Rock Cafe run by sports geeks, and you have a pretty good vision of the sports and

rock memorabilia dominating the interior).

The fare is fairly eclectic for a theme restaurant: There's Ty's Cobb Salad, the Ryne Sandburger, and the Megadeth Meatloaf. Cooper's Town does its own smoking on the premises, so the ribs are recommended. Fans of home cooking will appreciate the tuna-noodle casserole made from Mama Alice's recipe. And yes, Alice Cooper does spend quite a bit of time hanging around.

If you're famished, consider The Big Unit, a two-foot-long hot dog named after the Diamondbacks' Randy Johnson (an original investor in the restaurant). We're not going to go into the homoerotic aspects of eating a Big Unit, but be prepared for a fuss if you do: Sirens go off when a customer orders one. Alice Cooper's Town, 101 E. Jackson St., Phoenix; 602/253-7337; **alicecooperstown.com**.

In the same vein (sans the rock and roll, though) is Majerle's Sports Grill, also located in downtown Phoenix. Dan Majerle was a star forward for the Phoenix Suns, and when US Airways Arena was completed in 1992, Majerle went into the sports-bar business and opened up Majerle's in the oldest commercial building in downtown Phoenix. Majerle's Sports Grill, 24 N. 2nd St., Phoenix; 602/253-0118; **majerles.com**.

If you find yourself in the vicinity of Chase Field at night after a few cocktails, drop by Lo-Lo's Chicken and Waffles. Phoenix isn't known for its soul food, but Lo-Lo's is in a class by itself when it comes to that magic combination of chicken and waffles — a much better pairing than you'd think. Lo-Lo's Chicken and Waffles, 10 W. Yuma St., Phoenix; 602/340-1304; **lolochickenandwaffles.com**.

Considerably more upscale is the Barrio Cafe, which bills itself as modern Mexican. Reviewers near and far rave around the Barrio Cafe and are amazed that owner/chef Silvana Salcido Esparza decided to locate a haute-cuisine establishment in a transitional neighborhood.

The menu changes monthly, but there are some items always available. Be sure to have the Guacamole Casero, prepared tableside: It's a ripe avocado moistened with olive oil and mashed with onions, cilantro, tomato, and pomegranate seeds. As for the rest of the menu, mole fans will want to check out the enchiladas de mole, while the *cochinita pibil* (slow roasted pork with achiote rojo) is excellent. Wash it down with a *horchata*, a sweet Mexican drink made of rice, cinnamon, lime juice, and water.

It's a little unfair to doom the offerings at the Barrio Cafe to be haute cuisine: It's excellent food served at a reasonable price in a neighborhood cafe. The place is small (seating only 69) and fills up quickly; if you're not there right at opening time (5:30 p.m.), be prepared for a wait, even if you do make a reservation. Highly recommended. Barrio Cafe, 2814 N. 16th St., Phoenix; 602/636-0240; **barriocafe.com**.

For Mexican seafood, check out Mariscos Playa Hermosa. We think of Mexican cuisine as being a monolithic entity, but regional flavors are important south of the border. In the case of Mariscos Playa Hermosa, the cuisine is not only Mexican but specializes in the seafood cuisine found in Hermosillo. You normally don't think of great seafood when you think of landlocked Phoenix, but Mariscos Playa Hermosa shatters that stereotype. Mariscos Playa Hermosa, 1605 E. Garfield St., Phoenix; 602/462-1563; **mariscosplayahermosa.com**.

Phoenix has more than its share of steakhouses, and one of the more notable ones is Rustlers Rooste. Whether you buy into the mythology of the place — that the restaurant was formerly a hideaway for cattle rustlers — there's no doubt that the Rooste provides an impressive view of the Valley. Most will order steak; the adventurous will order rattlesnake. Rustler's Rooste, 8383 S. 48th St., Phoenix; 602/431-6474; **rustlersrooste.com**.

This doesn't even scrape the surface of good restaurants in Phoenix; we're not even going near the likes of Tarbell's or Tomaso's, both located in the Camelback Corridor.

insider's tip

Remember that all the spring-training facilities in Phoenix are fairly close together. It's easy to move around the city, so don't assume that just because an attraction or restaurant is Scottsdale or Tempe you should avoid it. Tempe, Scottsdale, Mesa, and Phoenix are all adjoining communities, as are Peoria and Surprise. We list hotels and restaurants by locale, but don't let these boundaries stop you from perusing the listings for all the ballparks in search of a restaurant or attraction. You're never really far away from anything in the Valley of the Sun.

SCOTTSDALE: UPSCALE MEETS KITSCH

Downtown Scottsdale is a curious mix of the kitsch and the artsy; it's where the hoi polloi in the region step out to buy a cowboy t-shirt for the grandkids and then dine at an upscale restaurant before hitting the well-regarded Scottsdale Art Museum.

Of course, another way to put it is that Scottsdale has something for everyone, ranging from a slew of touristy Old West shops in Old Town to the upscale department stores at the Scottsdale Fashion Mall. This all means you can easily entertain yourself for days in Scottsdale between spring-training games in the Valley.

There are four major districts to downtown Scottsdale: Fifth Avenue, Main Street, Old Town, and Marshall Way. Fifth Avenue features upscale shopping and dining; the Marshall Way Arts District features art galleries specializing in contemporary art from local artists, as well as a wide variety of regionally produced jewelry; Main Street is one of the largest concentrations of art galleries in the world; and Old Town features the aforementioned Wild West kitsch.

The San Francisco Giants play at Scottsdale Stadium, which we'll cover in its own chapter.

Two Spring-Training Traditions: The Pink Pony and Don and Charlie's

From the exterior, The Pink Pony is nothing fancy, looking much the same as it did when first opening in 1952.

And while the food is good — it's a red meat kinda place, with the steaks and prime rib especially recommended — you don't go to the Pink Pony for the food or the decor.

You go for the people, as did Ted Williams, Mickey Mantle, and Willie Mays. Dining at the Pink Pony is a Scottsdale tradition for Giants players and coaches and visiting players and coaches. A sports bar before there were sports bars, the Pink Pony opened in 1952 and has cultivated a reputation as the place to be seen in spring training (for dinner, that is; at lunchtime the place is fairly quiet). As you might expect, the walls are covered with sports memorabilia, mostly Giants-related, as well as pink pony statues. And the booths are real Naugahyde — what more could you want? If you go, ask for booth #3: It was Gene Autry's favorite. The Pink Pony, 831 N. Scottsdale Rd., Scottsdale; 480/949-8677.

Don & Charlie's dates back only to 1981, but it too has become a spring-training tradition. Yes, the menu is geared toward the masculine — ribs and steaks are the highlights — and owner Don Carson is a lifelong baseball fan who has covered the walls with sports memorabilia. You'll see Don working the room most nights during spring training. With a little prompting he may even sit down and share a few memories with you. Don and Charlie's tends to be pretty packed in spring training; a reservation is recommended, especially on the weekend. Don and Charlie's, 7501 E. Camelback Rd., Scottsdale; 480/990-0900; **donandcharlies.com**.

Scottsdale Dining and Drinking

Apart from the traditional choices, downtown Scottsdale features a wide range of dining and drinking options in all sorts of genres and price ranges. Though this is a fairly extensive list of restaurants and hotspots, it's by no means a complete list.

Our favorite spot before a Giants home game at Scottsdale Stadium is the Sugar Bowl Ice Cream Parlor. The specialty, as you might expect, is ice cream (try the Top Hat Sundae), but the menu also features tasty sandwiches and burgers. It's the most kid-friendly place in downtown Scottsdale. Sugar Bowl Ice Cream Parlor, 4005 N. Scottsdale Rd., Scottsdale; 480/946-0051.

Though there are several Zipps sports bars in Phoenix, our favorite is Zipps Sports Grill Camelback, in the middle of Old Town Scottsdale. It's a great place to follow March Madness; the outdoor deck features TVs and a firepit, perfect for viewing those evening basketball games. Zipps Sports Grill Camelback, 7551 E. Camelback Rd., Scottsdale; 480/970-9507; **zipps-sportscafe.com**.

The Blue Moose is another downtown sports bar of note. The half-pound burger will keep you filled for a day or two. Sit out on the deck before the game. Blue Moose, 7373 E. Scottsdale Mall, Scottsdale; 480/949-7959.

Bravo! Bistro is a downtown landmark featuring a Mediterranean/Italian theme. Chef and co-owner Tony Hamati trained at the Sorbonne in Paris and cooked for King Hussein in the Royal Palace of Jordan. 4327 N. Scottsdale Rd., Scottsdale; 480/481-7614; **bravobistro.com**.

If you like your Italian cuisine without a Mediterranean influence, Cowboy Ciao features modern Italian cuisine with a Tex-Mex twist. 7133 E. Stetson Dr., Scottsdale; 480/946-3111; **cowboyciao.com**.

More casual dining can be found at Flicka's Baja Cantina, especially on the 3,000-square-foot patio overlooking Scottsdale Road. Yes, it is a little odd to design a deck with a nautical look in the middle of the desert, but the approach works, especially when complimented by a menu that includes fish tacos and cheap PBRs. Flicka's Bar & Grill, 2003 N. Scottsdale Rd., Scottsdale; 480/945-3618; **flickasbajacantina.com**.

Old Town Tortilla Factory is located in a 75-year-old adobe home in the heart of Old Town Scottsdale and features a 1,200-square-foot deck. The margaritas served here have won national acclaim, and it's hard to imagine anything better than sipping an excellent margarita under a clear desert sky at night. Old Town Tortilla Factory, 6910 E. Main St.; 480/945-4567; **oldtowntortillafactory.com**.

Dos Gringos has a well-deserved reputation for being a place where hookups frequently occur. The patio is huge and perfect for mingling, while the beer is cheap. Dos Gringos, 4209 N. Craftsman Court, Scottsdale; 480/423-3800; **dosgringosaz.com**.

And then there's the Salty Señorita, which is basically Hooters with a Mexican accent. Perhaps that's not quite fair; the place also specializes in a wide selection of tequilas. But the atmosphere is definitely a party one. Salty Señorita, 3636 N. Scottsdale Rd., Scottsdale; 480/946-SALTY; **saltysenorita.com**.

Order yourself a man drink (scotches and bourbons dominate the drink menu) at AZ 88 and hang out with the sleek and sexy of Scottsdale on the gorgeous patio. North of the Scottsdale Museum of Contemporary Art, AZ 88 is the embodiment of Scottsdale chic. AZ 88, 7353 Scottsdale Mall, Scottsdale; 480/994-5576; **az88.com**.

The food (sandwiches, designer pizzas) at Furio isn't as hot as the clientele, but the beautiful people abound. A good place for martinis and Cosmos. Furio, 7210 E. 2nd St., Scottsdale; 480/945-6600; **furio.tv**.

Patsy Grimaldi's Coal Brick-Oven Pizzeria is definitely an oddity or a pleasant surprise, depending on your point of view. We're not exactly sure how one of the best pizzerias in Brooklyn ended up with a Scottsdale outpost, but we're too busy scarfing down the thin-crust pizza to care. For those who don't worship the perfect pizza, there are calzones on the menu as well. Patsy Grimaldi's Coal Brick-Oven Pizzeria, 4000 N. Scottsdale Rd., Scottsdale; 480/994-1100; **patsygrimaldis.com**.

After a day of noshing at the ballpark you probably won't want to tackle a huge dinner, so the tapas (Spanish finger food) at Pepin is a good alternative to a steakhouse serving up large slabs of red meat. Stick around for the flamenco dancers, who perform on Friday and Saturday nights.

Pepin, 7363 Scottsdale Mall, Scottsdale; 480/990-9026; **pepinrestaurant.com**.

Though not really within walking distance of any spring-training site, Fox Sports Grill nevertheless has earned the reputation for being a spring-training hangout. Located in the high-end Promenade of Scottsdale, Fox Sports Grill features a fairly standard sports-bar menu (ribs, steaks, chops, pasta) and an Arizona decor. Fox Sports Grill, 16203 N. Scottsdale Rd., Scottsdale; 480/368-0369; **foxsportsgrill.com**.

A cluster of great restaurants, including the Kona Grill and Z TeJas, are at the Scottsdale Fashion Mall, located at Camelback Rd. and Scottsdale Rd. The name is a misnomer: Though Nordstrom and Neiman Marcus are two of the anchor stores, there's much more than just fashion at this sprawling temple to shopping.

Old Town Scottsdale

Scottsdale is not a very old community: It began life as a housing development in 1894 when an Eastern banker named Albert Utley divided 40 acres of desert land into lots. The name Scottsdale comes from U.S. Chaplain Winfield Scott, whose promotional efforts attracted many of the earlier settlers.

Most of today's Old Town in downtown Scottsdale dates back to the 1920s or earlier, when the area experienced its first growth spurt. There are several remnants of the original Scottsdale in the Old Town area:

→ Cavalliere Blacksmith (3805 N. Brown Av.; 480/945-6262). George Cavalliere moved his family to Scottsdale in 1910 and opened a blacksmith shop on the edge of downtown Scottsdale. He originally set up shop in metal building, which he replaced with the current adobe structure in 1920. The Cavalliere family still operates the blacksmith shop.

→ The first post office in Scottsdale opened in 1928 and was a community gathering place when the mail was delivered from Phoenix. The building still stands and is now home to Porter's Western Wear (3944 N. Brown Av.; 480/945-0868).

→ Our Lady of Perpetual Help Catholic Church (3817 N. Brown Av.) is a striking white building in Old Town. It dates back to 1933 when local Mexican residents volunteered their time and money to construct the church.

→ The Little Red Schoolhouse (7333 Scottsdale Mall; 480/945-4499), now housing a local historical society, was built in 1909 as a two-room schoolhouse. It housed the school through the 1960s and was then used for a variety of civic purposes.

→ Los Olivos Restaurant (7328 E. 2nd St.; 946/225-6480), built in the 1950s, originally housed a pool hall and a church before becoming a Mexican restaurant.

→ The Rusty Spur Saloon (7245 E. Main St.; 480/941-2628) originally was the Farmer's State Bank of Scottsdale when the building opened in 1921. The bank didn't last long, closing during the Great Depression.

There's one other feature in Old Town worth checking out: the olive trees along Drinkwater Boulevard and Second Street. Chaplain Winfield Scott, the founder of Scottsdale, planted them in 1896.

OTHER SPORTS IN THE AREA

In the unlikely event you have a spare moment during your spring trip to Phoenix, there are plenty of other sports events to occupy your time.

Phoenix is a major-league city, and both NBA and NHL games are scheduled in March. The Phoenix Suns play at the downtown US Airways Center, one of the more intimate facilities in the NBA. Buy your tickets early; entering the 2008-2009 season, the Suns had sold out 117 con-

The right-field pool is a signature item at Chase Field.

You can catch future major leaguers at Packard Stadium, home of the ASU Sun Devils.

secutive games over three seasons. US Airways Center, 201 E. Jefferson St., Phoenix; 602/379-7800; **usairwayscenter.com**.

US Airways Center is also home to the ECHL's Phoenix Roadrunners. The ECHL is a second-tier minor league, so don't expect a high skill level (let's just say there are a lot of physical grinders in that league). But you can usually snare a great seat for a Roadrunners game with little notice, making it a great spur-of-the-moment excursion.

If major-league hockey is more to your liking, the NHL's Phoenix Coyotes play at Jobing.com Arena in Glendale. It always feels a little weird to us to be sipping cocktails in 80-degree weather and then heading into a hermetically sealed area to see ice hockey, but apparently there are enough expatriate Canadians and Minnesotans in the Phoenix area to support an NHL team. Jobing.com Arena, 9400 W. Maryland Av., Glendale; 623/772-3200; **jobingarena.com**.

A free evening could entail a visit to see the Arizona State University Sun Devils playing at Winkles Field-Packard Stadium at Brock Ballpark (known by most locals as Packard Stadium). It's a decent college ballpark, and generally speaking, the Sun Devil baseball program always features a future major leaguer or two. Sit along the third-base line or set up shop down the right-field berm; you can get a decent view if a typical gorgeous Arizona sunset is happening. Packard Stadium, 201 S. Packard Dr., Tempe; 888/SUN-DVLS; **thesundevils.collegesports.com**.

insider's tip

If you're in Phoenix during the end of spring training, check out a Diamondbacks schedule. Most years the team schedules one exhibition game at Chase Field right before the regular season, sometimes for charity. Spring-training prices apply to the seat tickets (but, alas, not to the concession prices). In addition, college games are occasionally scheduled at Chase Field in March.

PHOENIX/SCOTTSDALE AND THE WILD WEST

The mythology of the Wild West is still strong in Arizona: The state is an essentially conservative place where citizens take great pride in the frontier spirit exemplified in the Wild West ethos.

Where mythology ends and caricature begins is another issue, of course — not every pioneer was as funny as Gabby Hayes, as heroic as Tom Mix, as black-hearted as Wyatt Earp, or as tuneful as Gene Autry — but there's just enough truth to the tales of the Wild West to reverberate in today's culture.

There are many outposts in Phoenix celebrating one vision or another of the Wild West. To be honest, we've not visited them all (if you've seen one fight at the OK Corral, you've seen them all), so we can't vouch for their authenticity or entertainment value. Still, if you're bringing your kids to spring training, chances are pretty good they'd enjoy some exposure to the Wild West.

One of the bigger Wild West attractions in Scottsdale is the Rawhide Steakhouse and Saloon, a recreation of an 1880s Arizona town. This Wild West adventure includes train and stagecoach rides, outdoor cookouts, gunfights, and gold panning. Grownups will appreciate the cowboy steaks and cold beer at the Rawhide Steakhouse. Rawhide Steakhouse & Saloon, 5700 W. North Loop Rd., Chandler; 480/502-6500; **rawhide.com**.

For a more somber look at the Wild West, check out the Mesa Historical Museum: It contains the standard pioneer exhibits as well as a replica of the first schoolhouse in the area. Mesa Historical Museum, 2345 N. Horne, Mesa; 480/835-7358; **mesaaz.org**.

➙ chicago cubs

HoHoKam Park

Capacity 12,575
Year Opened 1997
Dimensions 340L, 390LC, 410C, 390RC, 350R
Surface Grass
Address 1235 N. Center St., Mesa.

From Phoenix, take 202 Loop east to exit 12 (McKellips Road), turn right on W. McKellips Road; and turn right onto N. Center Street. HoHoKam will be on the left-hand side of the street. From Tucson, take Route 10 North to 360 (Superstition Highway), to Country Club Drive exit north; turn right at Brown Road; turn left at Center Street; the ballpark is one block on the right.

The Heart of the Cactus League

We all know that Chicago Cub fans are on the rabid side — in a good way, of course. But the Cubbie passion travels well, as HoHoKam Park is *the* ballpark in the Cactus League where hometown fans so thoroughly dominate.

The only thing that would make you completely feel like you're at Wrigley Field would be Old Style on tap, though you can now get it in a cup. Otherwise, a Cubs game at HoHoKam Park is a pretty re-creation of a Friendly Confines experience: The fans cheer for the good guys and hoot the enemies, a celebrity (or someone with some level of name recognition, anyway) sings the national anthem, and home runs from the bad guys are thrown back onto the field.

The name *HoHoKam* ("those who vanished") can be traced back to a local Native American tribe formerly in the Valley of the Sun and the Tucson basin. In reality, HoHoKam Park is named after a local charitable organization key in luring the Cubs to Mesa's Rendezvous Park way back in 1952. (The Cubs have not been training in Mesa continuously since 1952; the team moved spring training to Long Beach in 1966 and Scottsdale in 1967 before moving back to Mesa in 1979.) HoHoKam Park is one of the hottest tickets in the Cactus League, as those refugees from the cold Chicago winters are only too eager to flee to sunny Arizona. And with a total capacity of 12,575 (including 8,000 fixed seats, 2,000 bleacher seats, and lawn capacity of 2,575), HoHoKam Park's large capacity allowed the Cubbies to set spring-training attendance records in the past.

Indeed, HoHoKam Park is really a Class AAA park masquerading as a spring-training facility. It certainly has one of the the largest scoreboards in the Cactus League: a 12'x16' instant replay video screen on a 32-foot high left-field scoreboard. The contours of the outfield wall are designed with the same dimensions of those at Wrigley Field — but, of course, there's no ivy or brickwork. It was designed by HOK Sport, designer of Oriole Park at Camden Yards (Baltimore), Jacobs Field (Cleveland), and Coors Field (Denver), so you know that there are retro touches throughout: In the case of HoHoKam, there are traditional steel trusses and a steel canopy above the upper deck.

In bad news for the Cubs and good news for you, attendance for Cubs spring-training games is actually off a little in recent years, making it easier to snare a seat.

(Note that both the Cubs and the city of Mesa use the terms *HoHoKam Park* and *HoHoKam Stadium* interchangeably. We'll use HoHoKam Park, as that's what it says on the sign at the ballpark.)

The rowdiness you see in the Wrigley Field bleachers during the regular season can be found at HoHoKam Park. The grass berm in left field is usually crammed soon after the gates open as fans maneuver for the best views. Wander through the concourse and you'll probably see Don Christiansen, who wraps himself in ivy to emulate the outfield wall in Wrigley Field. And you will not be able to avoid Cubs superfan Ronnie "Woo Woo" Wickers, who will compel

Fans cram into HoHoKam Park to see the Cubs.

Cubs fans to cheer by sheer force of will and effort.

If your only choice is between seats far down the line or the berm, go for the berm. The seats down each line are not oriented very well to catch the action, so you'll spend a lot of time twisting your neck to catch a pitch. The berm, which can be a serious sun field on a hot day (in other words, bring your suntan lotion), is much better for watching a game. It's also a better spot for watching the fans: There's usually a bevy of Sun Devils coeds on display.

The berm is also a good place if you want to be near the bullpens. They're unusual: The bi-level bullpens are in right-center field. The only shaded seating is right behind home plate, and it's limited at best.

During the rest of the year HoHoKam Park is also the home of the Arizona Fall League Mesa Solar Sox and the Mesa Cubs in the Arizona Rookie League.

insider's tip

The Cubs do not practice at HoHoKam Park. Instead, the Cubs practice at Fitch Park (655 N. Center St.), just up the road from HoHoKam Park. Practices begin at 9:30 a.m. Access to players at Fitch Park is limited, so arrive early and plant yourself next to a practice field and hope you can get the attention of a player.

This is actually the second HoHoKam Park; the first was built in 1976 at Fitch Park as the spring-training home of the Athletics, who quickly bailed on Mesa and made way for the Cubs to return in 1979. The new complex provides 25,000 square feet of team facilities, including a major league clubhouse, four practice fields, one practice infield, enclosed batting tunnels, batting cages, a maintenance facility, and administrative offices for the Cubs.

THE SPRING-TRAINING BALLPARK EXPERIENCE

Concessions

Like Wrigley Field, the food at HoHoKam Park tends to the basic, but very accessible: There are seven concession stands scattered throughout the ballpark. The $5 all-beef hot dog is overpriced, but then again so is almost every other hot dog in spring training. (In general the hot dogs are not very tasty at HoHoKam Park.) There are also Chicago red hots for those who want a real taste of Chicago in the desert; look for them on the third-base side of the concessions, and order one with the works. And, of course, Bud is everywhere, though in recent years the Cubs and concessionaire

Ovations added Old Style to the mix. For those with more refined palates, wine is available as well.

In general, the food choices at HoHoKam are not very inspired. The Cubs do not allow any outside food into the park, either, so eat before or after the game.

Autographs

The Cubs' clubhouse is on the first-base side of the outer ballpark, and you can snare autographs as players come and go. You can also hang around Fitch Park (655 N. Center St.) and hit morning practices, which begin at 9:30 a.m.

The best seats are in the shade.

Parking

There is adequate paid parking next to the ballpark — 3,000 spots, give or take. The cost is a reasonable $5. Interestingly, there's not as much tailgating before the game as you might expect.

Many fans drive into the surrounding neighborhood to park for free.

Getting into the ballpark is no great shakes: There are long lines if you're coming from the north on Center Street. Our advice is to loop to the south of the ballpark and make your way north on Center Street. You may also snare some street parking if you arrive early enough.

If You Go

Where to Stay

Mesa does feel like it is a separate area of the Phoenix region, and if you're a true Cubbie fan you'll want to spend as much time as possible hanging around the ballpark and practice facility. There are a number of hotels within two miles of the ballpark:

→ Phoenix Mesa Marriott, 200 N. Centennial Way, Mesa; 480/898-8300; **marriott.com**. Technically, this is the hotel closest to the ballpark.

→ Best Western Mezona Inn, 250 W. Main St., Mesa; 480/834-9233; **bestwestern.com**. We'd highly recommend the Mezona Inn; it's a traditional hot spot during spring training. It's also where the Cubs minor leaguers stay.

→ Holiday Inn Hotel and Suites, 1600 S. Country Club Dr., Mesa; 480/964-7000; **holiday-inn.com**.

→ Travelodge Mesa, 22 S. Country Club Dr., Mesa; 480/964-5694; **travelodge.com**.

→ Ramada Inn and Suites Mesa, 1410 S. Country Club Dr., Mesa; 480/964-2897; **ramada.com**.

RV Resorts Near the Ballpark

The ballpark is in the western part of Mesa, putting it a decent distance from the many RV parks in eastern Mesa and Apache Junction.

And there are an abundance of them, to be sure. Mesa is known in some circles as being the RV park center of the Phoenix area. That's not necessarily a bad thing. There are at least 16 RV parks in the greater Mesa area, and that's not counting more in Tempe, Gilbert, Chandler, and Apache Junction. Check out the likes of Tower Point (**towerpointresort.com**), Mesa Spirit (**mesaspirit.com**), and Good Life (**goodliferv.com**), but be warned that in general the RV resorts in Mesa are really snowbird camps.

Nearby Restaurants

Originally called Harry and Steve's Chicago Grill — named after former investors Steve Stone and legendary broadcaster Harry Caray — Sluggo's Grill is still a prime watering hole for Chicago Cubs fans after Ho-HoKam Park games. As you might expect, the emphasis is on Budweiser. Sluggo's Grill, 161 N. Centennial Way, Mesa; 480/844-8448; **sluggosgrill.com**.

The Blue Adobe Grille features the cuisine of New Mexico in an Arizona setting. Go figure. It's a popular spot, so make those reservations from the park before you head over. Blue Adobe Grille, 144 N. Country Club Dr., Mesa; 480/962-1000; **blueadobegrille.com**.

For Mexican, Rancho de Tia Rosa is recommended. The restaurant is designed to look like an old hacienda, and the menu is fairly standard — tacos, chimichangas, burritos — with signature items like slow-roasted pork (*carne asada*), salmon enchiladas, and chicken mole scattered throughout. If possible, sit out on the patio. Rancho de Tia Rosa, 3129 E. McKellips Rd., Mesa; 480/659-8787; **ranchodetiarosa.com**.

Another Mexican mainstay in the general area is Serrano's Mexican Food, with several locations throughout the Valley. The Serrano family has been in business in Arizona since 1919, but at that time the family business was clothing. In 1979 the Serrano family ditched the clothing and shifted into the Mexican restaurant business, keeping the Serrano logo. You'll find the usual Mexican fare at Serrano's, though there's a noted emphasis on seafood dishes like *pescado a la tortilla* (tilapia encrusted with tortilla) and *enchiladas de camarón* (shrimp enchiladas). Serrano's Mexican Food, 1964 E. McKellips Rd., Mesa; 480/649-3503; **serranosaz.com**.

The ballpark is north of downtown Mesa; while other communities in the Valley of the Sun are forced to create downtowns from scratch, Mesa has an old one. Downtown Mesa has its own historic districts and attractions. You could do worse than spend some time driving around and taking in a show or exhibit at the Mesa Arts Center (1 E. Main St., Mesa; 480/644-6500; **mesaartscenter.org**)

Spring-Training History

The Chicago Cubs have trained in a variety of locations: Selma, Ala. (1900); Champaign, Ill. (1901-02, 1906); Los Angeles (1903-04, 1948-1949), Santa Monica (1905); New Orleans (1907, 1911-1912); Vicksburg, Miss. (1908); Hot Springs, Ark. (1909-1910); Tampa (1913-1916); Pasadena, Cal. (1917-1921); Catalina Island, Cal. (1922-1942, 1946-1947, 1950-1951); French Lick, Ind. (1943-1945); Mesa (1952-1965, 1979-present); Long Beach, Cal. (1966); and Scottsdale (1967-1978).

Why Avalon on Catalina Island? (Catalina Island is located 20 miles outside of Los Angeles.) Because Cubs owner William Wrigley Jr. bought a majority interest in the island in 1919. Wrigley then constructed a ballpark on the island to house the Cubs in spring training: It was built to the same dimensions as Wrigley Field. (The ballpark is long gone, but a clubhouse built by Wrigley to house the Cubs exists as the Catalina County Club.) By 1951 the team had grown disenchanted with Catalina Island, however, and spring training was shifted to Mesa, Arizona, after the Cubs held a profitable series of games against the New York Yankees in Arizona. At the time Mesa was not seen as an attractive area for spring training, and in fact the Oakland Oaks of the Pacific Coast League failed to draw at all when the team held spring training at Mesa in 1952.

The move to Mesa was also promoted by Dwight Patterson, a Mesa rancher and builder who worked to bring spring-training games to the area. The Cubs were hesitant to move to Mesa with the New York Giants training only 20 miles away in Phoenix, so Patterson and a group of local businessmen formed the HoHoKams, who put up a $22,000 guarantee if the Cubs moved to Mesa's Rendezvous Park. (Fittingly, Patterson was the first "Chief Big Ho.") Today the HoHoKams exist as a charity. Rendezvous Park seated 3,000 when the Cubs moved there in 1952 but was expanded soon afterwards.

After the Cubs moved spring training to southern California in 1966, Mesa did not host any spring training until 1969, when the Oakland Athletics moved their training from Scottsdale. Charlie O. Finley was dissatisfied with the training facilities in Scottsdale, hence the move to Rendezvous Park. The A's were not a big draw in Mesa, however, and in 1976 Rendezvous Park was torn down.

→ cleveland indians / cincinnati reds

UNNAMED NEW BALLPARK

Capacity 8,000 fixed seats, 500 premium seats, 1,600 berm seats, 400-seat party area, 6 suites

Year Opened 2009

Surface Grass

Local Airport Phoenix

East of Estrella Parkway on Lower Buckeye Road, Goodyear

A Little Bit of Ohio in the Desert

The Cleveland Indians are returning to Arizona for a second stint in the Cactus League. For the team, it's a return to roots:The Indians and the New York Giants comprised the first Cactus League, so-to-speak, when Bill Veeck wanted spring operations closer to his ranch in the Tucson area and made arrangements accordingly.

The Indians will inhabit a new spring-training complex in Goodyear by themselves in 2009, followed by the Cincinnati Reds in 2010. The all-Ohio complex should play well for fans of both teams, who can carry their rivalries into intimate spring-training quarters.

The spring-training complex will include the ballpark, four practice fields, two half practice fields and batting practice areas. It's designed to be the centerpiece of a larger complex that includes retail, office space, and hotels. As of this writing the associated development was not yet in place.

Still, we expect the Indians (and later on the Reds) to run things in Arizona the same way they ran things in Florida. Indians and Reds spring-training games are always low-key affairs, with a few local food items on the menu. And it wouldn't be spring training if Indians great Bob Feller didn't set up a table by the front entrance and sell autographs.

Courtesy of HOK Sport.

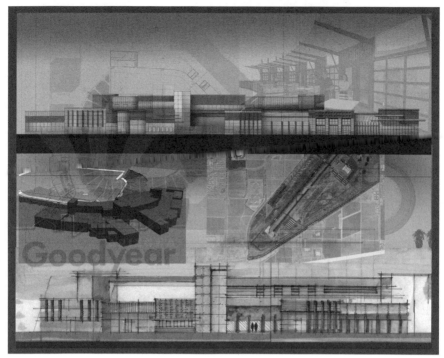

Courtesy of HOK Sport.

A Final Nod to Chain of Lakes Park

With the move of the Cleveland Indians to Arizona for Spring Training 2009, it's the end of the road for Chain of Lakes Park, known recently as the spring home of Indians but perhaps more fondly known as the former spring home of the Boston Red Sox. The Chain of Lakes complex is now slated for redevelopment, and it won't be long before the wrecking ball arrives.

Which is a shame. It's a classic Florida baseball venue; only Holman Stadium comes close to matching Chain of Lakes, in terms of fidelity to the era in which it was constructed. The ballpark hails from an era where a) sellout crowds were rare and b) fans were expected to stay in their seats for most of the game. The brickwork in the concourse was real — there was nothing retro about Chain of Lakes Park — and the scenic lakeside location made for a true Florida spring-training experience.

Nearby Attractions

There is not much within walking distance of the ballpark yet, save lots of housing developments.

223

SPRING-TRAINING HISTORY

The Cleveland Indians have trained in the following locations: Cleveland (1901); New Orleans (1902-1903); San Antonio (1904); Atlanta (1905-1906); Macon, Ga. (1907-1908); Mobile, Ala. (1909); Alexandria, La. (1910-1911); Mobile, Ala. (1912); Pensacola, Fla. (1913); Athens, Ga. (1914); San Antonio (1915); New Orleans (1916-1920); Dallas (1921-1922); Lakeland (1923-1927); New Orleans (1928-1939); Ft. Myers (1940-1941); Clearwater (1942); Lafayette, Ind. (1943-1945); Clearwater (1946); Tucson (1947-1992); Winter Haven (1993-2008); and Goodyear (2009-present).

→ kansas city royals / texas rangers

SURPRISE STADIUM

Capacity	10,500
Year Opened	2003
Dimensions	350L, 379LC, 400C, 379RC, 350R
Surface	Grass
Local Airport	Phoenix
Address	15850 N. Bullard Av., Surprise.

Surprise Stadium is located 1 1/2 miles west of the intersection of Bell Road and Grand Avenue (U.S. Route 60). Bullard Avenue is located off of Bell Road, 1 1/2 miles west of Grand Avenue, or 2 1/2 miles east of Loop 303.

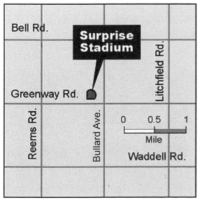

Surprise, Surprise

It's a little off the beaten track, but Billy Parker Field at Surprise Stadium may be the perfect place to see a spring ballgame: The sightlines are gorgeous, the concourses are wide, and the ballpark design is striking.

Built for the Texas Rangers and the Kansas City Royals, Billy Parker Field at Surprise Stadium features two 37,000-square-foot clubhouses with locker rooms, team kitchens, weight and training facilities and administrative offices. In addition, each team has a practice infield and six full practice fields.

With the full Phoenix sun out for most games, you'll want to carefully choose where you sit. Both teams draw well in spring training, so a little planning is in order. But it is worth while, as Billy Parker Field is one of the most pleasant venues in the Cactus League.

The ballpark features a main seating bowl, a second level that features both seats and luxury boxes, and outfield berm seating, with a concourse ringing the ballpark. The best seats in the house are on the second level and within the middle seven or so sections of the main seating bowl: These are the seats that are shaded for the majority of the game. The main level of seats extends all the way down each line. If the middle sections are sold out, you're better off sitting all the way down the line as opposed to a section facing the outfield, as the seats farthest down the line are angled to

The best views are from the berm. Photo by Jim Robins.

give you a direct view of the ballpark. Unlike most spring-training venues, there are cupholders at each seat, so you don't need to worry about some clumsy rowmate knocking over your $7 Dos Equis.

The design is modern and clean. It does have a little touch of the retro that's proven to be so popular in major-league parks like Oriole Park at Camden Yards, but not so much to distract you from your spring-training experience.

insider's tip

The Kansas City Royals and Texas Rangers both begin their days early: They schedule workouts at 9 a.m. daily.

Billy Parker, by the way, was a former major leaguer who worked with youth baseball programs before his death in 2003. He played parts of three seasons with the California Angels and hit a game-winning homer in his first game.

THE SPRING-TRAINING BALLPARK EXPERIENCE

Concessions

There is a plethora of concession stands along the concourse, with one big food court down the left-field line featuring Southwestern foods, burgers, ice cream, and fry bread. Down the right-field line the Johnsonville Brat area offers sausages, and there's a seating area where a band sometimes plays late in the games. The hot dogs are worth seeking out: They may be roller-grilled, but they're plump and flavorful. In addition, there's a separate concession area in back of center field for those watching the game from the berm.

The beer selection is fairly limited: Miller and Bud dominate the taps, but worth seeking out is Dos Equis on tap.

Autographs

The biggest flaw in Billy Parker Field is its lack of good autograph opportunities. Your best bet is to hit the ballpark when the gates open and try to lure a player to the stands. Also, players will sometimes sign autographs after they leave the batting cages located next to each side of the grandstand. But other than that the pickins are pretty slim.

A group party area brings in the crowds. Photo by Jim Robins.

Parking

When the ballpark opened, Surprise charged to park at the adjoining parking lot. After that plan met with much resistance from the locals, the decision was made to forego parking fees, but it was up for annual review. If you're lucky, there will be free parking this coming spring.

IF YOU GO

What to Do Outside the Ballpark

Quite honestly, there is not a lot to Surprise. It's on the far edge of the Phoenix metropolitan area, and it's still an area in transition: It's currently a mix of housing developments (the original Sun City development is due east, while new Sun City developments are within the city limits to the west) and big-box retailers. You're likely to find a field of cauliflower across the road from a brand-new set of houses. There's no downtown Surprise, and the big draw in Surprise is the ballpark. Even hardcore Texas and Kansas City fans may find it a little boring to spend entire days in the area, even when spending all morning hanging around the practice fields.

These days there's much more in the general area, you're still talking basic suburban sprawl here. And with some recent problems on the issue of a big development near the ballpark, this is highly unlikely to change in coming years.

Restaurants close to the ballpark include IHOP (13734 W. Bell Rd., Surprise; 623/556-2151) and Applebee's (13756 W. Bell Rd., Surprise; 623/544-0368), and there are several more chain restaurants at the corner of Bell Road and Hwy. 60 east of the park.

Worth a little farther drive is Macayo's Mexican Kitchen. We've discussed the Macayo chain of restaurants in previous chapters, but it bears repeating here. The Macayo's Mexican Kitchen chain dates back to 1948 and goes past a standard menu of tacos and burritos with specialties like chicken poblano and grilled salmon. Macayo's Mexican Kitchen, 6012 W. Bell Rd., Glendale; 602/298-8080; **www.macayo.com**.

Where to Stay

There is nothing within walking distance to the ballpark; the closest you'll come are some newer hotels closer to Peoria and Hwy. 101. You may want to check out our chapters on San Diego and Seattle regarding hotels in the Peoria area.

Because there are so many spring-training venues in Phoenix and you're more than likely visiting more than one ballpark, chances are pretty good that you don't necessarily need to be staying close to the ballpark. Phoenix is a relatively easy area to make your way around, so don't feel like it's essential you stay close to the park.

The entrance to Surprise Stadium is easily accessible. Photo by Jim Robins.

Flying In

The closest airport is Phoenix Sky Harbor International Airport, but it's quite a haul from the ballpark. It's served by all the major airlines, including United, America West, Delta, Northwest, Air Canada, American, Continental, US Airways, and Southwest.

SPRING-TRAINING HISTORY: TEXAS RANGERS

When the "new" Washington Senators entered the American League in 1961, they established a spring-training camp in Pompano Beach, Florida, and stayed there until 1986, when operations were shifted to Port Charlotte. The Rangers moved spring training from Florida to Surprise in 2003.

SPRING-TRAINING HISTORY: KANSAS CITY ROYALS

When the Kansas City Royals moved spring-training facilities to Arizona in 2003, it was the first time the team had not trained in Florida in team history. In 1969 through 1987 the team trained in Terry Park in Ft. Myers (a facility that's still around, if you want to visit), while in 1988 the team moved to the brand-new Baseball City in central Florida.

➔ los angeles angels of anaheim

TEMPE DIABLO STADIUM

Capacity	9,785 (7,285 seats, 2,500 outfield capacity)
Year Opened	1969; renovated several times since
Dimensions	340L, 388LC, 405C, 308RC, 340R
Surface	Grass
Local Airport	Phoenix
Address	2200 W. Alameda Dr., Tempe.

Take the Broadway Street exit off I-10 (coming from either direction); travel west on Broadway to 48th Street; turn left; Tempe Diablo Stadium is 1/2 mile on the left. Enter ballpark by turning left on Alameda.

Devils and Angels in Tempe

It is the most scenic ballpark in the Cactus League, bar none. With buttes beyond the left-field fence, a striking Spanish-style exterior, and a relatively remote location that paradoxically offers easy freeway access, Tempe Diablo Stadium is a gem, a must-visit for anyone hitting Phoenix in March.

The ballpark itself is very fan-friendly. Renovations in 1993 made the place a much more accessible venue, adding a concourse level above the bowl housing a wide variety of concession offerings, while a second set of renovations in 2006 expanded the training facility and provided a new entrance. Throw in easy accessibility to practice fields (located on the other side of the parking lot from the ballpark) and you have a great spring-training experience.

The two best things about the ballpark are its location and its layout. It's easy to get to — get on I-10 south, take the Broadway Street exit, and follow the signs — and there's plenty of cheap adjacent parking. Tempe is within 10 minutes of the Phoenix airport, which makes it easy to hop into the car and hit a game right after arrival. And, of course, Phoenix is an easy drive from Los Angeles, which allows passionate Angels fans the chance to see their team in action at a great, intimate facility.

And those fans have responses. A few years ago it was easy to snare an Angels spring-training ticket, but these days the Halos are one of the hottest spring-training tickets in the Cactus League. Plan ahead; the days

You feel like you're in the midst of the hills, thanks to the buttes.

of walking up and snaring a good ticket 30 minutes before game time are gone.

The original Diablo Stadium was built in 1968, but it was expanded in 1993 under the supervision of HOK Sport. The original playing field, seating bowl and visitors' clubhouse were incorporated into the new facility, which added a new clubhouse, enclosed batting tunnels, and more.

In addition, the renovation added five concession stands, a concourse-level plaza area, an observation deck, and a picnic area down the third-base line. It's worth getting to the park early to snare one of these picnic tables, as they're fairly close to the action; their usability is somewhat limited by the fact that the Angels don't allow any outside food at all in the ballpark.

The latest round of renovations added more training fields to the mix (six full fields in total), practice facilities and a minor-league clubhouse, as well as a new entrance to the ballpark. Previously the Angels had practiced at an offsite facility, but the latest expansion allows all the major- and minor-leaguers to train at the same location.

The layout of Tempe Diablo Stadium is standard, with most of the seating occurring in the grandstand, which are roughly half armchair seats and half bleachers. There is also lawn seating in left and center field. The best seats are the box seats down the first-base line: You're definitely in a sun field, but the view of the buttes beyond the ballpark is spectacular. There's a minimum of foul territory, so you're never too far from the action — which includes rubbing elbows with pitchers warming up in both bullpens down each line.

insider's tip

Not every seat is created equal, of course. In general, you'll want to sit in the last four rows of the grandstand behind home plate or on the first-base side if you want to avoid the sun; a canopy covers concessions, not seats. (Try the back of section 12 for a good, shaded seat.) Speaking of avoidance, don't sit in sections 23 or 24. Better choices are sections 21 and 22 — which feature raised bleachers — while sections 1-4 and 18-20 feature bleacher seating as well.

One underrated area of seating: the berm, which runs down the left-field line and wraps around the foul pole into left field. As a bonus, the berm seating overlooks the bullpens, and there's generally a lot of room out there.

As if you can't tell, we adore a spring game at Tempe Diablo Stadium. The Angels have kicked up their level of fan commitment and the fans have responded, making Tempe Diablo Stadium one of the great hot spots in spring training.

THE SPRING-TRAINING BALLPARK EXPERIENCE

Concessions

The one mandatory food item at Tempe Diablo Stadium is a mesquite-grilled hot dog. You can smell those pups from the parking lot, so beware of heading to the ballpark on an empty stomach. Diablo Dogs are actually brats topped with jalapenos.

Then again, maybe you should go to the ballpark with an empty stomach, because there are a wide variety of foodstuffs on the menu, ranging from Mexican specialties and pad Thai to root-beer floats and fresh-squeezed lemonade. You can even find an espresso stand on the concourse.

Most of the beer stands feature corporate swill, like Budweiser. Near Section 13 there's a stand with a wider variety of microbrews, including Fat Tire, Fosters, Tecate, and Widmer.

Autographs

If you get to the ballpark early enough you should hang out in the parking lot: Players practice in the adjoining practice field in the morning and must cut across the parking lot while heading to the clubhouse. The Angels rope off a walkway for players, but you can wait alongside it and snare some autographs.

Inside the park, plant yourself next to sections 21 and 22. These sections are located next to the tunnel leading to the clubhouse, so players and coaches have no choice but to walk past fans here. Also, players are known to hang around the bullpen before games, so you should head down there and snag an autograph. If you're seeking the autograph of a visiting player, head down the right-field line after the game and catch the attention of players heading for the team bus. The parking lot to the east of the ballpark is secured, so you can't seek autographs next to the bus or the right-field gate.

Parking

There are two main parking lots on the east and west sides of the ballpark, but in general the west lot is reserved for players, the front office, and VIPs. Unless you come to the ballpark really early, you'll be shuttled down to the east lot or other lots of Ajo Way. Some businesses also sell parking, but don't be gouged: Generally the parking offered by the Angels

No, no one has ever hit it out as far as the butte.

is cheaper ($5 in 2007). There is also limited street parking in the area, but be warned: The area is crawling with cops, and you will be towed if you're parked illegally.

Because the Angels have grown into a hot Cactus League ticket, it's in your best interest to arrive at the ballpark early. During our last visit we arrived at the ballpark an hour early and we still were presented with a huge traffic jam on Ajo Way.

IF YOU GO

What to Do Outside the Ballpark

There's really nothing within walking distance of the ballpark before or after the game. There are some fast-foot joints on Broadway (Whataburger, etc.) and 48th Street, but they're not the sorts of places where you'll spend a lot of time.

Built in the old Tempe Railroad Depot, Macayo's Depot Cantina is the Tempe outpost of a popular locally owned chain. The specialties of the house: margaritas, freshly made tortillas, tacos, and enchiladas. Happy Hour (4-7 p.m.) rocks at Macayo's; a few visits to the complimentary buffet will fill you up. Sit out on the deck if you can. Macayo's Depot Cantina, 300 S. Ash Av., Tempe; 480/966-6677; **macayo.com**.

El Tlacoyo Restaurante Mexicano isn't the easiest place to find — it's behind an Asian grocery and not visible from the street — but it's worth the fuss. The food is authentic beyond belief: A tlacoyo is made from masa stuffed with pinto beans and then cooked on a griddle, while the weekend finds consume de birria (kid goat soup, basically) on the menu. El Tlacoyo Restaurante Mexicano, 2535 E. University Dr., Tempe; 480/894-9543.

If near-authentic Mexican food isn't your thing, you're in luck: Downtown Tempe is a short drive away. Tempe is a college town, and as you might expect from a school with a party atmosphere, there are a fair number of establishments in the downtown area for those who imbibe, most centered around Mill Avenue. (The university is located northeast of the training complex. To get there, head east on Broadway Road and then north on Mill Avenue.) At night you can easily wander in and out of the many watering holes and fast-food joints (and they are plentiful, good, and cheap in the Mill Avenue area). While you can find fine dining in the Arizona State area (House of Tricks, for instance), here are the more casual places a spring-training fan will find most appropriate at the end of a long day in the sun.

Beer fans will want to check out Four Peaks Brewing Co., a brewpub and restaurant known for its patio, fresh beer (have the Hefeweizen if it's on tap), and good food. Expect a crowd, even if you're visiting during spring break. Four Peaks Brewing Co., 1340 E. 8th St., #104, Tempe; 480/303-9967; **fourpeaks.com**.

It's a chain, but it's a damn fine chain: The beer at the Gordon Biersch Brewery is great, and the garlic fries are to die for. In fact, a combination of a seasonal beer and the garlic fries is really all you need at dinnertime, especially if your spouse isn't along on the trip. Go for the deck, which gives you some great people-watching on the second floor. Gordon Biersch, 420 S. Mill Av., Tempe; 480/736-0033; **gordonbiersch.com**.

At first glance, Rula Bula is an oddity: It looks like an old Wild West saloon with an Irish theme. But go in and you'll see what you assumed to be a Wild West saloon is really a Irish saddlery, taken down from its original location in Waterford, Ireland and then reassembled in Tempe. Yeah, it's a bit odd, but the exotic construction means this is an Irish bar through and through. You can nosh on traditional Irish dishes like fish and chips or purported Irish delicacies like Irish spicy lemon shrimp. Rula Bula, 401 S. Mill Av., Tempe; 480/929-9500; **rulabula.com**.

Another oddity: pasties in Arizona. Pasties are usually associated with Eastern European immigrants — you normally find them in northern Minnesota, Wisconsin, and Michigan's Upper Peninsula — but the Cornish Pasty Company takes the humble pastry and charges them up with a variety of creative fillings, including lamb vindaloo and carne adovada.

Wash it down with a Hoegaarden White Ale or Mickey's Malt Liquor; both are on the eclectic drink menu. Cornish Pasty Co., 960 W. University Dr., #103, Tempe; 480/894-6261; **cornishpastyco.com**.

Begin your day at Chompie's, the closest thing to an authentic deli in the Valley of the Sun. With bagels, blintzes, latkes, and a full breakfast menu available in the morning, Chompie's is the place to load up before heading to the ballpark. Chompie's, 1160 E. University, Tempe; 480/557-0700; **chompies.com**.

The kids will enjoy a visit to Fiddlesticks, a 20-acre amusement park that includes go-karts, batting cages, miniature golf, bumper boats, and a video arcade. Fiddlesticks, 1155 W. Elliot Rd., Tempe; 480/961-0800; **fiddlesticksaz.com**.

Where to Stay

The Buttes (now a Marriott property) is the closest hotel to Tempe Diablo Stadium, within easy walking distance of the complex. It's also one of the more scenic hotels in the Valley of the Sun: From the freeway it looks like some sort of futuristic neo-Wrightian extension of the hillside. The extension is the Top of the Rock restaurant, and it offers some great views of the area at sunset. Wyndham Buttes Hotel, 2000 W. Westcourt Way, Tempe; 602/225-9000; **wyndham.com**.

Also within walking distance (albeit a long walk on some unfriendly terrain) is a Hampton Inn. There's really nothing more to say about it. Hampton Inn, 4234 S. 48th St., Phoenix; 602/438-8688; **hamptoninn.com**.

As the training complex is close to Sky Harbor International Airport, any of the airport hotels (and there are many) would be convenient as well, as would any Phoenix hotel, for that matter.

RV Parks

Apache Palms RV Park (1836 E. Apache Blvd., Tempe; 480/966-7399; **apachepalmsrvpark.com**) is less than four miles away from the ballpark. It's not in the best of neighborhoods, so you may want to look to Mesa or Scottsdale for a better RV park experience.

Flying In

As mentioned, Phoenix Sky Harbor International Airport is close to the training facility. We discuss it in our chapter on Phoenix.

You may also want to consider flying into Tucson and then driving to Phoenix if the fare to Tucson is significantly cheaper. The drive is 117 miles and takes a couple of hours on I-10, but it's a pretty drive if you like desert scenery.

SPRING-TRAINING HISTORY

The major-league Los Angeles Angels began playing in 1961 under the ownership of Gene Autry. The team's first spring-training home was Palm Springs, where their home was the Polo Grounds (later renamed Angels Stadium).

In 1966 the Angels partially shifted spring training in Holtville, Cal., and 10 days to two weeks at the four-diamond complex from 1966 through 1979 (splitting time with Palm Springs), before returning on a full-time basis to Palm Springs in 1980. The Angels then reverted back to a split schedule in 1982 and 1983, dividing spring headquarters between Casa Grande, Arizona, and Palm Springs.

In 1992, Angels spring training shifted fulltime to Tempe Diablo Stadium.

➜ los angeles dodgers / chicago white sox

GLENDALE SPRING TRAINING COMPLEX
GLENDALE, AZ   NOVEMBER 19, 2007

Unnamed New Ballpark

Capacity	13,000 (10,000 seats, 3,000 berm seating)
Year Opened	2009
Surface	Grass
Local Airport	Phoenix
	107th Avenue and Camelback Road, Glendale

Expanding the Cactus League in Glendale

As this book goes to press there's much up-in-the-air regarding a new Los Angeles Dodgers and Chicago White Sox spring-training facility in Glendale: the name of the facility, for instance, or to what extent the White Sox will be there in 2009.

So let's begin with what we know. The Los Angeles Dodgers will spend Spring Training 2009 at the new facility. The Chicago White Sox may or may not join them, depending on their lease situation with Tucson. (Check **springtrainingonline.com** for up-to-the-minute information on the spring-training situations.)

The other thing we know: The Glendale spring-training complex will be one of the largest in the majors. The site, organized around a central connecting path and lake, hosts two stadium entries: One at home plate and a more prominent entry at center field. Located on a 141-acre site with a three-acre lake, the stadium has the capacity to host 13,000 fans. It includes more than 118,000 square feet of major and minor league clubhouses as well as four major league practice fields, eight minor league practice fields, and two practice infields. Each team has a replica major league field to emulate their home ballpark.

The Glendale ballpark is slated to be surrounded by retail and office space. Renderings courtesy of HKS.

A Final Nod to Dodgertown

Spring Training 2009 will be the first spring training since 1948 that the Los Angeles Dodgers have not trained in Vero Beach's Dodgertown. Yes, it seems odd that a West Coast team would have continued training in Florida year after year, but until now the right deal never came along, and the unique nature of Dodgertown kept the team from pulling the trigger on any possible earlier moves.

With the Dodgers as a tenant, Dodgertown was the most historic venue in spring-training history. Walking through the grounds of Dodgertown was a timeless experience: You were likely to run into the likes of Tommy Lasorda or Sandy Koufax checking out the latest phenoms, while the ghosts of Don Drysdale and Walter Alston were hanging back in the shadows. The place didn't change much in the last 30 years — which was both a good thing and a bad thing.

The Dodgers were attracted to the area by Bud Holman, a local entrepreneur and director of Eastern Air Lines. He persuaded Buzzy Bavasi (then the farm director of the Brooklyn Dodgers) to consolidate spring training for the Dodgers and their 30-plus farm teams. The city of Vero Beach wasn't sure this was a good idea — as a matter of fact, the city refused to put in a swimming pool that Holman requested — so technically the Dodgers contracted with Holman, who in turn leased the land from the city.

The Dodgers were so pleased with spring training in Vero Beach that by 1952 the Dodgers signed a 21-year lease with the city of Vero Beach for a true Dodgertown at a former Naval air base. As part of the lease, the Dodgers agreed that the entire major-league club and 50 percent of the Dodgers' farm teams would train in Vero Beach. The players were put up in former Naval barracks.

The Dodgers then furthered their commitment a few months later by investing $100,000 in a new stadium, named Holman Stadium. 1,500 steel chairs were brought from Ebbets Field in Brooklyn when the stadium was constructed. Holman Stadium has an impressive lineage: It was designed by Normal Bel Geddes (designer of the Futurama building at the 1964 New York World's Fair) and engineered by Captain Emil Praeger, who also engineered Dodger Stadium in Los Angeles.

The future of Dodgertown is up in the air: Indian River County and Vero Beach officials hope to lure another team to the area. For those with long spring-training memories, the loss of Dodgertown as a Grapefruit League stop will make Spring Training 2009 a much lesser experience.

Nearby Attractions

There is not much within walking distance of the ballpark yet, save lots of housing developments.

Within a short drive is a classic Valley of the Sun resort, the Wigwam Resort and Spa. Built on a former Goodyear cotton farm, the resort opened in 1929 with enough rooms for 24 guests. Over the years the emphasis changed to golf and spa living, and in that time the area around the resort morphed from open country to suburbia. A part of that 1929 building is still in use as a reminder of the resort's past. Wigwam Resort and Spa, 300 Wigwam Boulevard, Litchfield Park; 800/327-0396; **wigwamresort.com**.

Spring-Training History

The Los Angeles Dodgers have trained in the following locations: Charlotte, N.C. (1901); Columbia, S.C. (1902-1906); Jacksonville (1907-1909); Hot Springs, Ark. (1910-1912); Augusta, Ga. (1913-1914); Daytona Beach (1915-1916); Hot Springs, Ark. (1917-1918); Jacksonville (1919-1920); New Orleans (1921); Jacksonville (1922); Clearwater (1923-1932); Miami (1933); Orlando (1934-1935); Clearwater (1936-1940); Havana (1941-1942); Bear Mountain, N.Y. (1943-1945); Daytona Beach (1946); Havana (1947); Ciudad Trujillo, Dominican Republic (1948); Vero Beach (1949-2008); Phoenix (2008); and Glendale (2009-present).

→ milwaukee brewers

MARYVALE BASEBALL PARK

Capacity	8,000
Year Opened	1998
Dimensions	350L, 400C, 340R
Surface	Grass
Local Airport	Phoenix
Address	3600 N. 51st Av., Phoenix.

Take 51st Avenue (Exit 139 off I-10) north. Maryvale Baseball Park is on the left just before Indian School Road.

Maryvale: Far From the Madding Crowds

Hate crowds? Want to feel close to your favorite ballplayer, even if they don't play for the Brew Crew? Then look no further than Maryvale Baseball Stadium, the spring-training home of the Milwaukee Brewers. This ballpark is the great secret of Cactus League spring training: Because the Brewers don't draw very well on their own (though attendance has been rising in recent years, thanks to a competitive team and the likes of young stars like Ryan Braun and Prince Fielder), there are usually good tickets available for almost every spring-training tilt. That's why fans of visiting teams often outnumber Brewers fans for games against popular teams like the Cubbies or the Giants.

And no matter where your team allegiances lie, you'll find Maryvale Baseball Stadium to be a pleasant place to take in a baseball game. Despite the name, this stadium is actually within the city limits of Phoenix: Maryvale is a neighborhood in western Phoenix, bumping up against Glendale. It is a spacious ballpark: Designed to accommodate two teams in the spring (à la Peoria or Surprise) but housing only the Brewers, there's plenty of space surrounding the ballpark, as well as ample seating (7,000 seats, plus 1,000 or so on lawn seating) within.

The layout should be familiar to anyone who has visited a newer ballpark in the last decade: It utilizes the familiar plan of a concourse with ample concessions behind the seating area, so you're never out of view of the action. The 56-acre complex features five full major/minor league

During a practice everyone is close to the action.

Be prepared with some sunscreen at Maryvale Baseball Park.

practice facilities, two half-field practice facilities, a major-league club-house, and a minor-league clubhouse. The minor-league facility is open before home games, so feel free to wander around and see the future Brewers in action.

There's really nothing spectacular about the ballpark, but nothing seriously wrong, either. You have easy access to concessions and you can stretch your legs throughout the course of a long game, and most fans don't need more than that.

To avoid the sun, sit on the first-base side or in the right-field berm. A favorite tactic is to buy a berm seat, have a couple of beers while hanging around the outfield berm and concourse, and then claim an unused seat for the remainder of the game. If an average crowd is on hand, you can move to open seating by the sixth inning or so. But we've also gone both ways on the seating level: It's not impossible to snare good seats next to a dugout a week or so before a game. (For the record, the Brewers occupy the first-base dugout.)

Maryvale Baseball Stadium is an afterthought for all but hardcore Brewers fans, but it's definitely worth a visit if your favorite team happens to be the visiting team.

Berm seating down each line is a popular option.

THE SPRING-TRAINING BALLPARK EXPERIENCE

Concessions

The mandatory food item at Maryvale is the $2.75 mesquite-grilled Klements hot dog, considered among the best in the Cactus League: charred and smoky, cooked over an open flame. Top it with the mandatory sauerkraut and spicy mustard. This being the spring home of the Milwaukee Brewers, there are also several other wursts and dogs available, as well as BBQ pork and chicken-breast sandwiches. And, of course, there's MGD and Miller Lite on tap, though the beer prices are on the high side (a 12-ounce premium beer runs you $7, while a 16-ounce MGD or Lite costs $6 as well). On a hot day, a frozen banana or shaved ice can be refreshing. Most of the concessions are located behind the grandstand, but there are stands down each line as well, where you can find exotic delicacies like soba noodles and Mexican fare.

Autographs

There's no designated autograph area at Maryvale Baseball Stadium, so your best bet is to arrive early to the ballpark and attract the attention of the players as they head from the clubhouse to the field.

One nice touch: There's definitely a laid-back vibe at Maryvale Baseball Park, a vibe that seems to infect opposing teams as well. You'll usually find both teams milling around their dugout before a game, and both coaching staffs will engage in friendly chats with fans. As an organization, the Brewers have cultivated openness with the fans, and that attitude is certainly on display at Maryvale Baseball Park.

The entrance to the clubhouse is down the right-field line, so they must walk in foul territory after leaving the game. This is the place to buy a ticket and try to snare a player before or after the game.

Another game plan: Arrive at morning practice. The Brewers open workouts at 9:30 a.m. in the adjoining practice fields. You can try to snare a player to or from workouts.

Parking

The city really does have you by the throat when it comes to parking. Your choices are to either pay $8 to park at the complex or take your chances parking in the surrounding area, which presents its own set of issues. Our advice: Bite the bullet and pay for the parking.

IF YOU GO

What to Do Outside the Ballpark

Maryvale is not one of the more upscale areas of Phoenix (as a matter of fact, it's a transitional area, which is a polite way of saying that the neighborhood could go to heck in the next few years), so chances are pretty good you won't be spending much time in the area. Your dining and entertainment options are severely limited: There's nothing nearby, save a Sizzler or Denny's. If you're a golfer, you can get in nine or 18 holes at the nearby Maryvale Golf Course (5902 W. Indian School Rd.), considered to be a pretty decent municipal course.

However, you are on the western edge of Phoenix, which means you're close to Glendale and Peoria. Check out our chapters on San Diego/Seattle, Kansas City/Texas, Los Angeles Dodgers, and Cleveland Indians

The lobby at the Biltmore.

for more information on what to do in those areas.

Where to Stay

There really is no reason to stay near Maryvale Baseball Stadium. There are no attractions in the surrounding neighborhood, no hot and trendy restaurants in the area, and no hotels within walking distance. You will find some hotels close to I-10 within a few miles of the ballpark (in the city's Midtown area), but we're not talking about plush and scenic resorts. We're talking Super 8, Motel 6, and Red Roof Inn. Sitting next to the freeway, to boot.

Instead, you should look to stay either in nearby Glendale or downtown Phoenix. (We discuss downtown Phoenix hotels in our previous chapter on Phoenix.) Glendale is a suburb located north of the Maryvale neighborhood, between Phoenix and Peoria. It's the new home of the Los Angeles Dodgers, with a spring-training facility slated to open in 2009. It's also home to Jobing.com Arena, the home of the NHL's Phoenix Coyotes, as well as University of Phoenix Stadium, home of the NFL's Arizona Cardinals.

Glendale is not exactly party central, but it does have its own charms: Antique lovers flock to the 90 antique shops in downtown Glendale, while anyone with a sweet tooth appreciates a tour of Cerreta Candy Company. Yes, any chocolate-factory tour is merely an excuse to devour samples at the end, and the Cerreta Candy products are worth the wait: French mints, milk and dark chocolates, caramels, truffles, crunches, and nut clusters. Cerreta Candy Company, 5345 W. Glendale Av., Glendale; 623/930-9000; **cerreta.com**.

SPRING-TRAINING HISTORY

The Milwaukee Brewers have trained every spring in Arizona, a stretch beginning when the team was the Seattle Pilots: In 1969 the team's history began with spring training in Tempe, which lasted through 1972. This was followed by springs in Sun City (1973-1985), Chandler (1986-1997), and then Phoenix (1998-present).

→ oakland athletics

PHOENIX MUNICIPAL STADIUM

Capacity	8,500
Year Opened	1965
Dimensions	345L, 410C, 345R
Surface	Grass
Local Airport	Phoenix
Address	5999 E. Van Buren, Phoenix.

The ballpark is located northeast of I-10 Exit 153 (48th St.). Take HoHoKam Expressway to Van Buren Street, right on Van Buren two miles.

Improving the Muni

It is a low-key venue, to be sure. But it may be one of the most beautiful venues in the Cactus League despite being one of the oldest, a ballpark tucked into the foothills of the Papago Park recreation area. What was once a dumpy, old ballpark with uncomfortable bleacher seating and a minimalist approach to comfort is now one of our favorite places to catch a spring-training game, especially at night.

A 2004 renovation of Phoenix Municipal Stadium was designed to add some comfort to the ballpark, and it did: Chairbacks were installed behind home plate, and a new second level contains luxury boxes and press facilities (which, admittedly, were nicely integrated into the ballpark) were added as well.

But more importantly, the ballpark renovation was designed to give a sense of place to what was once an anonymous facility. There's a strong architectural tradition in Arizona going back to the days of adobe buildings, a style with an emphasis on natural building materials and integration with the buttes that dominate the area. In the case of Phoenix Municipal Stadium, accents made from decorative stones placed adorn the entryways of the stands, while the general feeling in the concourse echoes the Papago Park surroundings. As a bonus, embedded in the concourse are tiles illustrating the history of spring training in Phoenix, which dates back to 1929.

The best time to visit Phoenix Municipal Stadium is for a night game. Photo by Jim Robins.

250

insider's tip

The Athletics do not train at Phoenix Municipal Stadium. Practices take place at nearby Papago Park (1802 N. 64th St., near the corner of Galvin Parkway and McDowell Road). Traditionally, morning practices begin at 9 a.m. To get there from the ballpark, take Galvin Parkway north across McDowell Road, hanging a left on Walter A. Haas Jr. Parkway. (Haas is a former owner of the A's.) Go all the way to the end of the road and park in the appropriate parking area.

Be warned that the practice — which includes eight practice field and a clubhouse — has minimal facilities. The main practice fields (that is, the diamonds where the major leaguers are most likely to be) feature limited seating and some shade. Autograph hunters love the openness (and they can usually be found dashing from practice field to practice field, three-binder notebook crammed with photos and cards in hand), and regular fans will love spending some time seeing their favorite A's in a more relaxed environment.

Night games at Phoenix Municipal Stadium are a special treat: The A's usually schedule one each spring, and the colors off the rock formations beyond center field are just spectacular. There's always something special about an Arizona sunset, and the reds of the rock formations in the Papago Park recreation area contrast nicely with the yellows and pinks of the night sky. True, the rock formations make a nice backdrop to the action during a day game as well, but at night the colors come out.

Phoenix Municipal Stadium dates back to 1965, built to house spring training and minor-league baseball. All of the seating is located between the foul poles (no outfield grass berm seating here), and it's a mix of chairbacks and backed bleachers. The concessions are located in back of the grandstand and down the left-field line. It is also one of the only spring-training complex to feature a kids' play area.

Traffic jams at the ballpark are common: If the ballpark is close to sold out you can expect crowds

All ages enjoy spring training. Photo by Jim Robins.

The entrance to Phoenix Municipal Stadium a little tight. Photo by Jim Robins.

milling around the entrance and next to the concession stands. It's not a place where you can walk around and view the game from different vantage points; the only open area is down the third-base line, next to a makeshift picnic area.

BALLPARK HISTORY

Phoenix Municipal Stadium was the home of the Phoenix Firebirds until 1992, when the team moved to Scottsdale Stadium and played there before the arrival of the Arizona Diamondbacks. It also served as the spring home of the Los Angeles Dodgers for two weeks in 2008, when the Dodgers left Vero Beach early to play a series in Japan and then spent the remainder of spring training in Phoenix.

THE SPRING-TRAINING BALLPARK EXPERIENCE

Concessions

Phoenix Municipal Stadium receives good marks for the quality of its hot dogs and Polish sausages. More substantial fare includes cheeseburgers and grilled chicken-breast sandwiches. Prices are actually lower than they were several years ago, which makes a game at Phoenix Municipal Stadium a better proposition for families.

There is a decent selection of beers — Fat Tire, Sierra Nevada Pale Ale, Coors, Pyramid Hefeweizen — ranging in price from $4.75 to $7.50.

Also, there are only two main concession stands in the ballpark, so be prepared for some long lines.

Autographs

Without a designated autograph area, you're reduced to begging players to come over to the dugout areas and sign. Position yourself down the right-field line; A's players warm up in the area and tend to hang around there before the game.

Parking

There's really no avoiding the $5 charge for parking in a lot across the ballpark. Unless you're there early, you'll be parking quite a distance from the ballpark as well, so bring your walking shoes.

IF YOU GO

What to Do Outside the Ballpark

With food so expensive at the ballpark, you'll want to grab a bite before or after a game.

Honey Bear's BBQ is a Phoenix institution, scoring a slew of local awards after opening in 1986. It's billed as Memphis-style ribs and chicken, although the smoking tends to be on the subtle side and the sauce is pretty sweet. There are multiple Honey Bear's locations, but this is the one closest to the ballpark. Don't leave without ordering the sweet-potato pie. Honey Bear's BBQ, 5012 E. Van Buren St., Phoenix; 602/273-9148; **honeybearsbbq.com**.

Stockyards Restaurant is also a Phoenix institution, albeit for much longer: The original bar has been around since 1889. As you can guess from the name, Stockyards is a steakhouse, but it's also known for its seafood. 5001 E. Washington St., Phoenix; 602/273-7378; **stockyardsestaurant.com**.

And then there's Papago Park itself, a 1,200-acre recreational area with hiking trails, a golf course, fishing ponds, and picnic areas. It also contains the Phoenix Zoo and the Desert Botanical Garden, which we discussed in our earlier chapter on Phoenix.

Papago Golf Course is continually one of the top-rated municipal golf courses in the country. It's not an easy course, carrying a 73.3 championship rating, but it is extremely popular, so reserve your tee times as early as possible (they can be made up to four days in advance). Papago Golf Course, 5595 E. Moreland, Phoenix; 602/275-8428; **www.phoenix.gov/sports/papago.html**.

And, of course, you're not too far from Tempe or Scottsdale. East-bound Van Buren Street actually turns into Mill Avenue before heading into downtown Tempe. We describe this party and bar area in our Los Angeles Angels of Anaheim chapter. From the ballpark, heading north on Galvin, east on McDowell Road, and north on Scottsdale Road will bring you into downtown Scottsdale in practically no time.

Nearby Hotels

There are many hotels north of the airport that are within two miles of Phoenix Municipal Stadium. They're virtually all corporate — Marriott, Springhill Suites, Hampton Inn, Doubletree, Crowne Plaza, Residence Inn — but not necessarily overpriced during spring training. You could do worse than adopting a Phoenix airport hotel as your base of operations for spring training.

Scottsdale and its wide variety of hotels is only a short drive away as well.

Nearby RV Resorts

There are no RV resorts in the area. The closest ones are in Tempe and Scottsdale.

Spring-Training History

The Oakland Athletics franchise dates back to the beginning of the American League in 1901. Spring-training sites have included: Philadelphia (1901, 1919); Charlotte, N.C. (1902); Jacksonville (1903, 1914-1918); Spartanburg, N.C. (1904); Shreveport (1905); Montgomery, Ala. (1906, 1923-1924); Dallas (1907); New Orleans (1908-1909); Atlanta (1910); San Antonio (1912-1913); Lake Charles, La. (1920-1921, 1938-1939); Eagle Pass, Texas (1922); Ft. Myers (1925-1936); Mexico City (1937); Anaheim, Cal. (1940-1942); Wilmington, Del. (1943); Frederick, Md. (1944-1945); West Palm Beach (1946-1962); Bradenton (1963-1969); Mesa (1969-1978); Scottsdale (1979-1983); and Phoenix (1984-present).

→ san diego padres / seattle mariners

PEORIA STADIUM

Capacity	12,882
Year Opened	1994
Dimensions	310L, 385LC, 410C, 385RC, 310R
Surface	Grass
Local Airport	Phoenix
Address	16101 N. 83rd Av., Peoria.

From I-17, take Bell Road and go west to 83rd Avenue.

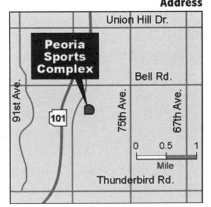

Party Time in Peoria

Peoria Stadium is a newer facility that's considered by many to be among the best ballparks in the Cactus League, despite being one of the biggest. The Seattle Mariners and the San Diego Padres share the stadium, so if you visit Peoria — a suburb of Phoenix — during any point in spring training, you will undoubtedly find a game going on, with tickets available for most dates.

The ballpark itself isn't very distinguished, with an exterior done up in Arizona adobe brown. And the design is questionable at times: The interior concourses is crowded for most games, the outdoor concourse is usually filled with standing-room-only types, and the seating can be on the cramped side. So what makes a game at Peoria Stadium such a great experience? Because the fans get so enthused about their team.

There is outfield grass seating; you won't want to sit there during the day unless you brought your SPF 30 suntan lotion, but if you do you'll have a great view of the action. (Arrive early to claim a good spot: The best spots in the outfield go quickly.) All in all, the ballpark is very accessible, has good sight lines, and can accommodate larger crowds very nicely.

The complex was the first MLB spring-training facility shared by two teams. (There had been situations where two teams played games in the same ballpark, but they maintained separate training facilities.) Today, of course, almost every new training camp in the Cactus League is built for two teams.

The berm is packed for most games.

The Peoria Stadium complex contains two 40,000-square-foot club-houses, indoor and outdoor batting tunnels, 12 major-league-sized practice fields (two lighted), and two half-fields. The extensive facility allows both teams and their minor-league squads to practice simultaneously.

More than any other Cactus League facility, any spring-training game at Peoria Stadium feels like a real event. There's always a lot of traffic and excitement surrounding a game — both the Padres and the Mariners draw well during spring training — and the games certainly sport a carnival-like atmosphere. There are some who decry the location of the ballpark (set, essentially, in the midst of a series of strip malls), but fans seem to love the wide variety of restaurants within walking distance of the park. The ballpark and the games also feel like they are part of the local community: You can expect to see many members of the Peoria Diamond Club — the "Red Shirts" at games — who raise funds for local charities.

insider's tip

There's not a lot of shade at Peoria Stadium. Your best bet for relief from the sun lies in the area around Section 208, closer to the back of the grandstand. Otherwise, you'll face lots of exposure to the sun — so bring plenty of sunscreen.

There's virtually no difference to how a spring game is run here. No matter who's the home team — and the first week of the season it won't matter a lot, as every spring the Padres and Mariners face off against each other several times — the games are run the same. You can always expect crammed seating, a berm area teeming with families and drunken expatriates, and a crowded concession concourse. The only difference may be the fans are paler when Seattle's in town; San Diego residents always look tanner and healthier than their pasty Puget Sound compatriots.

If you can, definitely hit a Padres or Mariners game in Peoria: It is one of the essential experiences in Cactus League spring training.

insider's tip

Both the San Diego Padres and Seattle Mariners begin practices at 9:30 a.m. in the outlying practice fields.

There are plenty of places to just stand around. Photo by Jim Robins.

BALLPARK HISTORY

Peoria Stadium was built for the Seattle Mariners and San Diego Padres, first opening in 1994.

THE SPRING-TRAINING BALLPARK EXPERIENCE

Concessions

The food selection at Peoria Stadium is amazingly varied. Yes, there's the normal selection of ballpark foods — John Morrell hot dogs, hamburgers, nachos, pizza, pop, etc. But if your palate runs to the more refined, you can seek out more exotic offerings like vegetarian Gardenburgers, gyros, Philly cheesesteaks, flame-broiled burritos, teriyaki chicken and noodles, Cajun-style turkey sausages, Miss Karen's Frozen Yogurt, or fry bread. Try the Dingleberry: a strawberry on a stick, dipped in chocolate.

The beer selection is OK (it includes Red Hook and Alaskan Amber Ale), but be prepared to pay a lot more for a premium selection. More bang for the buck can be found with the $5.50 margaritas.

You will also find it difficult to pass up BBQ from Randy Jones's BBQ stand located out in right field, as the smell of BBQ ribs and chicken will be assaulting your nose all game long. Randy Jones is a former star pitcher with the Padres, and although it's a trendy gimmick for a concessionaire (in this case, Aramark) to place a player "in charge" of a ballpark rib stand (i.e., Boog Powell in Baltimore, Greg Luzinski in Philadelphia), the formula seems to work in Peoria: You can expect to wait in line to order ribs here.

Alas, most of the concessions are located in back of the grandstand, so you'll miss some of the action if you decide to closely peruse the offerings.

insider's tip

Look for Rick "The Peanut Man" Kaminski in the stands. He's one of the true characters of the Cactus League.

Autographs

There is no formal autograph signing area at the ballpark and you can't get at the players after practice, so your best bet is to arrive early to the ballpark and attract a player or two to the edge of the stands. The Padres tend to gather near Section 122 before a game; we've never been to a game where a few players didn't head over to sign autographs.

A good place to position yourself is down the right-field line, in foul territory. Players enter and leave the ballpark from this area.

You can also set up shop near a dugout before the game. The Padres' dugout is on the first-base side, while the Mariners' dugout is on the third-base side.

Parking

There is a sea of paid parking adjacent to the ballpark. However, if you want to save a few bucks and grab a meal, dine at one of the many surrounding restaurants and then walk over to the game.

IF YOU GO

Where to Stay

Staying in Peoria is problematic. On the one hand, there are many hotel rooms available within two miles of the ballpark (some are located in Peoria, others in Glendale). But tour operators, who combine a hotel room with game tickets, reserve many of those rooms months in advance. The rooms that are available typically go for $150 or more a night — which is a *lot* to pay for a room during spring training.

To be within walking distance of the ballpark and have an affordable room, you'll need to make a hotel reservation almost a year in advance or else buy a package from a tour operator. Here are the places within a mile of the ballpark:

→ La Quinta Inn & Suites Phoenix West Peoria, 16321 N. 83rd Av., Peoria; 623/487-1900; **laquinta.com**. This hotel is located directly next to the complex; you'll have to deal with a lot of traffic, but you'll also have a ridiculously short walk to a game.

→ Comfort Suites Peoria Sports Complex, 8473 W. Paradise Ln., Peoria; 623/334-3993; **comfortinn.com**. Again, we're talking ridiculously short walk.

→ Residence Inn Phoenix Glendale, 8435 W. Paradise Lane, Peoria; 623/979-2074; **marriott.com**.

→ Hampton Inn, 8408 W. Paradise Lane, Peoria; 623/486-9918; **hamptoninn.com**.

→ Holiday Inn Express, 16771 N. 84th Av., Peoria; 623/853-1313; **holiday-inn.com**.

→ SpringHill Suites Phoenix Glendale, 7810 W. Bell Rd., Glendale; 623/878-6666; **marriott.com**.

An alternative, should you not want to stay in the midst of a suburban strip mall, is just to stay somewhere else in the Phoenix area and then drive to the ballpark. In the middle of the day the freeways of Phoenix are not packed, so there's usually very little advantage to staying close to the ballpark.

RV Resorts Near the Ballpark

There is an abundance of RV Resorts in the general vicinity of the complex and a short drive away from the ballpark. A few are located in adjoining Sun City, and the remaining resorts close to the ballpark are located south on Highway 60, which can be a traffic nightmare. (No, there's no resort within walking distance of the ballpark.) In general, these resorts are geared toward season snowbirds and not necessarily for short-term stays, so do some homework and call ahead before assuming there will be a spot for you.

What to Do Outside the Ballpark

There are some who decry the suburban nature of Peoria, and indeed the area surrounding the ballpark does have a suburban feel, as chain restaurants sit comfortably next to local establishments.

But you don't need to go to Hooters before a game to catch a meal; there are many outstanding establishments within walking distance of the park. Most are located across 83rd Avenue, a short walk from the ballpark. Sadly, our favorite after-game hangout, The Monastery, closed down in early 2007. But there are still plenty of places to catch a brew before or after the game.

McDuffy's is everything you'd expect from a sports bar: a slew of TVs showing popular sporting events (the place to be for March Madness in the ballpark area), an extensive menu, and a patio. It's already notorious in baseball circles: It was there that Padres first-round draft pick Matt Bush was arrested for disorderly conduct in 2004. McDuffy's is all lights and action; it's also the place to hit if you want to find a broadcast of the NCAA basketball tournament within a close walk of the ballpark. McDuffy's, 15814 N. 83rd Av., Peoria; 623/334-5000; **mcduffys.com**.

Also recommended is Abuelo's. Though it's a chain (there are Abuelo's in Texas, Oklahoma, Ohio, and beyond) and the décor is a little over the top, the food at Abuelo's is marvelous. Go for the cilantro lime soup as an appetizer and the stuffed chicken-breast medallions as an entrée. It's also the perfect place to eat before the game, as you can dine and then leave your car there while you walk a block to the ballpark. Abuelo's, 16092 Arrowhead Fountains Center Dr., Peoria; 623/878-8282; **abuelos.com**.

Also within walking distance of the ballpark is the Elephant Bar, which offers an extensive menu (i.e., there really are no specialties of the house) and huge portions. Elephant Bar, 16160 N. 83rd Av., Peoria; 623/776-0100; **elephantbar.com**.

For ribs and BBQ, try Dillon's. It is definitely not a chain, but be warned that it's very popular, so you might need to wait. Try the smoked turkey. Dillon's, 8706 W. Thunderbird Rd., Peoria; 623/979-5353; **dillonsrestaurant.com**.

New to the area is Lis Doon Varna, an Irish pub in the midst of the desert. It's one of those "authentic" Irish outfits where a pub was built in Ireland and then sent far, far away from Ireland. The menu features a long list of Irish specialities, but we're looking forward to cocktails there: Guinness, of course, will be on tap, as well as Harp and Bass. Lis Doon Varna, 16100 Arrowhead Fountains Way, Peoria; 623/979-0730; **lisdoonvarnapub.com**.

The official pizza of the San Diego Padres is served at Oggi's Pizza & Brewing. (Of course, Oggi's is headquartered in southern California, so the link isn't that absurd.) Featured are microbrews and trendy designer pizzas. Oggi's, 6681 W. Beardsley Rd., Glendale; 623/566-8080; **oggis.com**.

Families will enjoy the comfort food at the 5 & Diner. On the menu: burgers, pork chops, meatloaf, chicken-fried steak, pot roast, and waitresses with attitude. You get the idea. 5 & Diner, 7541 Bell Rd., Peoria; 623/97903073; **5anddiner.com**.

If you want something more mainstream, there are a number of chain restaurants close to the ballpark, including Buca di Beppo, P.F. Chang's, Hooters, Krispy Kreme, and In-N-Out Burger.

Other than dining, drinking, and golf, there aren't too many other attractions in Peoria. One attraction perfect for the entire family is the Challenger Space Center, which features exhibits on the history of America's manned-space program from Project Mercury through the space shuttles. It also contains Arizona State's Center for Meteorite Studies. Challenger Space Center, 21170 N. 83rd Av., Peoria; 623/322.2001; **azchallenger.org**.

SPRING-TRAINING HISTORY: SAN DIEGO

The San Diego Padres have trained in Arizona since their National League inception in 1969: From 1969 to 1993 the team trained in Yuma, while in 1994 the team moved to the new ballpark in Peoria.

SPRING-TRAINING HISTORY: SEATTLE

The Seattle Mariners have trained in Arizona since their American League inception in 1977: From 1977 to 1993 the team trained in Tempe, while in 1994 the team moved to the new ballpark in Peoria.

→ san francisco giants

SCOTTSDALE STADIUM

Capacity	12,000
Year Opened	1992
Dimensions	360L, 430C, 360R
Surface	Grass
Local Airport	Phoenix
Address	7408 East Osborn Road, Scottsdale. The stadium is located at Osborn Road and Civic Center Drive, 1/2-mile east of Scottsdale Road.

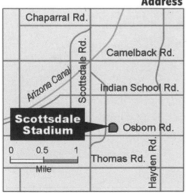

263

The Southwestern Atmosphere in Scottsdale

With a pleasant Southwestern design scheme and an efficient layout, Scottsdale Stadium is located in downtown Scottsdale and is one of the hottest tickets in the Cactus League. It's one of the best spring-training experiences in Arizona: You should plan on devoting a full day to walking the streets of downtown Scottsdale and taking in a Giants game.

Scottsdale bills itself as being a true Wild West town. Located outside of Phoenix, Scottsdale has a totally different look and feel than the rest of the Valley of the Sun: There's some genuine history in downtown Scottsdale, and over the years Scottsdale has evolved from being a kitschy little outpost outside of Phoenix to an affluent suburb. When you visit Scottsdale Stadium, be prepared to do some battle with Hummers and Audi convertibles on the roadways.

The centerpiece in the spring, of course, is Scottsdale Stadium. Today's ballpark is a renovation of the original Scottsdale Stadium (the former Cactus League home of the Baltimore Orioles, Boston Red Sox, Chicago Cubs, and Oakland A's.). Its renovation was overseen by HOK — of course — and it has all the retro decorative touches you'd expect from an HOK park, including lots of wrought iron and brick façades. It features 8,500 fixed seats, with room for 2,000 on outfield berms.

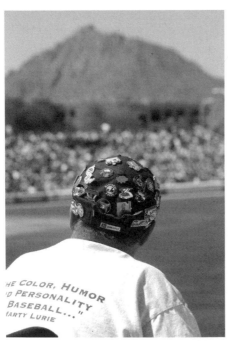

There's a scenic view from every seat in Scottsdale Stadium.

HOK gets a lot of criticism for building retro-style ballparks for both major- and minor-league teams, and Scottsdale Stadium certainly fits within this mold. But one other signature feature of a HOK ballpark doesn't get as much attention: HOK's propensity for breaking down a ballpark into very discrete elements. This means that fans can view the action from many different and unique viewpoints, an approach that works very well at Scottsdale Stadium. Most fans will want to camp out in the grandstand seating (which is fairly shaded from the Arizona sun), but for those wanting a more casual viewpoint there's a larger picnic area down the third-base line, outfield berm seating, and a casual standing-room-only area down the first-base line. (Indeed, we love heading to the right-field corner and hanging out with the casual fans and the cacti. It just screams Arizona.) There really is not a bad seat in the house.

insider's tip

The outfield berm is a great place to watch a game. Be prepared for a steep walk out there, though. Our favorite spot in the outfield is in center field; a beer guy patrols the area so you never have to leave.

Scottsdale Stadium is relatively subdued (instead of the loud rock music blaring before a game, you'll hear an organist playing ballpark-type music), but it's still a great experience for the fan.

Another great thing about Scottsdale Stadium is its location: on the edge of downtown Scottsdale. Your best bet is to arrive early to the game and park for free in a city-owned covered parking ramp directly north of the ballpark. Your car will enjoy the respite from the hot Arizona sun, and you'll have a chance to walk the two blocks to downtown Scottsdale.

insider's tip

Scottsdale Stadium is also home to the Arizona Fall League Hall of Fame and the Scottsdale Sports Hall of Fame. The Arizona League is where major-league teams send prospects after the regular season to play under elite conditions, and members of the Arizona Fall League Hall of Fame include the likes of Todd Helton and Derek Jeter. The Scottsdale Sports Hall of Fame honors notable locals, including Jim Palmer.

Despite the loss of Barry Bonds and a decline on the field, the San Francisco Giants are still a major draw for spring training. The local community supports the team, Giants fans still make the trek to Scottsdale, and the ballpark environment is the best in the Cactus League. And don't be seduced by the declining attendance at Scottsdale Stadium: When a traditional rival is in town — like the Oakland A's or the Chicago Cubs — the place is packed. Be sure to buy your tickets before you leave the ballpark.

Workouts
The Giants practice at Scottsdale Stadium. Workouts start at 9 a.m. Most of the time the major-league squad can be found in the ballpark; occasionally you'll see some specialized practices on an adjoining diamond.

Minor leaguers work out mornings at the expanded facilities Indian School Park, 4415 N. Hayden Rd. (at Camelback Road). This is more than just a workout facility: it's a great, new complex designed both to showcase players and provide comfort to fans as they watch a practice.

To check on a practice schedule, call the complex at 480/990-7972.

THE SPRING-TRAINING BALLPARK EXPERIENCE

Even the beer vendors are entertaining at Scottsdale Stadium.

Grub

The one bad thing about the ballpark is that you can't visit the concessions and watch the ballgame, as virtually all the major concession stands are located behind the grandstand.

Now, having said that, the concessions at the ballpark are pretty well laid out: Each section has its own limited concessions area (in other words, you're never too far away from a beer vendor), so you should plan on grabbing your food while en route to your seat. Or you can take a break from the action and bring some good down to the many picnics located down the left-field line.

Among the more notable offerings: roasted sweet corn (for $5), John Morell hot dogs and Johnsonville brats, and fresh fruit (the strawberries and cream is a particularly nice delicacy). The beer is fairly expensive, but the selection is excellentYou can find Fat Tire, Anchor Steam, and Sam Adams on tap. If that's not strong enough for you, blended cocktails are also available.

Picnic tables are located in the left-field corner if you don't feel like bringing that burrito or burger back to your seat.

Autographs

The best time and place to score an autograph is before the game; Giants players are pretty good about coming over to the first row of seats and signing autographs (head for Section 129 when you arrive at the ballpark). Also, Giants players will stop in the walkway next to the dugout (leading to the clubhouse) and sign autographs before the game.

Parking

Arrive early to score a free parking spot in the covered parking ramp directly north of the ballpark, next to the public library. From there you can walk into the ballpark or walk a few blocks to Old Town Scottsdale. As a bonus, many of the entrepreneurs reselling tickets set up shop outside the parking ramp. The Giants are still a good draw, but not the great draw they were in the Barry Bonds era, so you may be able to snare a decent seat from one of these entrepreneurs at a decent price.

Otherwise, there are many ramps and lots close to the ballpark, but there's more than enough free street parking in the area as well if you're prepared to walk. We've never had issues parking in downtown Scottsdale on a game day.

insider's tip

You don't need to park near the ballpark; you can catch the free Giants Shuttle to the ballpark. The shuttle runs between the Fifth Avenue Shops and Loloma Station Transit Station (2nd Street between Goldwater and Scottsdale roads) and the ballpark. It runs beginning 90 minutes before each home game and runs every 10 minutes up to game time. It then runs 30 minutes after the end of the game. For more information, call 480/312-7696.

If You Go

Where to Stay

Scottsdale is a great hotel town. In recent years the chain offers have been upgraded to the boutique-hotel class. Add the resorts outside of downtown and you have a great assortment of lodging options to choose from.

Your first call should be to the Hotel Valley Ho, an impressively retro facility within walking distance of the ballpark. This was the spring base for the Chicago Cubs when that team trained in Scottsdale in the 1960s, and it's still a favorite base for Cubbies fans on spring break. The hotel opened in 1956 and still retains a lot of that Eisenhower-era ambiance, though it's been modernized since; turquoise is still the color of choice in many rooms. Go for the retro feel, stay for the pool and spa, and have a nightcap at Trader Vic's during the evening Tiki Time. Alas, another former Cubbie hangout in Scottsdale is now gone: The frumpy Hampton Inn is now Hotel Indigo, another boutique hotel with attitude. Hotel Valley Ho, 6850 E. Main St., Scottsdale; 866-882-4484; **hotelvalleyho.com**.

Five hotels are within a half-mile of the ballpark, giving you the chance to set up camp and walk to the ballpark every day. Comfort Suites is typical of that budget chain; just be prepared to pay a premium if you can get a room. Comfort Suites, 3275 N. Drinkwater Blvd., Scottsdale; 480/946-1111; **choicehotels.com**.

The Courtyard by Marriott belies that chain's reputation as a mid-priced location and charges more than $200 nightly during spring training, if you can snare a room. Courtyard by Marriott Scottsdale Old Town, 3311 N. Scottsdale Rd., Scottsdale; 480/429-7785; **marriott.com**. Similarly corporate and similarly situated: the Holiday Inn Express and Suites. It's popular, clean, and easily accessible. What more do you need? Holiday Inn Express, 3131 N. Scottsdale Rd., Scottsdale; 877/863-4780; **holiday-inn.com**.

A more upscale offering is the Mondrian Hotel, located north of the training complex on Indian School Road. The Mondrian chain just screams boutique; if you can't take a dose of attitude with your room, you probably should pass. Mondrian Hotel, 7353 E. Indian School Rd., Scottsdale; 480/308-1100; **mondrianhotel.com**.

A good choice for families is the Homestead Suites, which features kitchenettes and multi-bedroom accommodations. Homestead Suites, 3560 N. Marshall Way, Scottsdale; 480/994-0297; **homesteadhotels.com**.

Otherwise, there's a larger assortment of lodging in the greater Scottsdale area, and you should not feel compelled to stay in downtown Scottsdale. Resorts in Scottsdale are among the best in the world, and we like two in particular.

The Camelback Inn is a flagship resort for the Marriott chain, featuring over 450 casitas (essentially, guest houses) with private patios. Before or after the game you can sun yourself beside one of the three pools. It's not cheap — try getting a room under $500 per night — but it does sell out. Camelback Inn, 5402 E. Lincoln Dr., Scottsdale; 800/242-2635; **camelbackinn.com**.

The Phoenician is a pure luxury resort featuring a 27-hole championship course. You're paying for the privilege of being away from the madding crowds. The Phoenician, 6000 E. Camelback Rd., Scottsdale; 800/888-8234; **thephoenician.com**.

RV Resorts Near the Ballpark

The Scottsdale Trailer Corral is about a half mile from the ballpark, a very easy walk on any given day. Scottsdale Trailer Corral, 3202 N. Scottsdale Rd., Scottsdale; 602/947-8532.

What to Do Outside the Ballpark

The ballpark is directly adjacent to the Marshall Way Arts District, which includes the Scottsdale Civic Center, the Scottsdale Center for the Arts, and the Scottsdale Museum of Contemporary Art. The mall between these buildings is a nice calm spot and well worth a stroll before the game. Right off the mall is a slew of restaurants and watering holes.

Otherwise, we cover the charms of the area in our Phoenix overview and its section on Scottsdale.

SPRING-TRAINING HISTORY

The San Francisco Giants have held spring training in the following locations: New York City (1901-1902); Savannah, Ga. (1903-1905); Memphis (1906); Los Angeles (1907, 1932-1933); Marlin Springs, Texas (1908-1918); Gainesville, Fla. (1919); San Antonio (1920-1923, 1929-1931); Sarasota (1924-1927); Augusta, Ga. (1928); Miami Beach (1934-1935); Pensacola, Fla. (1936); Havana (1937); Baton Rouge (1938-1939); Winter Haven (1940); Miami (1941-1942, 1946); Lakewood, N.J. (1943-1945); Phoenix (1947-1950, 1952-1983); St. Petersburg (1951); Scottsdale (1984-present).

Worth a drive on an off-day: a drive down I-10 to Casa Grande to see the former spring-training home of the Giants. Francisco Casa Grande is still around and retains many of the unique touches that made it such a charming spot for spring training.

Be warned: It still feels like the middle of nowhere, so imagine how remote Francisco Casa Grande must have felt in 1962 when the San Francisco Giants launched spring training at the brand-spanking-new $2 million resort. The resort, located outside of small

In the shadow of the Scottsdale buttes.

Casa Grande, was designed to be a total self-contained environment for the Giants, featuring its own airstrip, 18-hole championship golf course, pool, and multi-field complex. Next to it is a 3,000-seat ballpark used occasionally for exhibition games, although the Giants frequently traveled to Phoenix for the majority of their games.

For Giants owner Horace Stoneham, the hotel and training complex was an investment in Casa Grande's future: It was to serve as the training camp for the Giants in February and March, and a luxury resort the rest of the year. It was also highly speculative: Stoneham hoped (and probably assumed) the new interstate highway would be located near town, making his resort a short hop from the freeway. Alas, Interstate 10 was built quite a ways to the east, consigning Casa Grande to a future with limited growth (the 2000 census put the population at 25,224). Stoneham's future of a prosperous resort never came true, and by 1980 the Giants shifted spring-training operations totally to Phoenix.

Today the resort still stands and is a pleasant diversion should you need a break as you drive between Phoenix and Tucson: It's 50 miles south of Phoenix and 70 miles north of Tucson. It was renovated in 2004 — to the tune of $8 million — and it still retains some of the charming baseball touches in the original design. The pool is still shaped like a baseball bat, while the parking lot is laid out like a catcher's mitt. (Go up to the rooftop for the best view.) Within the resort are pictures from the days when the Giants trained there. Despite the renovation, the resort still has an early-1960s feel, and you'll want to spend a little time wandering the lobby and the grounds.

Gone are the practice fields and the ballpark. The watching stand at the center of the practice fields still stands, as shown below; you can imagine Alvin Dark or Herman Franks hanging out and measuring the spring progress of Willie Mays, Juan Marachial and Gaylord Perry.

→ tucson

Tucson: Peace in the Valley

If Phoenix is Party Central in the Cactus League, Tucson is the quiet cousin sitting at the edge of the action. Home to three Cactus League teams — Arizona, Chicago White Sox, and Colorado — Tucson is an easy drive from Phoenix and offers enough to serve as your spring-training home.

In many ways, Tucson is a smaller version of Phoenix, with many of the same attributes. (Yes, the Tucson tourism folks will hate to see this statement expressed so starkly, but it's true.) Present-day Tucson was founded on Aug. 20, 1775, with a Spanish settlement called Presidio de San Augustin. (The structure no longer stands, but the El Presidio neighborhood still exists in downtown Tucson.) Tucson has been part of the United States since 1853, except for a brief period when Confederate soldiers invaded the area and declared it Confederate territory.

Tucson is a gorgeous city, where you can count on sunny days and spectacular sunsets. The emphasis in Tucson is on outdoor activities: hikers and walkers will delight in the many offerings of the city, while nature lovers will enjoy spending time in the Sonoran Desert. And while Tucson is a university town, it doesn't necessarily feel like one.

Even though Tucson is in the midst of the desert, you'll want to pack for cooler weather for a spring-training trip. The average March high is 75 (but feels much warmer if you're from the north and not used to a warm spring sun), but lows dip down to 45. There's a smattering of rain during the month as well.

Tucson Activities

You won't spend all your time at the ballpark, so here's a selection of other activities in the area.

Located west of downtown, Sentinel Peak (sometime called "A" Mountain because of the University of Arizona "A" at the peak) was inhabited for thousands of years by the Hohokam Indians. Hohokam, which means "the vanished ones," farmed the area, but they inexplicably disappeared from the area, replaced by other Native American tribes. Today you can drive to the top of the mountain and see some great views of the entire Tucson basin. (Yes, it's the same Hohokam tribe honored at the spring home of the Cubs.) Sentinel Peak, Sentinel Peak Road.

271

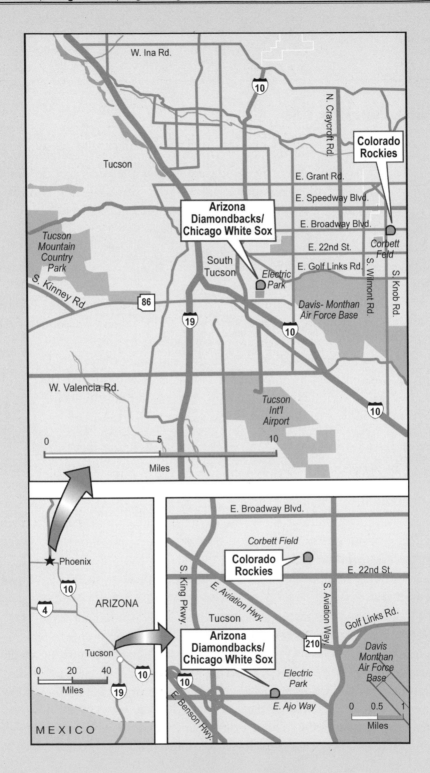

In 1692 Father Eusebio Francisco Kino made the first of his many trips to the area. Kino, an Italian missionary for the Spanish church, established a string of missions in Arizona and Sonora, with the most famous being San Xavier del Bac Mission, the "White Dove of the Desert," founded in 1694. It didn't start out as a white structure when constructed in 1797, but a 1900s renovation led to the repainting of the exterior in brilliant white, which is stunning in the desert sun. It still features regular masses as a Catholic parish. San Xavier del Bac Mission, 1950 W. San Xavier Rd., Tucson; 520/294-2624; **sanxaviermission.org**.

It's not Vegas, but gamblers will enjoy the games at Desert Diamond Casino: slots, live blackjack, keno, bingo, and the newest trendy game — poker. Four restaurants round out the experience. Desert Diamond Casino, south of Tucson on I-19 at Pima Mine Road; 866/DDC-WINS; **desertdiamond.com**.

The city of Tucson runs five municipal courses; you can reserve at any of them at 520/791-4336 or **tucsoncitygolf.com**. There is also an abundance of public and private courses throughout the area; you can check out rates and listings at 866/360-4653 or **visitTucson.org**.

The Spanish Missionary style dominates the local architecture. To see a good selection of historic buildings of that era, hit downtown Tucson. Some of the best examples are government buildings, like the State Building (416 W. Congress St.) and the Pima County Courthouse (15 N. Church Av.), while others formerly were private residences, like the Manning House (450 W. Paseo Redondo) and the Stevens House (150 N. Main Av.).

Old Town Artisans is the city's largest collection of locally produced Native American art, clothing and jewelry. Turquoise tends to be the order of the day here, although there's a wide selection available. Once you're done shopping, lunch at the cantina on the grounds or wander through the El Presidio Historic District. Old Town Artisans, 201 N. Court Av., Tucson; 800/782-8072; **oldtownartisans.com**.

The Arizona-Sonora Desert Museum is the place to see the entire local ecosystem in one shot: Over 300 animals and 1,300 plant varieties are on display on 21 acres. Arizona-Sonora Desert Museum, 2001 N. Kinney Rd., Tucson; 520/883-2702; **desertmuseum.org**. *Adults, $13; children (4-12), $4.25.*

Tombstone is the site of the legendary gunfight at OK Corral, where the Earps and Doc Holliday fought the Clantons and McLaurys. Today the city (located south of Tucson on state Hwy. 80) is preserved with a downtown historic district that features many original buildings, stagecoach rides and daily reenactments of the famous gunfight. Located south of town: Boothill Graveyard, where many of the local gunslingers were laid to rest. OK Corral,

Tombstone; 520/457-3456, 888/457-3929; **ok-corral.com**, **tombstone.org**.

Bisbee and Douglas are two mining towns south of Tucson featuring nicely preserved Victorian architecture dating back from the turn of the century, when these cities were rollicking mining towns. Baseball fans may want to check out Warren Ballpark in Bisbee: It's reportedly one of the oldest baseball fields still in use, though the surrounding ballpark is not that old.

Tucson Dining

Tucson is known as a town with great food: Southwestern cuisine came from Tucson, so it's not hard to find a good restaurant.

The Sakura Sports Bar is probably one of the most unique sports bars in the nation: It's a combination Japanese steakhouse, sushi restaurant, and sports bar — not a mix that one would intuitively make, but it seems to work for owner Mr. An. Have some toro while watching the NCAA basketball tournament. Sakura Sports Bar, 6534 E. Tanque Verde Rd., Tucson; 520/298-7777.

A more traditional sports bar is Bob Dobbs Bar & Grill, a neighborhood joint near the University of Arizona campus where the beer is cold, the burgers are huge, and the sound system is unobtrusive. The Bob Burger is a half-pounder flavored with garlic and Worcestershire sauce. And yes, the bar is named for J.R. "Bob" Dobbs, the founder of the Church of the Subgenius: Give me slack, or give me food, or kill me. Bob Dobbs Bar & Grill, 2501 E. 6th St., Tucson; 520/325-3767.

For pure Mexican food, there is the El Charro Café, with two locations: downtown and on the east side of Tucson. El Charro Café is touted as being the oldest Mexican restaurant in continual operation by the same family in America, dating back to 1922. Try the Carne Seca Beef. El Charro Café downtown, 311 N. Court Av.; 520/622-1922; **elcharrocafe.com**.

Cafe Poca Cosa is Mexican, but it is frequently described as Nuevo Mexican, which means that it's a lot more ambitious than tacos and burritos. It's located in the ground floor of the Clarion Hotel in downtown

Tucson. The chicken mole — prepared in a very unauthentic fashion with Kahlua — is to die for. It's a small place, so dinner reservations are highly recommended. Cafe Poca Cosa, 110 E. Pennington St., Tucson; 520/622-6400; **cafepocacosatucson.com**.

If you tire of Mexican or Southwestern cuisines, a welcome break can be found at The Dish, where the food is American eclectic and the wine selection impressive. It's a small place — only 12 tables — so reservations are recommended. The Dish, 3200 E. Speedway Blvd., Tucson; 520/326-1714.

The Fourth Avenue stretch near the University of Arizona features a variety of eateries and bars in a wide range of prices. Caruso's has been serving inexpensive Italian food to UA students since 1938, with three generations of the Zagona family at the helm. Pasta — and lots of it — dominates the menu. Sit outside on the patio if you can. Caruso's, 434 N. 4th Av., Tucson; 520/624-5765.

If casual is your style, try Gentle Bens Brewing Co. This brewpub, located near the University of Arizona campus, is the largest in the area. Recommended: the Red Cat Amber. Gentle Bens Brewing Co., 865 E. University Blvd.; 520/624-4177; **gentlebens.com**.

Where to Stay

Tucson hotels tend to be concentrated in downtown, near the University, and adjoining the airport. For those attending spring-training games, the downtown and airport areas offer the easiest access to the ballparks. Tucson is the second-largest city in Arizona, but it does not have an abundance of hotel rooms, so you may find your selections to be somewhat limited. However, spring training is not a huge event in Tucson (most games are mostly populated with locals and hardcore teams fans, not a general spring-training audience), so it's not difficult to find a hotel in your price range. We won't list all the available hotels here, but we will note the hotels closest to the ballparks on individual team pages.

Keeping in mind you probably won't be staying near the ballpark, we do have a recommendation if you're in search of interesting lodgings. Perhaps the most unique hotel in Tucson is the Hotel Congress, originally built in 1919 to serve passengers on the Southern Pacific Line. The rooms are inexpensive — $89-$119 for a double, $69-$99 for a single — and are outfitted with vintage fixtures like wrought-iron beds and antique radios. It's not for everyone (you won't be pampered by today's standards, and forget entertaining the kids with Cartoon Network), but for those in search of a unique travel experience, Hotel Congress rocks.

Jerry Kindall Field at Frank Sancet Stadium.

Inside the lobby of the Hotel Congress is the Cup Café and the Tap Room. The Cup Café isn't as old as the rest of the hotel (it dates back to 1990), but it's worth a visit even if you're not staying in the hotel. The dining theme at dinner is a fusion of Southwestern, Asian, Mediterranean, and more; sit at the bar for a unique experience. Better yet: breakfast, where $7 gets you a filling meal. The Tap Room, however, has been open continuously since 1919 and is simply an old cowboy bar, complete with paintings from noted cowboy artist Pete Martinez. Check out the jukebox as well.

Hotel Congress, 311 E. Congress St., Tucson; 520/622-8848, 800/722-8848; **hotelcongress.com**.

Other Sports in Tucson

The University of Arizona is the 800-pound gorilla in the Tucson sporting scene. If a University of Arizona basketball teams makes the NCAA tournament, you can expect the media and fans to be focused on the Wildcats.

A nice baseball alternative is the University of Arizona baseball team, which plays its home games at Jerry Kindall Field at Frank Sancet Stadium. Located on the southeast corner of campus (east of Campbell Avenue, north of 6th Street, next to the football stadium and arena), the home of the Wildcats is an average college baseball facility: not much shade and limited concessions. One nice touch, however, is a picnic area down the left-field line honoring Wildcats greats, including Jack Howell, Chip Hale, J.T. Snow, and Terry Francona.

Transportation

You'll need a car to see most of the sites in Tucson. Although there is public transportation in the form of Sun Tran (**suntran.com**), Tucson tends to be a sprawling metropolitan area. If you're not driving in, you can rent a car at the airport: All the major car-rental companies are located either inside the terminal or at a nearby facility.

Flying In

Tucson International Airport is located on the south side of town and is fairly close to the TEP, where the D-Backs and White Sox train. Most major airlines (Alaska Airlines, American, Continental, Delta, Frontier, Northwest, Southwest, US Airways, and United) fly into Tucson, although there are a limited number of nonstop flights. It's also a rather fetching airport: It was built in 1963 and the main terminal still has a classic Southwest façade.

Tucson International Airport, 7005 S. Plumer Av., Tucson; 520/573-8100; **tucsonairport.org**.

→ arizona diamondbacks/chicago white sox

TUCSON ELECTRIC PARK

Capacity	11,500
Year Opened	1998
Dimensions	325L, 405C, 325R
Surface	Grass
Local Airport	Tucson
Address	2500 E. Ajo Way, Tucson.

Tucson Electric Park is south of downtown Tucson, a stone's throw away from I-10. If you're coming from the north, take the Ajo Way exit (which is also marked as the Kino Parkway exit) and head east, following the signs.

TEP: D-Backs and Snakebites

Tucson Electric Park used to be an example of a spring-training facility done right. But it has not aged especially well, and as other newer spring-training facilities have surpassed the TEP — like Peoria Stadium and Surprise Stadium — it's become an OK-but-not-great place to take in a spring-training game.

It is amazing how a facility designed for the desert can have so little shade. During our last visit — a White Sox/Diamondbacks game, naturally — we noted poor, pasty White Sox fans having little chance of escaping harm under the hot Arizona sun, burned to a crisp by the end of the fifth inning. (Except for those in the limited number of level-200 suite-level seats, of course.) If it's not blazing hot, it could be raining (and rainouts do happen in Tucson), and there's usually nothing subtle about a March Tucson rain.

But there is a lot to love about how the Arizona Diamondbacks and Chicago White Sox put on a spring game. The vibe is relaxed, to be sure: There's real music from an organ played before the game, none of this loud canned music you find in most other ballparks. The crowd can be found milling the concourse right up to the start of the game, partaking of the tasty concessions. Families are relaxing on the outfield berm, while kids line up next to the dugout, looking for autographs. It is a prototypical spring-training vibe.

insider's tip

There's no difference in how a Diamondbacks game is run and how a White Sox game is run. If you're not necessarily a fan of either team but want a fun spring-training experience while visiting Tucson, feel free to attend a game hosted by either team. Of course, you may run a good chance of seeing the pair face off, especially if you head to a game early in March.

After parking in the adjoining parking lot (on loose gravel, no less) for $3, you enter TEP at ground level and look down to the action from a concourse level; the playing field is below grade. The main grandstand area features theater-style seats, while there are two levels of bleachers down each line.

The outfield area is noteworthy in that there's not a single bleacher seat; instead, the designers wisely put in grassy areas on both sides of a concession area in dead-center field. The 3,000 berm-seating tickets are

Tucson Electric Park features a panoramic view from the grandstand.

inexpensive and among the best bargains in the Cactus League. It's a great area for families to throw down a blanket — the kids can run around and play catch, while the adults get a great view of the action. The bullpens are in front of the center-field concession stand, and you can look down at them from the outfield grass. A concourse rings the entire playing field, so you can wander throughout the stadium through the course of a game.

One popular place for fans to gather is next to the walkway out of the ballpark down the right-field line. It's one of the better places to snare an autograph. It's also one of the better places to heckle a visiting player (when the Diamondbacks are in town, that is). If you go, spring for a grandstand seat or sit out in the outfield grass. Don't mess with the metal seating unless you must; they get hot on a March afternoon and are fairly uncomfortable. There are club seats on the second level of the grandstand, but these are quite a ways from the action and are not recommended unless you absolutely must be in the shade.

insider's tip

The White Sox draw slightly better than the Diamondbacks do, especially now that the Pale Hose are winning. You won't run into many sellouts, however; spring training in Tucson just isn't that big a deal, so don't be afraid to just head to the ballpark at the spur of the moment.

THE SPRING-TRAINING BALLPARK EXPERIENCE

Concessions

Only Peoria Stadium comes as close to TEP when it comes to food variety in the Cactus League. There are six main concession stands as well as smaller standalone booths. We're big fans of the pulled pork sandwiches from the Authentic Hickory grill down the first-base line, while the tacos and burros from El Saguarito, a local caterer, are to die for. Those wanting a different experience should seek out the fried soba noodles (as well as other Asian delicacies), fry bread, BBQ sandwiches, espresso, and turkey legs. And, of course, there are always standard ballpark items like hot dogs, burgers, fries, pizza, and soda. In the past you could find *horchatas* (a nice rice-based drink) at the ballpark, but they were missing during our last visit.

The beer selection at TEP is equally outstanding: You can find Sam Adams, Foster's, Corona, Sierra Nevada, Tecate, Fat Tire, Bud, Miller, and other microbrews throughout the park, albeit at fairly high prices. Mixed drinks are sold at the ballpark; expect to pay $10 for a drink with any decent level of alcohol.

Fans get close to players in pre-game autograph sessions. Photo by Jack Kurtz.

Autographs

Both the White Sox and the Diamondbacks begin practice at 9:30 a.m., at the minor-league complex across Ajo Way. You can try catching players going to and from practice. At the ballpark you should head for the front row of Section 121, along the third-base line. This is where the players warm up, and one or two will usually wander over and sign a ball or two. The gates to the ballpark open at 11:30 a.m. for a 1 p.m. start.

As with most parks, a number of players will hang around the field and sign autographs for fans.

Bullpens are located next to the berm seating.

The TEP clubhouses are not located in the grandstand, but rather in a separate building down the first-base line. When players leave the game, they must walk to the clubhouse via an open walkway. Depending on their mood, some players will stop on their way to the clubhouse and sign autographs. Let's put it this way: Rarely will a visiting star stop to sign autographs on his way to the clubhouse, but many of the home Diamondbacks will take the time and do so.

If You Go

Where to Stay

TEP is within four miles of both the airport and downtown Tucson, which means that you can easily stay at one of the many chains represented in both locales and then have a short commute to the ballpark.

The airport hotels actually begin about a mile from the ballpark, so you can stay there and have easy access to the ballpark. But Tucson is not the sort of community where you want to do a lot of walking: There's nothing within easy walking distance of the ballpark (a Quality Inn is technically about a mile from the ballpark, but it's not an easy walk), so a car rental will be necessary for a visit unless you drove down from Phoenix.

RV Parks

There are a host of RV parks in the Tucson area. Most of them are on the outskirts of town (the better to view the Sonoran Desert, of course) and geared more toward long-term snowbirds. Don't expect to stay at an RV park close to the ballpark, however.

Flying In

Tucson International Airport is the closest airport; we discuss it more in our chapter covering Tucson.

You may also want to consider flying into Phoenix and then driving to Tucson if the fare to Phoenix is significantly cheaper. The drive is 117 miles and takes a couple of hours on I-10, but it's a pretty drive if you like the desert scenery.

SPRING-TRAINING HISTORY: WHITE SOX

The Chicago White Sox have held spring training in Excelsior Springs, Mo. (1901-1902); Mobile (1903); Marlin Springs, Texas (1904); New Orleans (1905-1906); Mexico City (1907); Los Angeles (1908); San Francisco (1909-1910); Mineral Wells, Texas (1911, 1916-1919); Waco, Texas (1912, 1920); Paso Robles, Cal. (1913-1915); Waxahachie, Texas (1921); Seguin, Texas (1922-1923); Winter Haven, Fla. (1924); Shreveport, La. (1925-1928); Dallas (1929); San Antonio (1930-1932); Pasadena, Cal. (1933-1942, 1946-1950); French Lick, Ind. (1943-1944); Terre Haute, Ind. (1945); Palm Springs, Cal. (1951); El Centro, Cal. (1952-1953); Tampa (1954-1959); Sarasota (1960-1997); and Tucson (1998-present)

SPRING-TRAINING HISTORY: ARIZONA

The Arizona Diamondbacks have trained in Tucson since their team inception.

→ colorado rockies

HI CORBETT FIELD

Capacity	9,500
Year Opened	1937; renovated in 1992, 1997 and 1999
Dimensions	366L, 410LC, 392C, 348R
Surface	Grass
Local Airport	Tucson
Address	3400 E. Camino Campestre, Tucson.

From I-10, exit at Broadway, head east and then turn right on Randolph Way. Hi Corbett is located on the right-hand side. There are signs pointing the way.

Hi Corbett Field: A Classic Oasis

Hi Corbett Field is the kind of older facility that either inspires awe or turns folks off because of its relatively old age. Much of the ballpark dates back to the 1930s, even though it's been renovated several times during the years (most recently in 1999, when a team store and a ticket office were added, and in 1997, when a $3.77 million renovation yielded new seating and expanded the clubhouses).

It holds 8,665, but the trouble is that only 4,000 of these seats are any good at all. The box seats behind home plate — which sold in 2008 for $17 — are a great value: The grandstand's pitch is severe enough to allow the seats in the back to be close to the action, and these seats are the closest to the concessions. When you get down each line, however, the seating isn't so hot: The metal bleachers are totally angled toward the outfield and are uncomfortable, to boot. The bleachers down the left-field line are called the Sandpile (it's a takeoff on the Rockpile at Coors Field) and cost $4 in 2008.

insider's tip

You can avoid the shuttle by parking elsewhere in Randolph Park and then hiking to the ballpark. There's plenty of parking on East Camino Campestre, adjacent to the minor-league complex.

The only shaded area is the back of the grandstand.

Parking is a bonus at Hi Corbett: It's free, provided you show up early enough to snare one of the spots in the small parking lot. (If you don't, you'll be sent over to the nearly El Con Mall and then catch a shuttle back to the ballpark.) Remember: Gates open two hours before gametime.

The ballpark is in an idyllic section of Tucson, on the fringes of a city park and golf course. You're far away from the city when you're watching the Rockies in action, even though you're physically in a very busy part of town. (You'll discover that fact when you drive down Broadway to get to the ballpark.)

And it certainly is scenic. The most recent renovation to Hi Corbett Field added a Southwestern motif to the ballpark, something that fits right into the Tucson ethos. Adobe has always been part of the spring vibe here (the original configuration had an adobe outfield wall where fans sat and watched the games for free). Add a clock tower to the mix, and Hi Corbett is surely one of the prettiest ballparks in spring training.

Scoring autographs is easy at Hi Corbett: the Rockies run a rope line outside the clubhouse down the right-field line. (You can't miss it.) Many players hit the line after they shower to sign autographs.

Hiram Steven "Hi" Corbett, by the way, was a former Arizona state senator who was key in attracting spring training and the PGA Tour to the state.

insider's tip

Bring your sunscreen. There's precious little seating that's not in direct sunlight.

BALLPARK HISTORY

Hi Corbett Field opened in 1928 as Randolph Municipal Baseball Park, the home of the minor-league Class D Tucson Waddies from the original Arizona State League. (Some of those Arizona State League teams had interesting names, including the Tucson Missions, Lizards, and Cowboys). Later on the ballpark housed the Tucson Toros of the Triple-A Pacific Coast League, and the University of Arizona played night games there as well in the 1960s. The Cleveland Indians trained at Hi Corbett Field from 1947 through 1992 thanks to owner Bill Veeck, who wanted the team close to his Arizona ranch.

Back in the day there was much more adobe in the ballpark. In fact, the outfield walls were adobe as well. Fans used to sit at the top of the adobe outfield walls and watch games for free.

The Colorado Rockies then moved into Hi Corbett in 1993 for the team's inaugural spring training.

The ballpark is named for Hiram Corbett, the president of the Tucson Baseball Commission and the man who worked with Veeck to bring the Indians to town.

insider's tip

With its park setting, the Rockies' spring-training complex is one of the most bucolic in the Cactus League. Take some time to wander back to the four practice fields west of the ballpark to watch minor leaguers in action. There's plenty of shade and a little seating. More importantly, you can see baseball played for the fun of it, for the most part.

THE SPRING-TRAINING BALLPARK EXPERIENCE

Concessions

The food is fairly cheap at Hi Corbett, though there's nothing truly notable. The foot-long brats are $6 and are enough to feed a family of four, and the carne asada burros at the El Saguarito Cafe have a decent bite. For the traditionalists, a Rockies Dog (a foot long served with grilled peppers, onions, or sauerkraut), a staple at Coors Field, is on the grill. The beer selection is decent. You can go low-end with Bud or higher-end with Blue Moon, Killian's Red or Dos Equis. (In general, the beer is much cheaper at Hi Corbett than other spring-training venues, but the lower prices are relative: You're still looking to pay at least $6.25 or so for a 16-ounce beer.)

Rockies are easily accessible during spring training.

Recommended: the Jose Cuervo Margarita, sold only at the bar/margarita stand between first and home.

Autographs

Arrive early to watch morning workouts: The Rockies are very accessible during this time, whether it's walking to or from practice or taking a break.

You can also count on a few players coming to the edge of the stands to sign before the start of the game. It's not easy to snare an autograph from here, as the stands are raised above ground level and it's a little awkward.

Finally, there's a formal rope line outside the clubhouse down the right-field line. (You can't

Clint Barmes pleases the crowd.

miss it.) Many players hit the line after they shower to sign autographs. And while we're not fans of harassing players after a game, you should know Rockies players usually park in the lot near the first-base line. Just be respectful and know their names.

IF YOU GO

What to Do Outside the Ballpark

Hi Corbett is part of a larger complex that includes Randolph Municipal Golf Course, Gene Reid Park, and the Reid Park Zoo.

Reid Park Zoo features over 400 animals, including anteaters and polar bears. It's also one of the more active breeding programs, with white rhinoceroses and ruffed lemurs on display.

Reid Park Zoo, 1030 S. Randolph Way, Tucson; 520/881-4753; **tucsonzoo.org**. *Adults, $5; seniors, $4; children (2-14), $2.*

Randolph Municipal Golf Course contains two courses. Randolph North is the former site for PGA Events and is the current home of the Welch's/Fry's LPGA Championship tournament, held every March. Because of the tournament, you may find it hard to snare tee times if you're visiting in the middle of May. However, if you can handle the distance (7,000 yards from the championship tees, 6,500 yards from the regular tees), Randolph North is a gorgeous course: The fairways are lined with eucalyptus tress and palms, and the mountains make a lovely backdrop. Randolph South is a shorter course (5,800 yards from the regular tees) and easier to walk, making it a more popular course. Randolph Municipal Golf Course, 600 S. Alvernon Way, Tucson; 520/791-4161; **tucsoncitygolf.com/randolph.html**.

Where to Stay
As Hi Corbett is nearer the center of Tucson than Tucson Electric Park, there are a few hotels within a mile or so of the ballpark:

→ Doubletree Hotel at Tucson at Reid Park, 445 S. Alvernon Way, Tucson; 520/881-4200; **doubletree.com**.

→ Clarion Randolph Park, 102 N. Alvernon Way, Tucson; 520/795-0330; **choicehotels.com**.

→ Lodge on the Desert, 306 N. Alvernon Way, Tucson; 520/325-3366, 800/456-5634; **lodgeonthedesert.com**. This hotel dates back to 1936 and was designed in a hacienda style with tile-covered patios and fireplaces.

In addition, there are a host of hotels near the University of Arizona and downtown Tucson, both of which are less than five miles away.

RV Parks
There are a host of RV parks in the Tucson area. Most of them are on the outskirts of town (the better to view the Sonoran Desert, of course) and geared more toward long-term snowbirds. Don't expect to stay at an RV park close to the ballpark, however.

Flying In
Tucson International Airport is obviously the closest airport; we discuss it in our opening chapter on Tucson.

You may also want to consider flying into Phoenix and then driving to Tucson if the fare to Phoenix is significantly cheaper. The drive is 117 miles and takes a couple of hours on I-10, but it's a pretty drive if you like the desert scenery.

SPRING-TRAINING HISTORY
The Rockies have trained at Hi Corbett since the team's inception.

→ las vegas

Nothing Like the Smell of a Casino in Springtime

Not every spring-training game is played in Florida or Arizona. During the last weekend of spring training you'll find many teams scattering for points across the country; some (like Houston) traditionally play a pair of home games during that last weekend, while others use the occasion to take on a minor-league affiliate.

Traditionally there are MLB exhibitions at Las Vegas's Cashman Field during the last weekend of spring training as well. In recent years the format has slipped from four teams to two — usually the Chicago Cubs and the Seattle Mariners — and there's no guarantee the series will continue. But it's worth a check to see if the Vegas games are on the spring schedules, as the end of March is a slow travel period and you can snare a cheap fare to Sin City — as well as a last chance to see the boys of summer under the sun before they head to cloudier and cooler climes.

The games take place at Cashman Field, the regular-season home of the Triple-A Las Vegas 51s. As far as ballparks go, it's pretty much strictly utilitarian: Built in 1993, Cashman Field is an intimate, low-key stadium.

For the most part, the ballpark looks like a standard-issue Pacific Coast League facility: All of the seating is between the foul lines, a second level

Not much shade down each line at Cashman Field.

contains press facilities and suites, and there are some decent views of mountains beyond the outfield fence.

By late March there's a good chance of picking up a nasty sunburn at such an open ballpark, so the key to choosing a seat at Cashman Field is finding something in the shade. During a day game, Row L is the first row of the shaded area, with section 9-15 (theater-style seating with drinkholders) under the overhang. Any seat down the line will be open and hot, as metal bleachers dominate the area.

Should you not be able to score seats in the shade, we'd recommend sitting down the line and scoring a picnic table in the group area. Your view of the game won't be great — it won't be once you're past the dugouts, in any case — but you'll be able to better socialize with your friends.

If you feel overheated, head to the Plaza Seating area in the grandstand and take advantage of the misting system.

The attraction of Cashman Field isn't in the surroundings or amenities — it's the chance to see your favorite team in intimate surroundings. Any team playing there on the last weekend of spring training will feature lineups filled with regulars. If you go, expect competitive games in a relaxed atmosphere.

PARKING AND TRANSIT

There's plenty of parking in the area, but be warned it's a long haul from your parking spot to your seat. (Then again, this is Vegas: There's usually a long hike between the front desk and a hotel room.) Most of this is due to the unique layout of Cashman Field: You need to negotiate a large area between the parking lot and the actual grandstand, followed by a two-story concourse leading to a mezzanine level. From there, you go down to your seat. The mezzanine level contains most of the concessions.

But you can also get to Cashman Field via public transportation. The 301 (Deuce) line runs up and down Las Vegas Boulevard — the Strip, basically. You'll need to transfer at the downtown Las Vegas transport center and hop on the northbound 113 bus line. Be warned it takes about an hour to get from the corner of Flamingo and Las Vegas Boulevard to the ballpark via bus. Given how cheap and ubiquitous cabs are in Vegas, you may want to take a taxi instead.

The closest hotel to Cashman Field is the Best Western Parkview Inn (921 Las Vegas Blvd. N.), across the street from the Cashman complex. It is also resoundingly dull, and you don't go to Vegas for dull.

The closest cluster of decent hotels close to Cashman Field is in downtown Las Vegas, where most of the larger joints are about a mile from Cashman Field. (The walk between downtown and Cashman Field isn't

Watch out for those metal bleachers on a hot day.

the most scenic and sometimes a little creepy, although it's generally not unsafe.) There are some who swear by downtown Las Vegas — mostly older folks who have been going there for decades — and there's a certain Rat Pack quality to the area as well, though there's far less of that hip vibe downtown than the Las Vegas marketers would have you believe.

The Golden Nugget is the largest downtown hotel/casino, and it's also the swankest — but that's not necessarily saying a lot. It certainly is expensive for a downtown hotel: $144 on weeknights and $175 on a weekend. Better buys include the El Cortez (600 E. Fremont Street), the Four Queens (202 Fremont Street), Binion's (128 E. Fremont), the Golden Gate (1 Fremont Street), and the Plaza (1 Main Street). There's certainly plenty to do if you decide to stay downtown, though you may get tired of the Fremont Street Experience and the endless come-ons to visit the Girls of Glitter Gulch after a day or two.

As you might tell, we're not huge fans of staying downtown, particularly if you are bringing the kids over a long weekend. Given the huge number of hotel rooms in Vegas and the need for transport to and from the ballpark anyway, we'd recommend staying at one of the huge resort hotels on the Strip — the Flamingo, Bally's, Harrah's, Treasure Island — that don't cost an arm and a leg but still offer plenty of entertainment and dining options.

→ world baseball classic

The World Meets for a Classic

One complicating factor for spring training in 2009 is the World Baseball Classic. On the one hand, the tournament will expand the amount of baseball in March, and that's always a good thing. Plus, MLB has changed the format to ensure the tournament is less disruptive when it comes to regular spring-training games: No spring-training camps will be used for WBC games, and the impact will be limited to the loss of stars leaving their team camps to take part in the tourney games.

Because WBC games won't be played at any spring-training camp, we don't expect many regular attendees to make a huge effort to head to a game. But we expect some readers of this book to attend games in their area, hence the information about the tourney.

First-round games will be held at the Tokyo Dome, Puerto Rico's Hiram Bithorn Stadium, Toronto's Rogers Centre, and Mexico City's Foro Sol Stadium on March 5-12. Second-round games are slated for San Diego's Petco Park (March 15-19) and Miami's Dolphin Stadium (March 14-18). All have strong baseball traditions.

The Tokyo Dome hosted games in the 2006 edition of the World Baseball Classic, several major-league exhibitions and regular-season games. It is the home of the Yomiuri Giants, the leading (and oldest) franchise in Japanese professional baseball. (Home-run king Sadaharu Oh was a Giant for his entire playing career.) The ballpark is part of a larger entertainment complex featuring a high-rise hotel, entertainment complex, retail, and the Japanese Baseball Hall of Fame. Competing at the Tokyo Dome: China, Chinese Taipei, Japan, and Korea. 1-3-61 Koraku, Bunkyo-ku. Tokyo, JP 112-8562; **tokyo-dome.co.jp/e/**.

Hiram Bithorn Stadium is named for Hiram Bithorn, the first Puerto Rican to play in the major leagues when he pitched for the 1942 Chicago Cubs. His major-league career was short, limited by arm troubles to four years, but he's a national treasure in Puerto Rico, and his high-kick delivery was imitated by hordes of youngsters, including Juan Marichal. Over the years the ballpark has hosted a slew of major-league exhibition and regular-season games and, for two seasons, Montreal Expos "home" games. Competing at Hiram Bithorn Stadium: Dominican Republic, Netherlands, Panama and Puerto Rico. Hato Rey, San Juan.

Foro Sol Stadium is the regular-season home of the Mexican League's Mexico City Red Devils It is an interesting facility, to be sure: It was really designed as a concert facility and a racetrack, so the sightlines can be skewed at times, particularly in the left-field corner. Competing at Foro Sol Stadium: Australia, Cuba, Mexico, and South Africa. Viaducto Piedad y Río Churubusco S/S Cd Deportiva.

Rogers Centre (the former SkyDome) is an imposing presence on the Toronto skyline, located at the base of the CN Tower. The regular-season home of the Toronto Blue Jays, Rogers Centre has been upgraded in recent years by new owner Ted Rogers; there's less stress on the concrete and more on the amenities. With the weather still cool in Toronto in March, you can bet games will be played with the roof closed. Competing at the Rogers Centre: Canada, Italy, United States, and Venezuela. One Blue Jays Way, Toronto; **rogerscentre.com**.

Semifinals are slated for Petco Park and Dolphin Stadium. If the United States makes the second round, the team would compete at Miami's Dolphin Stadium, an easy drive for those attending spring-training games on the Treasure Coast or Fort Myers. Dolphin Stadium is the regular-season home of the Florida Marlins, a football stadium somewhat awkwardly configured for baseball. Bring the sunscreen; there's little shade at Dolphin Stadium. 2269 Dan Marino Blvd., Miami Garden; **dolphinstadium.com**.

It's a five-plus-hour drive from Phoenix to San Diego, so we're guessing it will be mostly locals taking in the semifinals at Petco Park. Too bad, as the home of the San Diego Padres is one of the nicest ballparks in the majors. Virtually every seat in Petco Park is a winner, but some locations are especially desirable. The choices are a bit dizzying with no less than 16 categories at 11 price points. If you can find them available and are willing to pay, the top-shelf Terrace Infield seats are the best in the house — sections 202-210. 100 Park Blvd., San Diego; **petcoparkevents.com**.

The finals are scheduled for Dodger Stadium, one of the grand old venues in professional baseball. The regular-season home of the Los Angeles Dodgers, Dodger Stadium is nestled in Chavez Ravine and is a scenic place to see a game, a little oasis in the sprawl of Los Angeles. There are not too many bad seats in the house, but at Dodger Stadium it's better to go upstairs than down the line. The finals are scheduled for March 21-23, 2009. 1000 Elysian Park Av., Los Angeles.